Fly Leaves
and
Waterside Sketches

To David,

with best wishes,

Gordon Mackie.

December 29, 1998.

Fly Leaves
and
Waterside Sketches

GORDON MACKIE

Illustrated by Jane Vaughan-Wilson

ROBERT HALE · LONDON

© Gordon Mackie 1998
First published in Great Britain 1998

ISBN 0 7090 6144 7

Robert Hale Limited
Clerkenwell House
Clerkenwell Green
London EC1R 0HT

The right of Gordon Mackie to be identified as
author of this work has been asserted by him
in accordance with the Copyright, Designs and
Patents Act 1988.

2 4 6 8 10 9 7 5 3 1

Typeset in North Wales by
Derek Doyle & Associates, Mold, Flintshire
Printed in Great Britain by
St Edmundsbury Press Limited, Bury St Edmunds
and bound by
WBC Book Manufacturers Limited, Bridgend

Contents

Foreword by Bernard Venables MBE   9
Preface   11
List of Illustrations   13

Part One

 1 A Fisherman's Journey   17
 2 A Galaxy of Bright Waters   22
 3 Springtime on the Usk   25
 4 The Torridge at Eastertide   28
 5 Two Hampshire Stillwaters   31
 6 A Shropshire Brook   33
 7 Insects Don't Read Books   36
 8 Trout Streams at Bluebell Time   38
 9 Chalk-stream Baptism   41
10 Jewels of the Downland   45
11 Where the Five Rivers Meet   48
12 Carnival Time in Wiltshire   53
13 In the Heart of the Cotswolds   57
14 Early Days on the Kennet   59
15 Holiday Time on the Teign   62
16 Mayfly Wrinkles   65
17 Pieces of Heaven   67
18 Food for Thought   71
19 The Wilton Diaries   74
20 The Height of the Season   77
21 Mayfly Holiday   81
22 A Week with Vincent Marinaro   85
23 Chalk Streams on a Shoestring   89

24   The Darlington Years   93
25   Mental Block   96

Part Two

26   A Latticed Bridge   99
27   Duty Calls   102
28   Spiritual Prostitution?   106
29   Follow My Leader   108
30   Kentish Glory   110
31   Treasures Beyond Price   113
32   The Golden Hours   115
33   An Evening in Summer   119
34   BWO Mysteries   122
35   Sunset Specials   124
36   Dawn Patrol   127
37   The Record Trout   129
38   Salmon are 'Keeper's Perks'   131
39   A Humble Brook   134
40   Nymphing Subtleties   136
41   Calculating Fly Density   140
42   Echoes from an Ancient Valley   142
43   Back-end Adventures   145
44   Grayling on the Shallows   148
45   Grayling, Pride of Autumn   151
46   Chasing Shadows   154
47   Winter Quarters   157
48   The Grayling Factor   160
49   Grayling Catches 1969–95 (August–November)   163

Part Three

50   Fisherman's Torment   167
51   Where Life Begins   169
52   Loafer's Luck   171
53   Media Hype   173
54   Cuthbert's Last Stand   175
55   What's It All About   177

56	Fishy Business	179
57	Wasted Years?	181
58	Man of the Riverside	183
59	A Triumph of Nature	185
60	Country Ways	187
61	Worker's Playtime	189
62	Trout Catches 1966–89	191
63	A United Front?	193
64	As Others See Us	195
65	Firing from the Hip	197
66	Stillwater Policies	199
67	On the Beat	201
68	Appliance of Science	203
69	A Lost Civilization	205
70	To See, and to Hear	207
71	Annie Alicia Oak 1898–1989	209
72	First Trout of the Antipodes	211
73	Sleepy Old Town	214
74	Magic Moments	216
75	A Sweet Finale	218
76	Archie's Farewell	220
77	Archie and a Lone Bellbird	222
78	Archie's Nirvana	224
79	Wild Trout of the South Pacific	226
80	One Last Chuck	232

◆ Foreword ◆
by Bernard Venables MBE

We live in unquiet times. Never since nature created the human species, thus to throw into disarray the harmony of all else of her making, has there been such cacophony. It assails us from birth till we die. How could we have guessed when, in relative peace this century began, what was to come? Who could have foreseen the outrageous offence that was to be?

It should have been foreseeable. We are nature's children, born of Earth: our acknowledgement of that must never cease if we are to live in health of mind and spirit. But we live without tranquillity, removed from earth's natural gifts. Such is the torment of our times that the soul sickens and must be anaesthetized: we must be so deafened that we cannot hear its suffering voice.

We are in danger of acceptance: so harangued are we in our every minute by salesmanship, propaganda, traffic's roar, every spurious clamour, that we may accept it as rational, that it may safely continue. We would delude ourselves. Utterly it is irrational; it can lead only to disaster. Never has nature tolerated unconforming species – species that multiply excessively, so bearing injuriously on others. Nature is highly jealous of the lovely intricacy of the balance of her making. Rogue species must be eliminated. We are a rogue species, astonishingly clever, but, day by day, the more dangerous for that. We threaten disaster for ourselves and for all others with whom we must share this earth. In our deadly brilliance, our electronic marvels, we persuade ourselves that we are masters of nature – and how lethally fatuous that is.

But, quietly, nature still goes her ways. It is by her inviolable rules that we shall continue or join the dinosaurs in extinction. We in the small time we have occupied earth have grossly changed it: nature established her rules some thousands of millions of years ago. She has not changed them. Still, day by day, the soil, earth's soil, feeds us; still

9

by nature's air we must breathe – though we have so striven to poison it. Wrap the world in electronic knitting as we may, the essentials of having life on earth are as immutable as ever they were. Not all those wonders of electronics will save us when by the damage we have done nature can no longer open her buds in spring.

But, so little heard under the insensate din, the attentive ear may hear quiet voices. Quiet as they are, they are gathering. They, if sanity is to save us, are the voices that shall make the future. It is such a voice that speaks from this book.

We must hope it speaks with prophesy, but so modestly does it speak, that it is unlikely that its owner claims any such intention. The author seeks no more than to record those days of angling that have been his contentment over the years: because their contentment has been so deep, so woven with the pulse of nature, their significance dwarfs promotion's vastest noises. The author, so truly of his kind, is no single-minded hunter of a quarry, unobservant of all else. His delight is of all that is of river valleys. He is, as good anglers are, a practitioner in applied natural history. His fishing days are abandonments of our technological obsessions; his soul thus freed from all those trivial falsities he sees with cleared vision the fundamental essences of life on earth. Perhaps he does not tell himself that in those straight terms: his delight is in the water, those rivers and lakes which by the mysterious life that is in them, culminating in the fish which are his quarry, so fasten his fascinated soul that so he must be for his life's length. By that he becomes a monitor: by how complete or partial is his pleasure is a measure of the health of the environment by which we must live.

It is the angler who sees the central truth of nature at work: water is the single clearest revelation. The author of this book tells us of the many waterside delights that have filled his days. So doing he reveals the unspoken fact of his intimacy with the delicate and most beautiful secrets of nature's workings. They should not be secrets, and would not have been so had we not dimmed our vision.

When anglers return contented from the water, all is well. When they come frustrated, with sad complaint, there should be sharp alarm.

ᥕᥬ Preface ᥉ᥭ

When I first tried my hand at gold panning, on a small stream in New Zealand, I was astonished to discover that beneath the gravel and assorted dross of the riverbed there were indeed a few tiny specks of metal languishing in the watery residue. There were also three very large trout poised on the glide, one of which sipped down my size 16 Olive Dun – but that's another story ...

Five years later I was sifting through another pile, this time of copy papers. Once again I found amongst the flotsam a handful of modest pieces which, on looking them over after some years – two decades and more in some cases – I felt might be of passing interest to today's trout and grayling fishermen. My friends had told me that before this material vanished forever I should make some of it available in book form. When the publishers also displayed a surprising level of enthusiasm for the project I was finally persuaded that I must press ahead before I, too, faded from the scene.

However, articles which I had thought would be fairly easy to gather up and collate in fact proved a wayward, ill-disciplined lot. Like leaves on an autumn wind they flew in all directions, refusing to settle comfortably alongside those nearby. Some were 'dated', in that they portrayed specific seasons, but many had no obvious home. There were anecdotal stories, humorous or pithy sketches, and a number discussed topical issues. Others were of a somewhat surreal flavour, or offered a cryptic message, while fictional characters flitted in and out as in some piscatorial pantomime.

Eventually, as the breeze subsided, a proportion of these papers began to fall into place. I decided to divide the book into three parts, the first two containing most of the episodical and descriptive writings depicting the fly fisher's season, before and after midsummer, while the third encompassed pieces of a more elusive or peripheral nature, plus a few about my New Zealand fishing adventures.

The content remains much as it was when it originally appeared, warts and all, and I have added a number of hitherto unpublished items in an attempt to weave the book into a reasonably presentable whole. Some revision has been necessary however, to avoid undue repetition, to update information or to iron out serious grammatical hiccups. Even so, you may find that certain phrases or short passages appear more than once, though this will not, I think, prove overly irksome to the reader. One or two contradictions may be apparent too; these reflect one angler's developing opinions, experience or knowledge as the seasons have passed. The original titles used over published articles have been altered as well in cases where new headings seemed appropriate.

Most of the material has been culled from back numbers of *Salmon Trout and Sea Trout* magazine, including several of my 'Random Casts' (written under the name Geoffrey Oaklands), and from *Fly Fishing and Fly Tying*, *Trout and Salmon*, and the *Journal of the Flyfishers' Club*. I wish to express my sincere thanks to the owners and editors of these publications for allowing reproduction. In addition, some works have been rescued from old titles which sadly no longer exist, including *Angling*, *Fisherman*, *Salmon and Trout*, *Wessex Life* and others.

My thanks are also due to the numerous friends and acquaintances who have helped me to get this book off the ground. In particular Roy Darlington, a veritable fount of knowledge, has always been there to curb my impetuosity, suggest an alternative approach and offer wise counsel. Indeed, the book would not have been completed were it not for the many hours of toil that Roy devoted to my bedraggled manuscript.

Over the years I have gained support and inspiration from many others – perhaps just by talking things over or sharing a rod – among them Merle Battle, with whom I first started fly fishing, John Bowden, Conrad Voss Bark, Mark Bowler, Ronnie Butler, Simon Cain, Mike Cridge, William Daniel, Ron Darlington, Lin Davis, Roy Eaton, John Ginifer, David Goodchild, John Goddard, Tony Hayter, Pam Hunt, Mike Kelly, Bill Latham, Geoff Lee, Bill Lees, Crawford Little, Denis Lofts, Norman Marsh, Roger Mills, Stewart Newell, Kenneth Robson, Raymond Rocher, Adrian Simmons, Norman Smith, Laurie Stokes, Alun (Taffy) Stephens, Jim Sumner, Graham and Joy Swanson, Jack Thorndike, Gordon Topp, Sidney Vines and Eric Williams.

It is my earnest hope that this book will provide an entertaining, chatty and thought-provoking read, and that it may, just now and again, touch some slender chord deep in the angler's soul.

✍ Illustrations ❧

Between pages 128 and 129

1 Dorset's major chalkstream, the Frome above Dorchester
2 Graham Swanson fishing a carrier of the Itchen near Winchester
3 May blossom-time on the River Ebble above Bishopstone Church
4 Gordon Mackie fishing the River Nadder in Wiltshire
5 November on the Heale Water of the Avon at Middle Woodford above Salisbury
6 A tricky cast on the Ebble near Coombe Bisset
7 The author hooks a good trout below Barford St Martin on the Nadder
8 High summer on the Itchen at Abbots Worthy, Hampshire
9 The tumbling Hoar Oak Water at Watersmeet, Exmoor National Park
10 Upper Teign FA water near Fingle Bridge
11 Cherry Brook, a tributary of the West Dart in the heart of Dartmoor National Park
12 The author wades a wooded stretch of the River Teign below Chagford in Devon
13 The upper Barle near Withypool on Exmoor
14 The sheltered valley of the East Lyn in North Devon

Illustrations courtesy of Graham Swanson

PART ONE

Perpetual devotion to what a man calls his business is only to be sustained by perpetual neglect of many other things – and it is not by any means certain that a man's business is the most important thing he has to do.

Robert Louis Stevenson

◦ 1 ◦

A Fisherman's Journey

Many people were uprooted during the hostilities of 1939–45. As the bombers gathered in the eastern skies our family moved west, to a flat near Plymouth Hoe – little realizing that the heart of that great city was about to be torn out by high-explosive and incendiary devices. Soon the centre of Plymouth had been flattened, and we had moved again, first to a house in Plympton and then to Russell House, next to the vicarage in the then small village of Plymstock.

These were harrowing days for my parents, what with food short-ages, blackouts and the wail of sirens heralding the next air raid. Even at 'Russell', some five miles from the main target area, we found the terror descending on us. Indeed I well remember my tears of anxiety as mother Katherine left the comparative safety of our Anderson shelter at night, spade in hand, to remove those devilish fire bombs which strayed onto our property. Father Rupert and his brother Gordon, great fishermen both, were away for most of the war; the former served in the Navy, while the latter endured a cruel sojourn in a Java concentration camp.

Both men survived, although time was no doubt deducted from their natural span. I often reflect on how, in the darkest days, they must have dreamed of fishing. But I think mother suffered a more last-ing distress, for it was some fifteen years later, around the time of her birthday on 20 April (which, ironically, she shared with a certain Herr Hitler), that she finally became lost and confused while on one of her country walks, and we knew she would require constant attention. Yet those post-war years were happy ones in many respects. We were at peace, and my parents could take pride in watching their children Helen, Richard and young Gordon stepping eagerly into a brave new world.

Such ramblings may seem to have little relevance to the subject in hand, yet it was these early years that most influenced the priorities I have held in later life. Had we remained in London it is doubtful whether I would have become so keen an angler, or whether the ways of the country would have become so familiar to me. It was those golden days spent walking along secluded lanes, across the fields to Radford Wood, or on the cliff tops at Wembury that led to my fascination with butterflies and other wild creatures, to a growing need to find peace in quiet places, and finally to the magical sights and sounds of countless river valleys.

The conversations around the dinner table are a hazy memory, yet I recall the name of our grandfather the Reverend G.E. Mackie being mentioned from time to time, though perhaps more in terms of ministering to trout than to his parishioners. He had taught his sons Rupert and Gordon to fish on the river Coln near Chedworth in Gloucestershire, where the family occupied the vicarage until his death in 1924. Many years later I learned that grandfather had fished with G.E.M. Skues, F.M. Halford and other great anglers of his time, taking over the presidency of the Flyfishers' Club from the latter in 1904.

Gordon junior, though, must have been a worry to all concerned. Unlike Helen and Richard I did not excel at school. They went on to university, gained good degrees and pursued teaching careers. Helen took up a post in Uganda, while Richard gained a commission in the Army, later becoming Headmaster of Ravenswood School near Tiverton, where he and I had been pupils during the war. Both my sister and brother have kept in touch with old friends throughout their lives, and each is now enjoying a happy retirement, the former in Cornwall and the latter with his wife Judy in Gloucestershire.

I was rather 'backward' and irresponsible by comparison, or maybe the functional brain cells had all been distributed before I appeared. I was never inclined to mix socially or foster close friendships, and I failed quite miserably in my exams. In the army I succeeded in advancing only to the heights of acting, unpaid Lance-Corporal. My achievements, such as they were, were on the games field, at cricket, football, hockey and high jumping, but I was too idle to continue participating in these sports after my National Service. Career-wise I was something of a failure too. Work was not difficult to find in the 1950s and 1960s, so I simply moved from job to job, each lasting perhaps two years or so on average. And there were girls, cars, coffee bars and juke-boxes, and of course I became an avid Plymouth Argyle supporter.

One day when I joined Dad on the river Erme, east of Plymouth –

it must have been in 1947 or 1948 – he handed me his Millward split-cane rod and suggested I throw the fly into a shallow ripple just down-stream, close to the near margin. There was a pluck, a boil at the surface, and a bright little eight inch trout came tumbling in to be swept unceremoniously onto the bank. This fish was no great shakes of course, certainly when compared with father's 5¼-lb sea trout caught here on 14 August 1953 (the pencilled outline of which still resides in my bottom drawer) but it seemed a fair whopper to me at the time. Strangely, this incident did not trigger any immediate enthu-siasm for fishing; my capture of a Pale Clouded Yellow and a Heath Fritillary, and mother's Silver-striped Hawk Moth were more note-worthy events. It would be some fourteen years, after both mother and father had died and I had taken a job in Bristol before I dug out the old rod and began to wonder where I might use it. I called at Veals tackle shop in Tower Hill, where I was enrolled as a member of Bathampton Anglers' Association and directed by Steve Wedlake to the Box Brook (known also as the By Brook) five miles east of Bath.

Here, suddenly, when I was 29, life took on a whole new meaning. The brook wound its way through lush pastures in a series of gravel runs, tight bends and deep, greenish pools. I had nearly three miles to explore, mostly overhung by trees and bushes. There were kingfishers, wagtails, water voles, dabchicks, toads, moths and a host of other insects along the riverside. And there were trout dimpling as they took small flies that floated on the surface, and the spinners danced in massed concentrations towards evening. I was in heaven. I crept through the undergrowth, stalking fish which I could see rising or poised up in the water. I switched the fly, or cast after a fashion, but more often I simply dapped. The trout were willing, provided I kept out of sight, and they were so numerous that I could afford to miss many and still enjoy some success. A 12-inch fish was a good one – most averaged about nine inches.

I drew up a detailed plan of the water, covering several sheets of foolscap. Every bend and straight was given a name: Big Stone Run, Sandy Pool, Two Trees, Snags Corner, Top Willow Bend. And as I met other anglers there was Hunt's Corner, Brian's Stretch, Donna's Chestnut, Upton's Patch, and so on. John Hunt, from whom I learned much in those early days, became my closest fishing friend, while Donna (Merle) was my girl friend at the time. That first season I recorded twelve trout, followed by 110 in 1964, 253 in 1965 and 381 in 1966 before John and I took ourselves off to more famous rivers, such as the Kennet, the Wiltshire Avon, and the Wilton Club's waters on the Wylye. We caught larger fish on these classic reaches, of course, yet our thoughts were never far from the little Box, nor were any of our captures more notable than John's grand trout of 1lb 4oz taken at the Wall Inflow on 31 May 1965. We fished further afield, too – in Wales, Ireland, Shropshire and Devon, but it was the Box with her ½–¾ pounders which would remain forever in our hearts.

Twenty-five years later, on 13 September 1992, I received a telephone call from Pam Hunt with the shattering news that her husband John had died quite suddenly that morning. He was only 59 and apparently in the best of health. I drove up to the Box Brook for old time's sake, fearing that after a quarter of a century it might have changed for the worse. But as I walked the length it all looked much the same. The descendants of those little trout hovered in front of the same stones and along familiar tree-lined banks. Upwinged flies came jinking around Big Elm Bend, the trout rose at Hunt's Corner as of old, and I spotted a beauty lying in the eddy below Donna's Chestnut.

Soon I came to the stone bridge where we had gathered long ago. I saw then just how far I had journeyed as an angler, and how little I had achieved in the eyes of my fellow men. My friends had successful careers, families to support, a house of brick, an index-linked pension. I too had held good positions, if only briefly. I too had enjoyed happy relationships, paid the mortgage and sought security, but somehow I always believed that lasting fulfilment lay elsewhere. There was another pathway which, if I could cast off the fetters of conformity, would lead me to a vast and largely undiscovered world beyond.

Sitting here on the bridge over the Box, I was shocked to realize how few old friends I could remember now. Perhaps some minor characteristic, some incident in which they had featured would return, but the names and the faces ... how elusive they had become. Yet those of every valley I have known are with me still; the tumbling hillsides, a cascade of oak, the glistening boulders, currents now sweetly gliding, now raging darkly in unbridled fury – such images will never desert me. Each river has a different song to sing, its individual profile, an unforgettable embrace. Perhaps I shall visit them again one day. But what of lost friends, and loved ones? Where are they now? Can I turn to them in my hour of need? The jobs, the motorcars and the houses where I once lived, these too have largely faded from my memory. People change, companies fold, and man's structures crumble as if made of straw – fleeting, transient, as though they had never been.

What remains are the ageless edifices fashioned by nature, works that withstand the ravages of time.

And so we enter a land of broad horizons and majestic skies, better appreciated alone perhaps, or with a single soul-mate; a landscape of fresh air, sunlight and pure water: eternal elements without which no life exists. Rivers are our everlasting joy, a source of wonder, of refreshment and of food; it has been so throughout countless generations since men first walked upon the earth. What comfort, if our only thoughts were of departed friends, the stresses of the workplace, an old home since demolished? How barren our lives if all we sought were the trappings of success, social standing, a secure retirement! We might have missed so much that life has to offer, so many uplifting messages. For beyond the ken of many is a vital force of which anglers, in their close communion with natural things, may gain the glimmerings of an understanding.

There is a constancy about rivers, and the unfailing cycles of creatures that have made their homes there. They embody a permanence and stability which appears increasingly lacking in man's acquisitive, rapidly changing world. Today I seek tranquility above all else, in places as untroubled as they were when my father and grandfather and those before them pursued their gentle art. Let us go fishing then, for I hear the whisper of quiet waters, and Spring is in the air.

ᔕᖇ 2 ᖇᔕ

A Galaxy of Bright Waters

Attempting to recall my greatest fishing adventure is like trying to pluck a star from the glittering firmament. As the years roll on, each thrill, each stolen moment and gasp of delight subtly merges into an exquisite whole from which it becomes increasingly difficult to single out one day, one river or a particular fish and say to myself 'that was the finest of them all'.

Should I invite my reader to join me in southern Ireland perhaps, on the mighty Shannon and her beautiful tributaries the Fergus, Maigue and Morning Star? We might go to Ennis and fish for large trout when the elvers are running, or up to Corofin where smaller fish rise all day to the floating fly. Then we might drive east to the Little Brosna, to Treacy's water, and catch a dozen 8–10 in. trout on a Partridge and Orange, several of which we fry for our supper. On the way back to Rosslare we may explore the classic Kings River and search the ruins of great mansions whispering still of an inglorious past. We catch few trout here, for each quickly seeks cover as we approach, but we take away grand memories of a wild day in wind and rain as the iron blues covered the surface.

We might go, too, to the border streams, where Arrow, Lugg, Clun and Teme come bustling eastward from the forests and mountains of central Wales. One day in March 1966 I caught three grayling from the Arrow; the largest was a mere 10½ in., so why do I remember this day so well? And over to the west, near Cenarth, the little Hirwen took me to her heart some years later, giving up many of her trout, fully mature at 5–6 in. These fish are totally in-bred, with big heads and skinny bodies, barely able to survive, and yet the long hours spent scrambling up the waterfalls on this Teifi tributary could so easily qualify as among the most memorable.

Some years earlier I had caught twenty trout of over two pounds

22

from the Itchen in a single season – but were those days at Abbots Worthy, Abbotts Barton, the Manor Water and the Alre happier, more remarkable times? Or the balmy evenings at Chew Valley and Blagdon lakes, when great fish sipped the buzzers or crashed at scuttering sedges? And what of those hot midsummer afternoons on London's Grand Union Canal, where the dace rose like gentlemen to my tiny Pale Watery while besuited business folk watched in amazement?

We can travel, too, to Devonshire, via the Dorsetshire Frome and the Piddle perhaps, and when we reach Dartmoor and Exmoor we will feel that little has changed since the last Ice Age. Indeed, the landscape here was not sculpted at this time, like that to the east, but fashioned millions of years before. Maybe the crags and boulders and rushing rivers will tell us so, and the surging salmon and sea trout remind us that it is we who are the newcomers in this ancient place. The East Lyn comes tumbling between narrow outcrops into pools of joy whose small brown trout dart at the fleeting fly, and sizzle over the camp fire towards evening. We will go fishing in the morning, or afternoon or at nightfall, both here and on the Hoar Oak Water or the Barle or Teign to the south, and we will find the wild trout rising gently all summer beneath the trees.

We may even board the jet plane bound for New Zealand, instead of just dreaming as anglers are apt to do. The books and magazines tell tales of Taupo and Tongariro, and we've watched videos of Rotarua and Rangitaiki. But we make for the South Island and its sparkling rivers hurrying down the slopes of the Southern Alps, or the crystal spring creeks of the west coast, topped up by forest seepage. Here we stalk big trout under a subtropical sun, and shake with excitement as they sip minute willow grubs from the surface.

We tramp for days into bush country to behold the stunning Karamea and tributaries such as the Crow and Roaring Lion, where fish average 4–5 lb and you can see them lying out ahead. In a clear pool forty feet deep on the Wangapeka I cast to one trout which must have weighed twelve pounds. He swung sideways on, showing all of his huge flank, but when I tightened there was no contact and the fish sank to the bottom, looking little more than a three-pounder at that great depth. But from a limpid pool above Crow Hut on the Karamea in December 1995 I caught one on a size 16 Olive Dun that scaled 5lb 13oz – and another, which weighed 4lb 10oz, I took from the Motueka near Baton Bridge one evening on a Sedge. What a fight they gave me, the heavier fish threatening to go down the boulder-strewn race below until I got waist-deep into mid-river with the rod under my arm so as to force him bodily into the net with bare hands. Was their vigour, their gameness any greater, pound for pound, than those little dace or the slender trout of the Hirwen? In truth I cannot say so.

When we return we might savour the southern chalk streams, where the ghosts of Francis, Marryat, Skues and Sawyer haunt the flower-decked meadows. I will take you to Plunket Greene's resting place, tucked between the banks of the Bourne and the cricket field at Hurstbourne Priors. Somebody has put a little box of flies on his stone, Iron Blues I suspect; and then we will take our lunch, as Halford did, in the thatched fishing hut a few miles to the south where the Dever meets the Test. One day on the Bourne above the Beehive Bridge I netted nine wild trout before my host joined me at 3p.m; he caught and returned forty trout and thirteen grayling after I left, which must be some kind of record. Is this the cream, then, or should we look to the Eden, Don or Tweed, or to lesser known streams such as the Shreen, Cerne or Till?

Then again, do our best days necessarily feature fish at all – or is the glory of the wider whole sometimes enough to satisfy the yearning spirit? The sight of a water vole chomping the weed or paddling across the river to its nest; the call of the flashing kingfisher or the piping of the wren; a blaze of buttercups, the may bush laden with blossom, and the beech as it turns to gold. Or the scent of the honeysuckle on a June night, the opening of a mayfly's shuck as the perfect insect emerges, and the sigh of the wind as the willows stoop towards the stream. How very powerfully such things work upon our senses, and how rich this life that we call fishing!

☙ 3 ❧

Springtime on the Usk

As you cross the Severn Bridge you seem to enter another world. First the waters of the mighty estuary stretch out below, then the Wye glides quietly by, and before you know it the motorway verges are a blaze of daffodils welcoming you to Wales, the land of the sewin, wild brown trout, the march brown, and of course Sweet's tackle shop.

On Sundays I would call at Lionel Sweet's house to collect my day ticket and hear tales of the Usk, of great salmon, and of folklore hereabouts. The soft voice, the squat, weathered features and those gnarled, gentle hands themselves told the story of a lifetime's experience on the river which no few words of mine can convey. Lionel has gone on now, yet his spirit haunts the banks still; and the little shop is just as it always was, save for the absence of Mollie Sweet (Sweet Mollie as I sometimes called her), so warm and friendly, whose exquisite flies are famous far beyond what was once called Monmouthshire.

Today, you will meet Jean Williams in Usk, behind the counter where Mollie used to be, and it will not be long before that sing-song laughter, ever close to the surface, will bubble forth to lighten your day. The flies are still made to Mollie's original recipe, and they catch fish here like no patterns I have known. The two-mile Town water is open to those spinning or fly fishing for salmon from 26 January to 17 October, and to trout anglers using wet-fly or dry-fly methods between 3 March and 30 September.

In March and early April, when I come here for brown trout, I find it difficult to decide whether dry-fly or the traditional wet-fly technique will be the more productive. Often, even though the fish are rising in their splashy early-season fashion, I have no luck with the surface fly, and the only takes are to my team of wets. Many a time I miss these too, so it's back to the dry fly – and so it goes on. Gradually, though, over some 27 years, I have formed my own theories about

25

these Usk trout, and while I confess that my results have never been startling, at least I can fish with some sort of strategy in view. And yet, it is important to keep an open mind.

Even though this is the Usk, and it is March, and Jean has sold you her March Browns (she sells everyone her March Browns) you may hardly see a fly all day. The heavier hatches generally occur in April, but even then you sometimes have to be mighty quick to take advantage of the mad march brown rise. I have known days when the hatch has been so brief – perhaps three or four minutes only – that it was almost over before I cast a fly. When the hatch has finished, you may have to wait up to two hours for the next, or the flies may not reappear at all. On other days it's like a heavy show of mayflies, lasting on and off for hours on end.

Clearly, you must be prepared. Just in case one of those short, sharp rises occurs, I make sure I have positioned myself somewhere close to fast, heavily broken water, where most of the activity takes place, and I have two or three artificials on my lapel, ready for a quick change of flies should it become necessary. You can shorten the odds by using a dry March Brown on the point, and a couple of wet patterns on droppers, which will simulate the hatching nymphs. Pitch these right into the tumbling water and let the current carry them downstream. The line should not be too tight, but allowed sufficient slack to ensure that the flies do not 'fight' the flow or remain on the surface. All the same, you should keep in touch with your flies, so as to feel the slightest pluck or to react rapidly to any visual indication.

There is no doubt that wet-fly experts develop what amounts to a sixth sense when it comes to detecting takes. I have not experienced this myself, but have watched Usk fishermen tighten into fish time and again, even though they will tell you they neither felt nor saw any take. Some Welsh wizards regularly use representations of several species of fly on the leader. The natural flies you will encounter in March may include large dark olives, black gnats, march browns, sedges and a variety of stoneflies, artificials of which can all be obtained at Sweet's. Sparsely hackled wet flies such as Greenwell's Glory, Gold-ribbed Hare's Ear, Partridge and Orange, and February Red are popular favourites, while Coch-y-Bonddu, Grey Duster, Blue Upright, Dogsbody and Kite's Imperial are excellent general-purpose dry flies.

One reason for my relative lack of success with the dry fly has been the difficulty of placing the fly with the required accuracy. In rippling water, where trout are rising only occasionally, and sometimes some distance away, it is not easy to pinpoint their positions. You approach to within casting range and drop the fly where you thought you spotted the rise, only to see the fish break surface a yard or more to one side. The trout here are seldom inclined to cruise, and so like the fly right 'on the button'; furthermore, they are not too impressed by a dragging dry fly. Yet, when you are using a wet fly or sub-surface nymph, the trout may take the active fly more readily than one which is fished inert, provided it moves in a natural manner.

My experience of fishing the evening rise on the Usk is limited, but it can be a most productive time from early June until mid-August. Perhaps I have been put off by my ducking one July, when, wading across the river in the dark, I slipped on the smooth stones and found myself completely submerged and being swept downstream rather too quickly for my liking. The waders had filled with water, and I was preparing for the worst and repenting my past sins when, lo and behold, I was washed up on a bank of shingle, from which I was able to squelch ashore. My car was parked in the gateway by a bend in the road, where the headlights of approaching vehicles picked me out with unerring precision. Fortunately I had a change of clothes with me, so I stripped off and dried myself as best I could before donning the dry apparel. What the motorists thought of that naked figure moving about in a field on a dark night I can only guess, but I can see the humorous side of the episode, now! And I had four trout to show for that evening, the best measuring 12½ inches. There are few trout, anywhere, which can compare for flavour with those of the Usk.

Everyone in Usk seems to know all about 'the fishing'. It is a fisherman's town, and Sweet's a kind of meeting-point-cum-information-centre. The river has her moods, of course, and the trout do not always oblige; the water may be too high or too coloured, or the fish may remain on the bottom. But if you are fortunate enough to come here on a day in March or April when the olives, march browns and stoneflies fill the air, the spring sunshine warms your back, and the trout are rising all down the river from Garcoed Pool to Llanbadoc Church, then you will have known the Land of Song at her very best. And when you return there will always be a special welcome in the hillsides, and in the valleys too.

✍ 4 ✍

The Torridge at Eastertide

An icy blast swept down the valley from the north-west, bringing wave upon wave of outsized hailstones. I could see each cascade approaching like a sombre grey curtain, and this allowed me time to reach the shelter of a nearby wood. Usually I left it too late, however, unable to resist a couple of extra casts, and was assaulted by stinging pellets as I ran the gauntlet towards my sanctuary.

I had been invited by a friend to fish for two days over the Easter period on his length of the upper Torridge, which lay on the left bank opposite the well known Half Moon Hotel beats at Sheepwash. This somewhat isolated North Devon village lies four miles upstream of the river's confluence with its main tributary, the Oakmont. The lower section of my friend's beat is about two hundred yards long, running slow and deep, while above I had more than half a mile of medium-paced, largely broken water, much of it wadeable.

There was little surface activity when I arrived, so I made for the top boundary and fished a pair of wet flies across and down the stickles, around the rocks in midstream and into likely pools and eddies. I felt a number of plucks, but nearly an hour had passed before a trout took hold. You have to keep well in touch with your flies here by fishing quite a tight line, for the little fish can eject the fly so quickly they are gone in a flash. This one leapt clear of the stream several times before coming to the net, a golden-brown beauty of nine inches with vivid red spots and the elegant, shapely fins of a true 'native'.

Four more trout of like size were hooked and returned in the following half-hour, but I wanted a brace for supper, and had set myself a ten-inch limit. I felt sure the larger fish would be lying in the deeper pockets where the water steadied beneath the elder bushes against the far bank. Access appeared much easier from the other side – it is ever thus – but I determined to have a go, for if I didn't those

Half Moon rods jolly soon would. The wet flies skated unnaturally from this angle so I moved six yards downstream, changing to a dry Stonefly pattern on a size 12 hook. Casting it up and across, I watched the fly float high on the ripple and down into the smoother bays.

Fish were rising here and there, but another violent hailstorm put paid to that. Then a ray of sunshine appeared, the wind abated to some extent, and for a moment or two spring smiled upon the valley. The Stonefly went under in a splashy rise, but my thoughts were elsewhere at that instant, and the trout was gone. I saw the next one coming to the fly a fraction of a second before he took; my rod arched over, and the reel-drum whirred as a lusty fish hurtled downstream, through the faster water and into his bolthole under the bank. The line was stuck fast, and the water was too deep at this point for me to wade across to try and clear it. In this situation you can sometimes free the line by paying off several yards from the reel and allowing the current to carry it down river, so that the pull is from a different direction. I was lucky this time, but rapid hand-lining was necessary to get the fish back on a tight line before he could bury himself in some other obstruction. These trout are tough fighters, but this one had tired by now, and the net soon received his 12½ inches. A fine fish by upper Torridge standards, and only a couple of ounces short of my best ever from this stream.

Between 1.30 and 3p.m. the trout lying in open water rose to the large dark olives with real enthusiasm, yet many of those along the margins were taking small black flies with similar relish. These little insects may well have been reed smuts, which often resemble the terrestrial black gnats and usually congregate near the bank. The angler should enjoy some success in these circumstances simply by offering a variety of patterns and relying on the law of averages, but he can save valuable time if he knows where the different species are likely to be found. I missed many more than I hooked, as often happens when fish are moving everywhere; even so, a total of eleven trout came to the net this day, most being returned unharmed.

The next morning found the wind still from the north-west, but the hail had given way to light rain showers, with longer spells of sunshine. Although I started at 10.30 a.m., earlier than one normally expects a hatch of fly at this season, the deep water at the lower end of my beat was littered with large dark olive duns. Here the density of the surface layer was such that the flies were having difficulty in freeing themselves from the clinging film, enabling the trout to take them down at will. My problem was not so much finding the right pattern (for I had every confidence that my Hare's Ear would do the trick) but in placing it in front of a feeding fish accurately, and at the right moment.

A dozen or more trout were cruising about sipping in the duns. Not every available fly was taken by any means, for the fish rose in definite rhythm, some six or seven seconds elapsing between rise forms. Some tipped up their noses a little more frequently than this, some less so, so that each trout had to be watched carefully and the cast timed to perfection. Two hours later I had been defeated by about eight of the trout, risen and missed two on the strike, and landed three of between nine and eleven inches.

Further upstream were two trouty-looking pools which I had not fished on the previous day, largely because they were so heavily shrouded by trees whose branches fingered the surface. By wading out into the stream however I was just able to snake the line up the tunnel into the head of the lower pool. The visibility was so poor here that I had thought it advisable to tie on a large Sedge, so that any take was likely to be seen, but when the rise came the audible 'gulp' was indication enough.

Shooting the fly up this dark alley had been such a challenge that I had given no thought to how I was going to play a trout in that treacherous tangle. Within about five seconds the pattern of my line across the surface resembled one of those maze puzzles seen in books, zig-zagging this way and that between branch, frond, root and twig. Of course, I had no chance of freeing that lot without a break, or so I thought. I was resigned to losing the fish, but I did want some of my tackle back, so with a switch here, a flick there, and a few mini roll-casts I managed to unravel all hitch-ups but the last (or rather the first, if traced back to the trout's initial rush-around). Somehow the line had draped itself over a partly submerged bough at a point about 4 ft above the stream, with the fly attached to something solid underwater. The line yielded slowly as I pulled, until there, hanging in mid-air, was my trout. I reeled in steadily, slid the fish over the top of the trunk and had him in the net, quite exhausted, within seconds. This was the best of the 27 caught this trip; 13 in. long and 14 oz. on the scale. I reckoned I had earned that one.

I feel closer to nature, more of a hunter, in such places than I do when fishing for trout which I know have been reared by man and turned in especially for me to catch in a largely artificial setting. Natural trout-streams abound in these islands. Often they teem with wild fish, are easier of access, and relatively inexpensive to fish.

ᥫᩤ 5 ᥫᩤ

Two Hampshire Stillwaters

Clear-water lakes have a special fascination for me, and if they offer some river fishing as well, that's an added bonus. Avington fishery nestles in a sheltered valley close to Itchen Abbas, Hampshire, with a side stream of the Itchen chuckling its way through the gardens, bisecting the main stillwaters, and flowing on parallel with the northern bank of the lower lake. The visitor's attention is taken at once by the sight of huge fish cruising in the lakes, so that possibilities on the little river tend to be ignored, even when the surface of the stream is bulging with rising trout.

The fish in the lakes were browsing in lazy fashion close to the bottom. Most appeared to be in the 2–4 lb class, but some were much heavier, and one I judged to be approaching 15 lb. Naturally enough, I stuck to the lakes and kept casting to these monsters for several hours, even though they were clearly not in a taking mood. By the time I finally withdrew to the stream it was mid-afternoon and the trout were rising less consistently, just dimpling gently here and there. Off came the heavy nymph, to be replaced by a size 15 Itchen Olive, and down went the angler on his haunches, trying his hardest to hide under a dock leaf, for this is real Red Indian stuff. The first six deliveries produced four rises, with two trout landed, and in the next hour a total of five fish came tumbling to the net after some hair-raising acrobatics. All were wild trout measuring 11–15 in., bar one which went to 18 in. and scaled 3 lb 3 oz.

Back on the top lake, with the fish at last feeding better, one rod had just taken a five-pounder, and I watched another land one of over 6½ lb. I had to leave by 6p.m. but just managed to secure another three-pound trout. A brace of this weight, plus a wild fish of 1½ lb, is a great day on any water – at any rate by my standards. But if I had timed my activities better and fished the river for the first few hours, spending the final two on the lakes, what great things I might have achieved.

Rooksbury Mill is an intimate, picturesque fishery on the southern outskirts of Andover. Here, too, a small chalk stream, the Anton, flows between two spring-fed lakes and on for a further four miles before joining the Test between Leckford and Chilbolton. The stream looked so inviting on this April day, with alternating glides and stickly shallows that I decided to devote my attention largely to this.

Around midday a few large dark olives appeared on the surface, and one or two fish began to rise. The air, however, was full of duns – which seemed strange, since I could not see such numbers emerging. But I concentrated on the few risers, soon connecting with a half-pound grayling, then another, and later two more. One sizeable fish was breaking surface intermittently, and I spent a further hour or more over this one without result.

I was nearing the top of this little river by now. It was after 3.30p.m., I was fishless, and I knew that at this season sport would soon tail off. I could see no flies hatching, but still there were many in the air. At last I twigged; these were pond olives, and they were coming off the upper lake just twenty yards away! Sure enough, the smooth surface was littered with them. The lake was clear and relatively shallow, and a number of trout were rising within range. The first delivery brought a big rainbow across at the fly; I could see his flank clearly, but I was too late and missed him. Then a swirl, a quick strike, and off went another, making the reel sing. This one came to the net easily enough, at 2 lb 2 oz. The next fish broke me, but before the hatch began to decline another two-pound rainbow, firm and brightly silver, toppled over the net rim.

At Rooksbury, as at Avington, I had again failed to interpret the signs which might have led to a bumper basket. But even when I saw the great catches weighed in by other rods, I found that my dreamy incompetence had detracted not one jot from my overall enjoyment of the day.

ᥱᥩ 6 ᥩᥱ

A Shropshire Brook

The alder fly scuttled up my left sleeve, causing me to lose control for an instant. Out of the corner of my eye I saw the darting rise form, but my timing was out and I missed on the strike. These trout of Shropshire and the Welsh Marches take like lightning compared with their larger cousins of the chalk streams.

I was fishing one of my favourite haunts, through Bluebell Wood, up to the weir and beyond into the deeper length above. Usually I visit the Cound Brook much earlier than this, at snowdrop time. Now it was just at the start of the mayfly, with the whole of nature bursting with life, the hawthorn ablaze with white and pink blossom and the woods ringing with birdsong. A kingfisher flashed downriver, wagtails danced at the edge of the ripple, and a dipper nodded his welcome to me from a rock in midstream. This year I had a bonus, for on a stump where the old horse used to idle away his days with the occasional scratch against gnarled timbers a little owl sat peering at me as I approached. I walked within four feet of its perch, but, save for a blink or two, the bird remained motionless and showed no fear.

Casting my mind back for a moment to congested Wessex, I thought how utterly peaceful it was here; no traffic noise, no low-flying aircraft, no dog-walkers treating the riverbank as their own, and the air so sweet I wanted to take lungfuls of it. Wading slowly along the margins with only wild creatures for company, I felt *this* was my rightful place, rather than that concrete madhouse where I must labour at meaningless tasks while life, real life, is slipping away. For a while I could forget about shopping precincts, digital 'bleeps', fast-food shops, yellow lines and loud-mouthed yobbos.

You fish by nature's timetable in these parts, knowing that a fine head of God's own trout exists, and that you will catch them if you fish well and are patient. There is no point in hurrying, for nature bestows her gifts in due time and in due season – a balanced scheme of things which has developed over countless centuries. If man becomes dissatisfied, seeking perhaps to improve his results, he could ruin this natural balance overnight.

A ten-inch trout came leaping to my feet, was twitched free and went scurrying off to rise another day. He had taken a Black Gnat, but I changed to a Mayfly pattern as a couple of splashy rises occurred beneath the trees. I use a barbed hook as a rule, but up here I often bend the barb over on a stone before starting to fish. The trout under the trees were not really 'on', unaccustomed as yet to feeding on these huge duns. Both lunged and missed, but another plump ten-incher furrowed his way across the shallows into deeper water before I could get him under the rod-tip and slide finger and thumb down the leader to ease him free.

I like to travel light on these streams, with neither fishing bag nor net; just my rod, two spools of point nylon, a small fly box, and a plastic bag in my pocket. Waders are essential, for it is difficult to fish where the banks are steep and heavily wooded. I created little disturbance ahead as I negotiated the quicker glides, but I had to be ultra cautious in the slow-flowing pools; my bow-wave spread several yards upstream no matter how carefully I inched forward, and trout would stop rising, even those a longish cast away. The only way to overcome this, silly though it may appear to the observer, is actually to lift each foot clear of the water before placing it back a short distance ahead so that at no time are you pushing against the current.

On one narrow stretch with little background cover, I had to kneel on the hard gravel in the river itself to avoid frightening my fish. Water trickled over my wader tops as I flicked the Mayfly a short cross-stream cast into the dark shadows under the opposite bank. My reward was a nine inch trout, hooked and returned within as many seconds, and a bright eleven-incher which went into the bag for supper. Catch-and-release policies are of value where there is a danger of trout becoming scarce, but here, as on any wild trout water where stocks are high and predators few, I would encourage anyone to take a brace or two – provided they are to be savoured at once with a little reverence, rather than stowed away in the freezer.

Trout are eager to feed at this season, but, as ever, the angler makes his own luck. Results depend as much upon approach work and presentation as upon using a closely imitative pattern. Wet fly, dry fly, up- or across-stream nymph, all are productive according to the conditions. When there is colour in the water, however, a little red in the dressing can work wonders, while in clear water outside mayfly time nothing beats a small Black Gnat – for me at any rate.

As we drove back towards Much Wenlock and the Wrekin, with Wenlock Edge towering to our right, we reckoned that in just under five hours of fairly leisurely fishing I had caught more than a dozen trout, taking three, and my friend John had fared much the same. Although the chalk streams were awaiting our arrival for the mayfly, we agreed that if the object is natural, unspoiled trout fishing, totally lacking artificiality – and in this sense 'real' sport – nothing compares with the multitude of lesser-known, often unsung streams which enter our great river valleys from the hill districts of the north and west.

ᦒ 7 ᦒ

Insects Don't Read Books

My angling diaries contain a somewhat disjointed hotch-potch of jottings and random observations, many of which have little relevance to fishing. Nevertheless, I am able from time to time to retrieve some useful snippet that will lead me to a trout or two in subsequent seasons.

On 17 April 1996 I had a rare opportunity to study the behaviour of that mysterious sedge fly the grannom, such a favourite with our forefathers, which in the past four or five decades has ceased to provide the kind of sport that brought fly fishers flocking to the river for a grand early-season carnival. Grannom hatches began to reappear on some rivers about fifteen years ago, but seldom in sufficient numbers for anglers to take its return seriously. Indeed on the day in question, when I was fishing the lower Avon near Fordingbridge, I had no recognizable pattern in my fly box.

As the diary records, 'from about 12 noon until 2p.m., the buff-coloured flies hatched in droves, struggling and skipping on the water for some seconds before becoming airborne. On emergence, each leaves a small (1–1.5 cm) pupa case on the surface, these floating down in thousands to form a brown mass along the margins. Vast numbers of resting or mating adults in the grass put up at every step. From 2 to 5p.m. clouds of females advanced in a huge procession upstream towards the shallows, coming down spent mostly between 3 and 4p.m. Amazing spectacle.' A few trout and many chub were rising, but it was interesting to note that most of the surface activity occurred not when the grannom were hatching, but while they drifted down spent around mid-afternoon. My catch was modest enough, although it included a five-pound chub, but next year the trout had better watch out!

On 29 April, unaccustomed to finding an evening rise in progress so early in the year, I was idling my time without a rod on the Wylye above Great Wishford when I was fortunate enough to witness the largest concentration of small spinners I've ever seen at this season. As if redressing the balance after a series of dry years during which ephemerids had declined sharply, nature produced 'hundreds upon hundreds of large olives, medium olives, blue-winged olives and small spurwings, plus clouds of tiny gnats, all flying quickly upriver, then massing around Kingsmead bridge and floating away at dusk towards the numerous rising trout.' I was surprised, to say the least, for one entomologist whose views I have never questioned has written that the female large olive spinner is seldom seen on the water, while some still believe the BWO only appears after mid-June. But insects don't read books, and seem to delight in breaking the rules on occasion. Either way, I shall be on the lookout for a repeat performance next season, and will have appropriate artificials to hand – and my rod.

One phenomenon that no longer catches me out, although I meet many dumbfounded anglers each year who have been bamboozled by it, is the curious second mayfly period that occurs in a few regions of Britain. On some streams in my area we have quite strong hatches at the end of July and in early August. In unsettled, rainy conditions especially, these can bring on a general rise of trout in the middle of the dog days, that includes the largest fish. This late summer mayfly hatch has given me some wonderful opportunities, with trout of 4 lb 13 oz and 3 lb 4 oz in the bag, and my early frustrations at not having a suitable pattern have led me to carry both dun and spinner dressings throughout the season today.

It has been suggested by some that our knowledge of trout and the insects they eat is now so extensive that there is little more to discover and 'it's all been said before'. I find this far from true, for it seems to me that almost every fishing day raises yet more intriguing questions to be answered.

❧ 8 ❧

Trout Streams at Bluebell Time

It's as well that I like to rise early, for the dawn chorus is under way just after 4a.m. at this season. And this was the start of a busy week, piscatorially speaking, in which I would cover nearly a thousand miles and explore five different rivers in widely varying geological regions.

My first port of call was Alveley, north of Kidderminster, where I was to pick up my pal John before driving to the river Lugg, just over the Welsh border near Presteigne. Here we found the stream in fine order, with a succession of twinkling shallows hurrying into picturesque, shaded pools; club members had been out clearing during the winter, wisely leaving sufficient shelter for the trout yet enough room for the stalking angler to make a horizontal cast beneath the trees. Although it was nearly mid-May, a few large dark olives were jinking merrily down the first stickle. The trout were accustomed to this daily feast and rose to the big duns in determined fashion, as if sensing that the hatching season of this species would soon be over. My freshly-tied pattern, featuring a mixture of grey/green seal's fur, primrose silk and five turns of blue dun hackle proved most effective, taking three beautifully marked, wide-tailed trout of ten or eleven inches in the first half-dozen chucks.

This was just the start I needed after my long journey. Now, thoroughly relaxed, I could enjoy wading quietly upstream beneath hawthorn and willow in the spring sunshine, with the swell of birdsong all about, picking up a trout here and there: in the ripples, along the margins and from dark, mysterious deeps. The diary records a dozen to my rod, with John catching a similar number, and in the evening we had two each for our supper, fried with mushrooms, and something to wash them down.

The following morning I bade John farewell and drove down to Usk, where I collected my ticket for the Town water and made my way to a parking spot upstream, close by the river. It's no bad thing to arrive early on the Usk, for a strong rise often occurs in the mornings at this time of year. Today, little was doing as yet, so I sat on a log and watched the grey wagtails bobbing about the margins while a pair of buzzards soared gracefully over nearby woods.

My daydream was broken by a splashy rise five yards ahead, but the fish was a 'oncer' and wouldn't come again. Then a sprinkling of medium olives appeared, encouraging two or three other fish to move at the surface. A good trout showed in the cushion immediately above a rock which jutted out from the near bank. Rise forms on the Usk are sometimes difficult to spot, but this fish was lying in relatively untroubled water. He rose again, this time to a smaller version of my Olive Dun, and sped down river into the turbulent current below. With 3-lb nylon I could afford to put on side strain, guiding the fish into a quiet backwater where the net performed its rightful duty. This trout weighed 1 lb 3 oz for his 14 in., a good one for the Usk, which usually furnishes an average of under 12 oz.

I was due at Stoodleigh in Devon for supper, so I made my way back to the M4 and onto the westbound M5 via the Severn Bridge. After a grand evening with old friends and relatives, and a dreamless sleep, I was raring to go the following morning – this time to Club water on the middle Exe. My start was delayed, for as I sat among the bluebells an otter appeared on the far bank. He sniffed the air and moved silently forward, followed by four playful cubs and the second adult at the rear. Greatly moved, I watched this innocent domestic scene for several minutes until the group departed. I had never seen a whole family before, and may never do so again.

With the scent of wild garlic filling my nostrils I made my way upriver, where half a dozen trout made rings on the gentle tree-lined pool. These fish were feeding on tiny reed smuts, too small to imitate, but the Olive was still on my point from the previous day and they accepted this readily enough. Of the six steady risers, five reached for my fly but only three connected, and another fish came from a speculative shot to a likely lie. Returning two ten inchers, and keeping a brace weighing 12 oz and 14 oz, I felt it was time to raid the sandwich box. Only an hour and a half had elapsed, yet I had enjoyed so many delightful incidents. As I dozed off, I thought of all the anglers who are searching for some kind of utopia. But our priorities are becoming so confused I wondered how many would recognize it.

Next day I visited a delightful stretch of the upper Torridge some thirty miles to the west. The last time I was here had been in August, fishing through to the early hours for the tearing, leaping peal. On balance, I enjoy hunting brown trout more than the chancy business of sea trout fishing at night, for all that the latter give you a fight you can never forget. I look for relaxing sport nowadays, and the opportunity to savour the wondrous sights and sounds of unspoiled valleys. On such streams in May you can cast as much or as little as you please to trout that are ever willing to rise, or simply sit and watch the glories of nature unfold before you. This day was quite idyllic, so that the catching of fish became almost incidental. The diary cannot adequately record such delights, but it reveals that my catch was nine trout for the day, four of which were received gratefully by my generous hosts.

Back on the Avon the mayfly was in full swing. Where the hatches are especially prolific, as they are around Amesbury, it pays to begin at midday before the trout have taken their fill. One fish was making a heavy swirl each time a dun came over him. He rose to my fly twice, but I failed to get a touch. When the fish boiled a third time the hook bit home, and he came to the net without much of a fight. I was surprised to discover it was a big grayling, a fish I seldom catch at mayfly time. Lacking the purple sheen of autumn, this was clearly a cock fish just recovering after spawning, and he went back to regain condition.

Trout were sipping down the large duns, making little more disturbance than they do when taking smuts. You have to give the fish time before striking when they behave like this, and even then they can be mighty difficult to hook. I pricked three good trout, which flopped off, and returned two smaller fish before setting the hook into a strong trout which tore line from the reel as he rushed towards the far bank. Dense ranunculus beds made it imperative that I play him hard, bullying the trout away from one weed patch, then another, each time reeling in madly to keep up the pressure and bring the fish yard by yard across the stream. By this time a group of my Salisbury and District AC friends had gathered to watch the fun and offer what I'm sure they meant to be constructive advice. As the fish showed his flank I hurried him into the net with a positive sweep of the rod, admiring the big red spots of a wild Avon two-pounder.

Driving home over the chalk downs, it occurred to me that, despite our technical advances, fly fishing remains so simple a pleasure. We see dramatic changes about us, both in economic and sporting attitudes, in management techniques, tackle design and tactical matters, and yet the essence of our sport is ever changeless.

ᔥ 9 ᔣ
Chalk-stream Baptism

Britain's motorway network enables us to explore areas we hardly dreamed of fishing two or three decades ago. My southern friends think nothing of travelling to Scotland in pursuit of salmon, or popping over to Wales for the sea trout, while all sorts and conditions of men and women converge on the world famous trout streams of the central south. This influx of fly fishers with fresh ideas has been healthy, for in piscatorial terms the Wessex region had become somewhat isolated, even blinkered. Yet now that the more rigid principles of the exact-imitation dry-fly school have gone, along with the knee-pad and shooting stick, I wonder whether some of those newcomers, themselves adhering to established techniques which evolved elsewhere, are failing to take full advantage of the wonderful opportunities these rivers can offer.

It used to be said that a budding chalk-stream fisherman should always serve his apprenticeship on other waters before daring to venture onto hallowed ground. Perhaps this idea was put about in order to discourage the masses, or simply because the incumbents did not want youngsters scaring their fish. Either way, I could not disagree more, for one of the major difficulties most of us face – having gone through the learning process on reservoirs, small stillwaters, spate rivers or meandering brooks – is then to modify our style and approach to meet a whole new set of conditions. Some of those conditions may be more challenging, some less so, but they are different. Suddenly, as we reach Marlborough or Salisbury, we find that nature has shifted the goalposts.

I recall seeking the advice of an acknowledged chalk-stream expert when I first came to these parts. He was one of those infuriating people who seem able to saunter out for half an hour and come back with a couple of fine trout after I've been labouring all day in vain.

'Well,' he said 'there's nothing wrong with your tackle or your casting, and those flies look OK. Maybe you are just not temperamentally suited to this game.' That comment hit me for six! It seemed almost insulting. And yet, as time passed and I watched others at work and tried to analyse my own performance, those words began to take on new meaning.

My early years on the rain-fed Box Brook, near Bath, had taught me how to study the contours of the stream, and so judge where trout were likely to be lying. I discovered that by systematically covering such areas with a dry fly or nymph I could induce fish to come up, even when no flicker of a fin was to be seen. Depending on my work rate and the number of hours I fished, I might catch up to ten or fifteen, even twenty wild trout in a day. Then, on the broken waters of the Usk, Exe and Torridge, I would simply cast out my wet flies, without attempting to conceal my presence, and let the currents carry them downstream over promising lies. I did not possess the skills of many, but the law of averages saw to it that I usually got some fish. While accuracy and delicacy of presentation would have improved my results, no doubt, I confess that neither appeared especially important, here or on the lakes I visited.

When I came to the Avon, Itchen and Test, and their tributaries, I found that much of my past experience was of limited value; indeed my methods were often counter productive. These rivers follow a relatively straight course, and apart from man-made structures, there were no rock outcrops or boulders to squeeze and push the currents this way and that, so the flows were pretty uniform from bank to bank. There were therefore comparatively few discernible lies, few natural pools and eddies, and the fish were more widely distributed over the width of the river. Since food was plentiful, the trout were seldom inclined to move more than a few inches from their chosen position and seemed to spend longer periods at rest. Moreover, when I did find a fish rising, or could see one nymphing in the clear water, it had the unfriendly habit of departing swiftly as soon as I came into view.

It was clear from the outset that fortune would play little part in fishing such water, and the law of averages would hardly enter the equation. I tried searching possible lies beneath the trees, or in the run against the far bank, but the trout were either not there or not interested in feeding. All I succeeded in doing was spooking fish out from the near margin, or there would be a bow-wave as my line fell close to those in midstream. Of course I told myself that the trout were gut

shy, or that I had the wrong fly on, but in my heart I knew these were
merely excuses. The fact was that the higher my work rate, the fewer
unsuspecting, and therefore catchable, trout would remain on my
chosen beat.

Contrary though it was to my lively nature, I was going to have to
curb my enthusiasm and cut out the action-man stuff. I must first
locate the trout, individually – which meant watching the water
intently for feeding fish, sometimes for a long time – and then creep
into a concealed casting position from which I could cover the lower
of those I had marked down. Spotting the trout's whereabouts was
relatively easy when there was a general rise, although even then I had
to take care not to frighten any non-risers nearby. At other times the
fish would go into hiding, and one could swear there were no fish in
the river.

I figured it would be wise to try and time my arrival to coincide
with likely feeding periods. These I noted down in my diary whenever
a good rise or sub-surface movement of fish occurred. If there
appeared to be nothing doing, I would find a spot where conditions
allowed me to see under water at some depth, and watch carefully for
any trout which might be tempted with a weighted nymph. This kind
of observation was far more rewarding than walking up and down the
bank or casting speculatively, but more rewarding still was making
sure I was on station when my diary, or a more experienced fisherman,
or the sight of a spinner procession suggested that the trout's dinner
gong was about to sound. Utterly absorbed over shorter periods, I
thus remained keen and alert, with the reflexes finely honed, and often
caught more and larger trout as a result.

I have since been fortunate enough to meet some of the world's
finest clear-water fishermen from America, France, Denmark, Italy,
New Zealand and elsewhere. What they have in common goes much
deeper than a mastery of tackle or their skill at the fly-tying bench.
Each is a true hunter, like the natural predator that remains still, ever
watchful, poised to strike with deadly efficiency only when the odds
are in its favour. A low casts-to-takes ratio is the hallmark of a great
fly fisher. He expects to take a trout with every delivery, otherwise the
rod stays motionless and his quarry undisturbed until that critical
moment of opportunity.

It is no accident that a number of distinct fly fishing styles have
developed in these islands, for each evolved quite naturally to meet the
conditions found in our various geological regions. Our methods have

little to do with blind conformity, or purism, just plain common sense. I shall continue to revel in the freedom of pitching my flies on spec into jinking ripples and pregnant pools when I'm in the West Country or the Welsh borders, and feel for those electrifying pulls as I sink-and-draw on stillwaters. But on the crystal streams springing from the chalk downlands ... well, I'm off to get myself a knee-pad and a shooting stick.

✍ 10 ଈ

Jewels of the Downland

While the major chalk streams are among the most productive rivers in the world, I confess a sneaking preference for those spring-fed tributaries which contain natural stocks and remain relatively unpampered. It is true that parts of the upper Itchen, Avon, Wylye and others maintain wild trout populations, but to my mind the most exhilarating sport of all is often to be found on the smaller chalk streams and sparkling rivulets known as winterbournes.

Anglers are sometimes uncertain as to what winterbournes are, and how they differ from the man-made watercourses. Carriers, sidestreams, runnels and drawns are all relics of the old water-meadow systems, in which water was diverted from the main rivers through a network of channels to irrigate low-lying fields. Irrigation for grass or crop production is seldom practised today, but many of these narrower waterways are kept open and cherished as trout waters. Usually running parallel to the parent river, they flow out of the main stream, via sets of hatch-gates, and join it again further down the valley. Winterbournes, on the other hand, are natural chalk streams in their own right. With an individual source high up on the downs, each follows its ancient course carved at the end of the ice age. Unlike the carriers and other artificial streams, winterbournes rely almost entirely upon spring water issuing from underground reserves in the chalk. As these reserves are depleted in summer, so the upper reaches become dry (hence the name), but under normal conditions the middle or lower reaches continue to flow throughout the season.

These little rivers are the very life-blood of the chalk-stream systems, supplementing flows with the purest water and acting as the principal nurseries from which watersheds are naturally stocked. This is not always apparent where rivers receive introductions of stew fish, but as levels on the winterbournes rise in late autumn and the native

45

trout are seen following their centuries-old path upstream, we realize what a vital role they play in the survival of wild populations. Salmon spawn here too, and some contain grayling, although coarse fish are seldom present, save for the occasional pike.

These jewels of the chalklands vary considerably in their size, the degree to which they become dry in their upper reaches, and to some extent in their geological make up. However, they are almost invariably as clear as crystal and teeming with aquatic life. Weed growth is prolific, with crustacea often more abundant than on major rivers. The weight and condition of trout can be quite remarkable, comparing more than favourably with those of the larger chalk streams.

Fish can be spotted without difficulty when one has learned how and where to look, enabling the angler to stalk them individually from a low crouching position at the margin, or by slow, heron-like wading. On stretches that flow between high banks, or are heavily bushed, a rod of 6 ft or less may be required, but a 7–8 ft rod is normally quite suitable. Short-range casting is often called for, in which a slightly heavier line weight is useful, with a relatively short leader of 8–8½ ft, tapering to a 3-ft point of around 3-lb breaking strain. Standard chalk-stream dry flies and nymphs will suffice, although where the quarry are wild, imitative patterns may prove more successful than the 'fancies' sometimes employed to lure recent stockies.

An accurate first cast is the ideal; three casts may be too many, causing a fish to bolt for cover. If a trout runs upstream, others in the vicinity usually sense danger. They may simply freeze, sink fractionally in the water, or inch closer to the nearest weedbed. Either way, any movement by the angler now can spell disaster. Two or three fish shoot forward, then another, and before we know it we've cleared the entire area. It is tempting to explore further upstream, but as we move ahead yet more trout may take flight. Better to remain perfectly still, perhaps for five to ten minutes, or until the fish are back and feeding again with total confidence. This game needs a lot of patience, and limbs may become cramped, but the satisfaction of securing a trout or two in such challenging conditions can be immense.

Access to a number of stretches may be readily obtained; others, which flow through farmland or private ground and may be virtually unfished, are worthy of investigation and polite enquiry. You can still rent short lengths cheaply, or get a day's free fishing, but as elsewhere this requires a degree of initiative. Clubs or syndicates such as the Ebble Valley Conservation FA, Gillingham AC and Salisbury and

District AC manage excellent stretches of the Ebble, Shreen and Bourne, while day tickets are available for the Upper Anton (Rooksbury Mill), Dun (Holbury Lane Fishery), Tillingbourne (Albury Estates), Upper Dever (Dever Springs), Sweatfords Water (Rockbourne), and Piddle (Wessex Fly Fishing) among others. Ticket waters are often stocked, though native trout will also be present; those controlled by clubs and private owners are usually full of wild fish averaging 12–14 oz, with a few reaching 2–3 lb.

As one watches young trout fry in the limpid shallow, their parents hovering nearby, and we note the eternal springs bubbling forth in the stream bed, one can spot among ancient flints the fossils of sea creatures deposited there in the long-forgotten past. Before me as I write I have a perfectly formed Micraster taken from the bed of the River Till which dates back 70–100 million years. The elemental forces are doubly apparent here, where the life forms of the chalk streams have their distant origin. It is not surprising, I think, that those who understand the nature of these fragile waters should be so protective of them against the ravages of modern man.

༒ 11 ༒
Where the Five Rivers Meet

Since its inception in 1941, when six local fishermen rented a length of the Wiltshire Bourne and a small lake nearby, the Salisbury and District AC has flourished to become one of the largest fishing clubs in Britain. With over twenty-five miles of river fishing and six lakes, members have an almost unlimited choice of waters: from lower Avon salmon beats, prime trout and grayling stretches on the upper Avon, Nadder, Wylye, Ebble and Bourne, to fine coarse fisheries on the Nadder, Avon and Dorset Stour.

The club's original resolve to provide unrestricted access to top-quality waters at reasonable cost has been carefully maintained, allowing many who would otherwise be unable to afford chalk-stream fishing to enjoy some of the best sport in the south. The club could have become as exclusive as others have done simply by increasing subscriptions and taking on few members. It could, with all this water, have become a highly profitable commercial concern, rather than operating on a break-even basis, ploughing any surplus back into fisheries and investing wisely on behalf of its members.

As it is, the fees are set so low as to seem positively overgenerous in this day and age. A full member, having access to all stretches and fishing whenever he chooses (365 days if he is able), pays just £90 for the year 1998. Senior citizens and juniors (12–16 years) qualify for a considerable reduction, while those not fishing on designated trout waters pay £50. The registration fee for new members stands at £15 for seniors and £5 for juniors.

Although the club has over 1,400 members as I write, more than seventy-five per cent of whom are game fishermen, the modest subscription rates and anytime access help to ensure that a number of stretches remain relatively lightly fished. Where fisheries restrict anglers to a single day per week or fortnight, and charge perhaps

£1,000 or more for the season, you can bet that few miss their prearranged outing, and each length thus receives continual pressure. Moreover, many of us have fishing on other waters yet retain our membership of the Salisbury Club as a delightful, inexpensive alternative. Some have joined just for the grayling fishing, which is considered to be some of the finest in the world.

Of course a fishing club, particularly a chalk-stream club, is only as good as the management policies it pursues. Chalk streams require constant attention, both in the care of stream-bed habitats and river banks, control of poachers and trespassers, sensitive balancing of stock levels, and the removal of harmful predators. Such responsibilities rest with Alex Amos, the Club Chairman, and General Secretary Ron Hillier, backed by Con Evans, the Treasurer, and a Committee of up to ten elected members, all working under the Presidency of Mr Tony Snook, a founder member of the Club. On the practical side a network of part-time bailiffs appointed to the various fisheries carry out much of the policing work and bank clearance under the overall direction of Laurie Stokes, the full-time keeper.

Laurie took on the post nine years ago when he moved down from Fleet Street, having been a member for twelve years before that. 'There was so much work to be done I hardly knew where to start,' he told me. The stews had to be completely rebuilt, bridges replaced and eroded banks filled in. Trees needed felling or dragging out of the river, and there were groynes to be put in place to narrow channels and increase flow-rates. Mowing, trimming, removing fallen fencing, clearing choked ditches, erecting signs – you name it and Laurie had to do it, in addition to regular tasks such as stocking, weed-cutting and keeping in touch with his team of bailiffs.

Much influenced by the writings of Frank Sawyer, Laurie has learned his keepering the hard way, hands-on fashion and in a remarkably short time. 'You manage to keep busy then?' I asked foolishly – with twenty-five miles of river and 1,400 members it could hardly be otherwise. But now he is settled into his house with his wife Mo and with three fly-fishing sons, he is a happy man. As he says 'Mo's a useful under-keeper; she's out stocking with me tomorrow. All my interests lie in the country. A bit of fishing, a bit of shooting, studying nature, insects, bird life. It beats the smoke every time.'

Given the lack of any formal vetting of applicants, it is encouraging to find standards of behaviour and general sportsmanship are high on these waters. All sorts and conditions of men and women come here. Generals and surgeons rub shoulders with cabbies, secretaries and supermarket staff, all equals when faced with a feeding trout. We fish dry fly only until 30 June on most of the trout waters, after which the upstream nymph may be used, and the daily bag limits are two trout and two grayling of over ten inches. Each member receives a yearbook detailing all the fisheries, including maps, at the start of every new season.

The following short profile of waters I know best, together with some random observations, may be of interest.

River Avon

Stratford and Town Waters, Salisbury. About two miles of main stream and carrier fishing. Mixed fishery with wild trout averaging ¾ lb. Dry fly, nymph or wet fly permitted throughout the season. Heavy grannom hatches in April, and fine sedge fishing at late evening, June to August. Winter grayling fishing with fly or bait until 14 March.

Durnford Fishery, Salisbury. Nearly three miles, mostly double bank. Main river and carrier fishing. Regularly stocked with brown trout up to 2 lb, with larger fish present. Record 8½ lb taken in 1986. Eighteen numbered beats available on a 'help yourself' disc system. Mayfly hatches starting mid-May, falls of black gnat in warmer conditions, and a good evening rise after sunset.

West Amesbury Fishery. Over two miles, mostly double bank. Fine head of native trout and grayling, supplemented by stocking. Excellent hatches of small fly, and heavy mayfly starting 8–10 May. Free-rising water throughout the season. Accompanied guests Monday–Friday, £15. Fly fishing for grayling continues to 31 December.

Countess and Ratfyn Fisheries, Amesbury. Two miles, mostly double bank. Good fly hatches with a heavy mayfly starting 8–10 May. Mixed population of wild and stocked trout, and many grayling. Fly or bait fishing for grayling continues on Countess only until 14 March.

River Nadder

Barford St Martin. A short, productive length accommodating three rods on a disc system. Excellent trout fishing, especially at late evening in summer. Few grayling present. Alternate shallows and deep pools, with good hatches of small flies and falls of land-bred insects. Wild trout supplemented by limited stocking.

Constable Fishery, Salisbury (includes part R. Avon). Nearly three miles of water, partly double-bank. Mixed fishery with large coarse-fish population. Dry fly, nymph, wet fly or spinning for trout, most of which are wild. Heavy hatches of grannom in April. Winter grayling fishing with fly or bait to 14 March.

River Wylye

Stapleford Water, Stapleford. Nearly one mile, single bank fishing. Fine head of native trout and grayling, supplemented by stocking. Free-rising water with excellent fly hatches, particularly blue-winged olive after mid-June. Mayfly season begins late May. Tremendous evening rise to sherry spinner and sedge, June to August. Limited to six rods on disc system. Fly fishing for grayling continues to 14 March.

River Bourne

Hurdcott, near Salisbury. Half a mile of crystal-clear winterbourne. Wild trout and grayling only, the trout averaging 10–13 in. with occasional larger fish. Trout feed very freely, but the challenging water requires a cat-like approach. Good hatches of upwinged duns and falls of land-bred insects. No mayfly hatch.

River Ebble

Bishopstone and Knighton. Three separate stretches totalling to some two miles available on disc system. Wild trout and grayling only, of good average size. Members are encouraged to return fish. Highly challenging waters, but trout rise well to small duns and spinners, especially during April and May.

Stillwaters

Ratfyn Lake, Amesbury. This small stillwater accommodates a total of six rods. Disc system operates. Regularly stocked with rainbow trout which feed well at or near surface level. Fly only, maximum length ¾ in. including the dressing.

I asked Laurie to sum up. How does he see the club's future, and its fishing? 'Things look healthy all round,' he replied. 'There's no denying that a combination of drought and water abstraction has lowered river levels considerably, but the quality of the sport remains consistently high. Additional stretches on the Ebble, Nadder and Avon have created a lot more work, but I get a good deal of help and advice from the Environmental Agency, and a number of the members are happy to put in a day's graft. Two of the hatchways at Durnford have just been rebuilt, and we've completed a major habitat-improvement project at West Amesbury. We turned up ten salmon on the upper Avon while electro-fishing for pike. All our rivers to the north and west of Salisbury seem to be stiff with trout and grayling. Yes, you can say my ambitions have been realized. This is a great club in a glorious part of the country, and I can't think of a more satisfying way of life.'

ᷔ 12 ᷓ

Carnival Time in Wiltshire

I have never allowed work, social functions or affairs of the heart to interfere with my fishing, certainly when the mayfly is up. In fact I've not missed this magical phase of the trout fisher's year since 1963, managing to be on the water during most of May and June throughout these many seasons. Of course, when fishing takes over your life to this extent you can end up lonesome, penniless, even something of an outcast – but, boy, are there compensations!

In 1995 I began my campaign on the main Wiltshire Avon at Lords Walk, a deep, narrow length two miles east of Stonehenge. Hatches start early in this area, with the trout coming well to surface duns by around 8–10 May. Today, 13 May, the fish were eagerly taking mayflies in cool, cloudy conditions when I arrived at 2p.m., and the trees along the far, left bank afforded some shelter against a brisk easterly wind.

Four trout were rising within range of my customary starting point, just above the Amesbury slip road from the A303. I knew I'd sink up to my knees in the boggy margin if I tackled the two fish lying under the opposite bank, but they looked to be sizeable and well worth the struggle. The back cast is difficult here, due to the presence of a large bush, but an inelegant switch somehow deposited the fly on its hackle tips close to the reeds, to be engulfed seconds later by a bonny native of some 12 in. As I tried to cover the second fish my fly caught up behind , which involved a tiresome wallow through the mud and a tip-toe job among the foliage before I could get back to work. Abandoning the switch cast I managed to place the fly near the bank via an overhanging reed stem by employing a low, horizontal cast which repeatedly clipped the surface to my rear. Not textbook stuff by any means, but effective. The fish reached for it, shot downstream, and leapt with a resounding smack in the darkness under the road bridge. I believe in using as heavy a nylon point as I can get away with (in this case 4 lb), so I soon persuaded the trout to join me and my landing net, despite two more displays of aerobatics on the way. Another glorious wild trout, with big red spots so characteristic of the Avon strain, this one measured 14 in. for his 1 lb 2 oz.

Freeing myself from the morass, I scrambled into a more comfortable position behind an unkempt willow just upstream, beneath whose trailing fronds two further trout were rising consistently. The nearer fish appeared quite small, but he had to be caught or otherwise removed, lest he should warn the larger one ahead. Fortunately he rose first chuck, and I was able to release a bright little ten-incher below me. The next cast was not so easy; it involved shooting under low-slung branches and then executing a curve to the left, so as to place the fly above another branch which dipped into the water. By arresting the line sharply as it extended, however, and with a little help from a friendly gust of wind, I pitched the artificial six inches to the right of the fish, which quickly grabbed it and rocketed into deep water almost before I could tighten on him. I had to play the trout hard, as weedbeds grow thickly in this spot, and there was no way I could wade in if he became entangled. This one scaled 1 lb 3 oz, making up two brace caught from twenty yards of water inside thirty-five minutes.

Several more trout were feeding ahead, but I decided to move on as far as the weir, in case a big one should be showing further upriver. I spotted no particularly large fish – a two-pounder is a real prize on the upper Avon – but succeeded in losing two middling-sized trout and returning two others of 11–12 in., along with a couple of grayling. All in all a good two-hour session I reckoned, with six trout landed, two of which came back for supper – and this from an open-membership angling club length where coarse fishers operate all winter.

Next day I fished just above South Mill on the club's West Amesbury water, where, against the bowl of a large willow on the far bank, a brown neb broke surface repeatedly, and dun after dun disappeared in a ring so tiny it might easily have gone unnoticed. My Mayfly pattern joined the procession of natural flies and went under at the second or third offer, only to come back fishless as the result of an ill-timed strike. The trout ceased rising, but I guessed he was keen to enjoy this veritable feast and would soon reappear. Meantime a string of trout in the sheltered bay above were asking for trouble. I wish I could tell you how selective or ultra-cautious they were, but in truth every one I covered properly took with enthusiasm. Two were stock fish weighing 1¼ and 1½ lb, another was a 1-lb native, and the fourth came unstuck at the net.

My friend under the willow had resumed feeding, so I crept back to my original position, giving the fish a few minutes to get into a regular rhythm before drifting the fly down his feed-lane. This time the hook bit home and a heavy trout bored deep, the leader getting held up in some unseen snag. Imparting as much side strain as I dared, with the rod held parallel to the surface, I managed to coax the fish downstream and out into the current, whereupon he buried himself in a nearby weedbed. Again I felt the jagging leader, but I had to risk everything before the line became immovable. Increased pressure from the rod brought my trout to the surface, luckily with a piece of river weed wrapped about his head; this effectively blinded the fish, which had little control over the subsequent proceedings. Only 16½ in. long, he scaled just over the magic 2 lb mark: as beautiful a native trout as I've ever seen.

After all this excitement it seemed hardly credible that it was still only mid-May, well before the mayfly period begins on some rivers close by. While the main hatches start about 15 May on the middle Test, those on the Kennet and Nadder would be approaching their height a week or more later, and those on the lower Wylye around the first or second week in June. Thus, by dodging from one river to another, I can extend my mayfly season from two weeks to five weeks. June the fifth and twelfth found me guesting on the Itchen above Winchester, where seven trout up to 2 lb 14 oz came to net, all on mayfly, but one of my most enjoyable days was spent on a public stretch of carrier fishing that branches from the River Wylye just five minutes' drive from home.

Some will tell you the carnival is over by 17 June, yet on this day, in cloudy conditions and with a fresh westerly wind, the fly came off in short flurries, bringing bursts of feeding activity between 2.45 and 5.30p.m. I crouched among the trees at the bottom end, but three young lads with float tackle soon flushed me out, and it was grand to see their faces light up as they began to understand what fly fishing is all about. I had them spotting rise forms for me, having learned how to move slowly and keep their heads down, while to hear something about the life cycle of mayflies and to watch the insects hatching from the shuck was a revelation. I returned five trout and a grayling, explaining that these would spawn and produce offspring in due season, and took three measuring some 12 in. apiece – one each seemed fair enough, and the river could spare them. I'll bet the boys' fathers had to fend off repeated requests for new gear that night, while their mums doubtless performed culinary miracles for the three budding fly fishers.

So the world keeps turning as new seasons come and go. As long as these streams keep producing such trout and nurturing all the aquatic life that makes up a healthy food chain, and as long as dedicated youngsters emerge to replace those who have gone before, then future generations will experience fresh peaks of delight when springtime turns to summer.

◌◔ 13 ◑◌

In the Heart of the Cotswolds

On 30 June 1968 I enjoyed an enchanted day on the little river Leach, which winds its way south through Cotswold limestone country before joining the Thames near Lechlade. This looked a perfect gem of a stream, full of wild trout, with numerous sharp bends and pools linked by sparkling gravel runs where fish hovered among bright ranunculus and starwort beds. Most were easy to spot in the clear water, and as easily put down by any sudden movement. My host, Ronnie Theakston, had drawn me a detailed map of the water, but in these circumstances the angler must advance so slowly and cautiously that it seemed doubtful that I would see much of it. Indeed the best part of the day was nearly over by the time I had reached the first stand of willows, but the sport with these little trout was utterly absorbing.

Few fish were rising, yet the sub-surface activity had been such that my Pheasant-tail Nymph was seized with enthusiasm whenever I presented it properly. Sadly this did not happen very often, and I remember thinking that a really skilful nymph fisherman could well have caught a couple of dozen from this short length. I watched help-lessly as several good trout went to cover, usually due to line shadow. Then, having added a four-foot point of fine nylon, I managed to secure a fish that measured 11¼ in. and had a partially healed heron stab across its back, and returned two bonny trout of around 10 in.

Up near the willows I spotted a number of larger trout, hooking two near-pounders which came unstuck and frightening others. I had cleared the area by now, but decided to wait in the hope that some would return and resume feeding. Soon I saw two fish back down-stream out of the shade and take up station in front of a weedbed. I held my hand a while longer, pitching the nymph well ahead of the nearer trout only when I sensed that both had fully regained confidence.

The nymph was about to pass a foot to the trout's left, so I imparted slight movement from the rod-tip to lift the fly fractionally in the water. The fish turned swiftly, opened and closed its mouth and was on. Risking a break I pulled the trout sharply towards me, praying that his neighbour over to the right would remain in position, and bundled him into the net as quick as a flash. This one weighed 14 oz for his 12¼ in, as plump and pretty a trout as I ever saw. Number two was still on the go, and this time the nymph came down so accurately as virtually to 'spoon feed' the fish. It did little more than lift an inch in the water, but I was learning fast and reacted instantly to this minor indication, setting the hook firmly home. The trout rocketed beneath the willows, making the reel sing, but I held him on a tight line as he tumbled towards the net, still full of fight. The scale pulled down to the magic one pound mark, and the ruler recorded his length at 13 in. exactly.

Ronnie was overjoyed by my modest success, although as an old hand I suspected he had fared better and bolted fewer fish than I. He told me of a large, dark trout further upstream which he wanted me to catch. The fish was feeding when we reached the spot, swaying this way and that in the centre of a small weir pool, and appeared to be well in excess of 1¼ lb. I cast the nymph some three yards ahead of the trout, but since it was difficult to judge the fly's whereabouts among the conflicting currents it was necessary to strike at any possible take, just in case. This I did a dozen or more times without making contact, and Ronnie did the same with a similar lack of response. When it was my turn again I hooked him at the third or fourth cast, but he kicked once and was off. Surprisingly, the trout immediately returned to its lie and continued to sway back and forth as before, but after a few more chucks we gave him best. I had my doubts whether the fish was in the best of condition, and wondered if he might have been blind or nearly so. It was a pity that I failed to land this old warrior, for he would clearly have been better killed at once than suffer the lingering fate which I felt sure awaited him.

If, when I am old and past my prime, I'm offered the chance to relive some of my happier fishing days, then the lovely little Leach, along with her better-known sisters the Coln and the Windrush, will be very near the top of my list.

༦ 14 ༧

Early Days on the Kennet

Making that first tentative delivery on hallowed water can be challenging enough, but to do so under the critical gaze of a hardened chalk-stream keeper was daunting in the extreme. Dennis Lofts had accompanied many skilled performers on the upper Kennet, and knew a duffer when he saw one. I was a new boy on the Savernake stretch; this was my big test, and I knew that if ever I had to get it right it was now.

Denis watched as I assembled my gear, tied on the trusty Hares Ear, and crept into position a few yards downstream. 'Sip' went the trout as I lengthened line over the glassy glide, and 'sip' again when my fly, aided by a friendly gust, settled ahead of the ring. The fish seemed to understand the importance of the occasion, for it took like a sportsman and shot out into midstream displaying all the antics of one expected to put on a show. It skittered and rolled and plummeted, in and out of the weedbeds, before deciding to make a wild dash for the open hatch gate some twenty yards below. I managed to avoid a break as I lowered the rod-tip, applied side strain, and coaxed the trout into a quiet bay where Denis, with the adroitness born of a thousand similar incidents, dipped my handsome prize ashore. Much to my disappointment he pronounced the fish to be 'a bit small' and slipped it quickly back whence it had come, but we exchanged warm smiles and I knew I had passed my initial examination.

Having driven back to the keeper's cottage and chatted awhile over coffee with Denis and his wife Doreen – the first of many such happy interludes – I was free to fish up the broad reach from Stitchcombe Bridge to Durnsford Mill. The Kennet produced some wonderful fly hatches in the 1960s, and today (16 April 1967) a procession of large dark olives came sailing down the stream around 1p.m., causing the trout to 'lock on' well, each in its chosen station. Accurate presentation was vital since so many natural insects were available that the fish didn't need to go searching (indeed I found my fly was ignored even when it passed within 3–4 in.).

Now, casting across the river, the breeze which had helped me to catch that first trout became something of a nightmare as I repeatedly failed to present the fly on the correct line. I noticed two or three rises close to my bank, the right, where the wind would once more be my ally, so, leaving the fish in midstream and along the far margin, I moved upriver and approached them. In fact there were four trout rising here, only a yard or so apart. Predictably, the lower fish proved to be the smaller, at 9 in., the next half an inch longer, and the third 10 in. The topmost trout took one look at my Hare's Ear and fled, but it was good to see so many small wild fish present. Later I learned to distinguish undersized trout from sizeable fish, by their rise forms or by the lie they occupy, but I had yet to adjust fully to the more selective approach normally employed on chalk streams; if it moved I chucked, without realizing that the law of averages seldom applies here.

Just below Durnsford hatches I spotted a number of rising trout. The river was shallower here, enabling me to wade out and cover those lying in awkward spots. One fish, visibly larger, was stationed above a thick patch of water buttercup, and another below and on the far side of the weedbed. Tackling the lower one first, I found that the cushion effect created by the obstruction caused the fly to drag at once, but that by wading two yards upstream I was able to place the line on top of the weed and away from the quicker current. Even so, I had only a foot of free drift, but with a slack delivery I could increase it to two feet. At the fourth attempt the Hare's Ear floated down just right, and a lively trout plunged into the mass of vegetation in a split-second. I felt the jar of a well-weeded fish, so waded across and commenced prodding the critical area with the landing net. The leader snapped and my trout was gone – a good trout too. But I had learned a valuable lesson: always to get the net, or hand or boot, beneath the weed growth and lift it, never to go in from above.

The trout at the head of the weed raft looked an easier target, but, here again, the flow acting on the line was faster than that where the fish was lying. The only way to overcome the resulting drag was to inch closer to my quarry while extending the arm well forward on the delivery stroke. I had to move much nearer to the trout than I would have wished, risking a spook, but luckily the fish accepted the first good offering and ran upriver, rather than down into the weed as I had feared. This one would certainly have provided a delicious supper, at 12 in., but here on the Kennet I guessed it was 'a bit small', so back it went.

In an area of slack water near my bank a brown neb appeared like clockwork as the large dark olives vanished one by one. So did my Hare's Ear, but the trout put up a poor fight despite his 14¼ in. The fish had clearly spawned and deserved a break, needing time to regain condition. The hatch of fly was petering out now, so I made my way back to the cottage, without my supper but delighted with my first day on this new water. The season of 1967 brought me 217 trout caught from the Kennet, 110 from the Box Brook, 25 from the Usk, 17 from the Avon and Bourne in Wiltshire, and two from the Test, a total of 371. As to weights, the Avon produced two trout of 1 lb 14 oz, and the Kennet seven of over 1 lb 8 oz, the largest scaling 2 lb 1 oz. Happy days!

ᐸᕄ 15 ᕄᐳ
Holiday Time on the Teign

Many of Devonshire's finest rivers have their source within 2–3 miles of Whitehorse Hill in the wilds of northern Dartmoor, among them the Tavy, Taw, Dart, Okement (which enters the Torridge) and one of my personal favourites, the Teign. Renowned for its outstanding beauty, this enchanted valley hosts an abundance of wildlife, from the otter and deer to the soaring buzzard and the fisherman's constant companion, the dipper. Brown trout are here in profusion, and sea trout shoal in the pools at midsummer, while salmon ascend in good numbers when water levels allow.

Fed by extensive peat marshes the two infant Teigns, North and South, flow for their first few miles across open moorland before joining forces a mile or so to the west of Chagford; the North Teign is the more substantial stream, much of the South Teign's watershed being drained by Fernworthy Reservoir. The river then runs in a more or less easterly direction towards Castle Drogo. Here it enters the spectacular Fingle Gorge, a steep, heavily wooded ravine of breathtaking grandeur which offers anglers a classic series of sharp stickles and smooth gliding pools down to the village of Dunsford, some ten miles below the confluence. Here the Teign turns southward, following a somewhat broader course past Christow, Ashton and Chudleigh towards its estuary at Newton Abbot.

Much of the Teign lies within the Dartmoor National Park, a major tourist attraction where fishing is not the only popular pastime. Scenic walks, nature reserves and camp sites may be found along the valley, yet the disturbance to the angler is minimal. Indeed, those accompanied by their families can fish in the knowledge that the rest of the party will enjoy a delightful day in the most blissful surroundings.

For fishing purposes, the Teign divides naturally into two main sections controlled by the Upper Teign and Lower Teign Fishing

Associations (UTFA and LTFA), whose boundaries meet near Steps Bridge, just upstream of Dunsford. Many LTFA members concentrate upon migratory fish, and the salmon season opens on 1 February and that for sea trout on 15 March; the season for both ends on 30 September. These fish may be taken on fly or by spinning in the early months, or on worm from 1 June. In practice, few salmon are taken on the fly, yet this method can be highly productive for sea trout – the Silver Stoat wet fly being a great favourite on the Teign. Salmon average 8–10 lb in the spring run, with grilse around 4 lb appearing in June. Sea trout weighing 3–5 lb are regularly landed.

While minor spates may occur after heavy rainfall, the Teign offers relatively stable water conditions compared with many hill and moorland streams. With Fernworthy Reservoir receiving much of the run-off from the southern catchment, and rain elsewhere being absorbed to some extent by the spongy marshland from which it later seeps, the river remains fishable for most of the season. Freshes are more common than outright spates, the water staying clear save for a tinge of sherry colour from the peat.

Brown trout are present in large numbers throughout the river, but it is generally agreed that the UTFA waters offer the cream of the fishing. Dry fly, nymph or wet fly may be used, the last proving more rewarding during the first six weeks of the season, which begins on 15 March. Thereafter, until 30 September, fish will be found rising below the stickles, in quiet runs at the edge of fast water, and in sheltered pockets along the margins. Hatches of upwinged duns may be relatively sparse, but falls of land-bred insects, particularly black gnats, occur on most days in summer, and wood ants, caterpillars, stoneflies and beetles feature in the trout's diet from time to time. Sedge flies hatch in considerable numbers, one of the most prolific being the grannom, whose appearance in the latter part of April and early May encourages some of the larger fish to begin feeding at the surface.

Size is relative, of course. Here, the Teign's acid nature means that trout are slow growing. A pounder is a very good fish, and the average length taken is around 8–10 in. Occasional trout of 2–3 lb are captured, usually by salmon or sea trout anglers, but the size limit of seven inches and bag limit of twelve trout reflect the upper Teign's capacity to produce a huge natural stock. Wading is necessary to cover the water effectively (felt-soled boots being the most suitable for added grip), but, this item apart, our normal trout tackle is likely to be adequate. The valley is well sheltered from the winds, and extra-long casting is seldom required.

Those accustomed to delaying the strike on other waters may miss nearly every take until an ultra-fast response has been developed; the fish rise like lightning, ejecting the fly in a split second. I still fail to connect with some fifty per cent of offers, never having mastered the quick tightening from the wrist that some have perfected. Not only is speed essential in the strike, so is lightness of touch, to avoid damage to the leader point, the hook or indeed the fish.

Permits to fish for brown trout on the UTFA water are available by the day, week or full season at a cost of £3, £12 and £27 respectively (1995) while anglers under sixteen pay £1, £5 and £10. Day tickets for salmon and sea trout cost £12 on the three miles of left bank from Chagford to Fingle Bridge. In addition James Bowden & Son, the tackle shop in Chagford, controls two short stretches at Chagford Weir, letting permits for salmon and sea trout at £5 per day. The main outlets for UTFA tickets are The Anglers Rest, a delightful restaurant at Fingle Bridge, and James Bowden & Son. The latter business has been run by the same family since 1863, and part of its premises is now devoted to a display depicting the old shop, together with tackle and other memorabilia from a bygone age.

The LTFA is limited to some sixty members, but tickets are available to visitors at £10 per day, to cover salmon, sea-trout and brown-trout fishing on one of three allocated beats on the lower Teign. One of the principal outlets for day tickets here is Drum Sports of Newton Abbot.

The M5 motorway takes anglers from the north and east to within fifteen miles of their destination, and these are covered quickly on the A30 Exeter–Okehampton dual carriageway. Then, driving along narrow lanes from Cheriton Bishop down into the Teign valley, you enter a magical, very different world, changeless these many centuries.

ન્ 16 ભ્

Mayfly Wrinkles

Mayfly fishing can be intensely exciting. Whether it is also rewarding often depends on how well we adapt our technique to cope with unfamiliar situations in which trout seem to break some of our accepted theories. Large fish may appear in spots where we least expect them, or they may indulge in a lot of 'oncing' or cruise widely in areas where trout normally remain on fixed station. Sometimes trout rise enthusiastically when few duns are hatching, yet refuse to budge when a mass of captive flies is available. I've fished almost every day in the mayfly period for thirty seasons past, yet, apart from learning a few minor wrinkles I cannot claim to have progressed much beyond first base in terms of understanding some of the more intriguing aspects of trout and fly behaviour.

One peculiar habit exhibited by mayflies is their tendency to emerge very rapidly from one river, causing trout to give up the chase, while on another they will linger on the surface for a considerable period, thus enabling fish to obtain an easy meal. This happens in identical weather conditions, and apparently regardless of surface density and flow-rate – so that when duns become airborne at once on the Wylye, for example, I sometimes nip over to the Avon to find them sitting on the water like gentlemen.

Regarding the unusual positions that trout take up, we should remember that mayflies hatch mostly from areas of silt and fine gravel close to the bank, where the nymphs congregate, and seldom from faster-flowing water. Flies which float down on the main current have often been blown from the margin, or have settled there after an unsuccessful attempt to take off. In rainy conditions they may flutter away in a series of six or eight hops, each time alighting again on the surface. Smaller trout in the main flow may grab at these more elusive insects, while larger fish occupy prime positions over the silt deposits where the nymphs emerge. Many a time I have cast to a trout in mid-river, only to disturb a big one as I approached the bank.

All is not lost when this happens, for half the battle at this time is locating the larger fish. When we know their lies we can creep back later and pop a fly over them. Likewise on days when only the occasional rise form is spotted, our chances of catching those fish are high, provided we have marked their position well. Even if the rise is seen from some distance, we can usually remember the spot by noting a grass stem, a flower on the bank or perhaps a strand of surface weed, and present the fly when we get within range. I remember the crafty old members of the Wilton Club on the Wylye twenty-five years ago, who would come down to stay in Great Wishford for three weeks, spending the first few days walking the river in order to note the lies of big trout. Then, drawing up a plan of action, each would systematically stalk a different stretch every day, sitting over known trout to await their feeding time. The heavier hatches usually begin around 3p.m. here, reaching their height at 5 or 5.30p.m., and most of the big Wylye trout are caught late in the afternoon, between 4 and 5.30p.m. However, if you go out at that time on rivers such as the Kennet or Avon the trout may have become gorged and ceased feeding.

Cruising fish can be exasperating, but they are often the larger ones. We should not get too close, but wait until we have determined the lower limit of their cruise path before approaching the bank, and cast only when we are fairly certain of the trout's whereabouts. Repetitive casting can be counter productive. Instead – and rather than reeling in each time between casts – we can lay the line on the grass behind, ready for an instant presentation when the fish shows.

✂ 17 ✂

Pieces of Heaven

The call of the cuckoo has a special message for the trout fisher, as if to remind us that nature is bursting at the seams, rivers are alive with promise, and we should be out there savouring every precious moment of it. Few of us need much persuading, given the opportunity. In 1994 I fished on thirty-two occasions during May and June, visiting nine rivers and one stillwater. I spent one or two guest days on limited-membership fisheries, others on public bits close to Salisbury, and some on hard-fished club and day-ticket waters, and the distinctions mattered not at all in terms of results or overall enjoyment. Indeed some of my most memorable outings featured the humblest stretches where few crack rods would care to be seen fishing.

One such, about 150 yards in length, flows beneath a large factory, with a car park on one side and a bowling green and playground on the other, down to the main road bridge carrying traffic into the city. Since the fishing is free, boys gather here with worms, bread and spinning gear, while small children paddle, families feed the ducks – numbering 64 at the last count – and dog-walkers stroll to and fro along the margin. Casting a fly can be a hazardous business, except on cold or wet days when few sane locals venture out, or at last light after the kids have gone home. But the top twenty-five yards or so, whose low-slung branches afford cover of a sort, is where I creep about when I feel the need to escape from finless or chinless wonders and return to my angling roots. I've never seen a stockie here, and the boys don't read much about fish culture or catch and release.

Arriving at 3.50p.m., I risked a wheel-clamp in the factory car park and ducked quickly into the undergrowth, lest the lads should spot me. I did not want an audience, especially as I'd seen a couple of rises against the bank. The branches were a problem, but wading around and beneath them I reached a position from which I could switch my fly across the stream the required seven yards or so. And by moving slowly up the shallow I would then be able to cover the rest of the run up to the factory wall, a total of some twenty yards.

A variety of aquatic and land-bred flies, including mayflies, were on the water in sufficient numbers to get the fish interested, yet sparsely enough to ensure that almost every one was accepted with enthusiasm. In cool, overcast conditions this looked the perfect scenario, and, sure enough, the first delivery saw a twelve-inch beauty boring and leaping away down river. Easing him free, I pitched the fly one yard ahead and hooked a second, and another yard upstream a third. Peas in a pod, all were true wildies with that characteristic dark brown/olive back, silver flank with a touch of old gold, and wide, delicate fins and tail.

I did not seek to emulate Kite's 'six fish with six chucks', but sat down for five minutes in case I should locate a big one. He duly showed right under a hawthorn bush opposite where no fly of mine could penetrate. However, I figured that, if he was keen, he would come out from his holt and reach for it. The fly bobbed down close to his lair, past it, and a great nose appeared two yards below the bush. I should have expected this, but my reaction was a hurried, mistimed strike. The pricked fish swirled and shot away, two pounds if he was an ounce. Another trout under the same thicket performed an identical manoeuvre, but this time I was ready and soon landed a glorious native fish weighing 1 lb 4 oz.

All the commotion did not disturb those feeding ahead, of which I netted two, missed two and lost one in a weedbed. By 5p.m. I was addressing four risers in the dark alley beneath the factory. One looked big, but vanished at the first cast. I had concluded that this little bit of Heaven could spare a few for the table, so the next two went into the bag, making up two brace averaging just under the pound. As I departed I wondered how an unkeepered, unstocked piece of free fishing like this can maintain a vastly greater stock than many managed waters elsewhere. Clearly it had to be for those very reasons, illogical though that may seem.

One week later I'd arranged for an old fishing mate and a friend of his to visit a day-ticket stretch some ten miles from Salisbury. I had known this length when it was packed with wild trout, but the new owner had thought it advisable to put in lots of large fish. This was to attract business I imagine, or to justify the charges. Either way, the result was that wherever my chum put his fly it seemed to be taken by a two-pound fish that had little fight, no guile, and felt soft to the touch when landed. He handed me his rod, and four lunkers came wallowing ashore. It was hilarious fishing, but I gave the rod back within twenty minutes, and neither of us wanted to carry on. Those trout bore no comparison to the bright and beautiful native fish of old. Some might suppose the latter had been fished out, but the truth is they had been stocked out – and for all the wrong reasons.

The following Saturday I spent an amusing afternoon fishing for a large trout I had spotted previously in the wide bend running around the cricket field in Wilton. A game was in progress, and it so happened that my casting spot was immediately behind the bowler's arm. Not wishing to destroy the batsman's concentration, I had to move several yards downstream each time the bowler operated from my end, and then creep back into position for a few casts as soon as the umpire called 'over'. Since the fish was cruising and rising intermittently over two yards of water, each presentation had to be carefully judged. I found I could make five deliveries per over, on average, but the trout eventually became fed up with my antics, as I'm sure the players had. When a slow bowler was brought on the overs became shorter, so I decided I would call another day. I never did, but maybe I shall find the fish rising again next season – hopefully in midweek.

Another of my favourite haunts at mayfly time is the millstream in Salisbury, which flows between the main car park and the city centre. The width of the river is restricted by concrete walls, so that it maintains a healthy pace all season with a fine carpet of ranunculus throughout. Several bridges enable pedestrians to cross back and forth, and a large proportion of them linger a while to feed the swans; if you don't catch a car or cyclist here, you'll probably hook an old lady on her way to the Post Office! Indeed I have found it altogether wiser to concentrate on the northern end and the adjoining carrier, where, although spectators abound, you may fish in comparative safety.

Rarely do I see another fly fisher on this water, but last year a very competent angler was exploring the shallow sidestream as I approached. Leaving him to it, I went over to the main river, where two or three trout were moving quietly in slow water beneath a flowering chestnut on the far bank. With a wide loop cast I was able to avoid the street lamp and advertising board behind me and pitch the fly against the wall, allowing it to bounce back on a loose leader. First a trout of about 1½ lb tore downstream under a footbridge and came unstuck, then another shot into the air, shedding the hook, and a third tumbled into the net after a desperate scrap among the weedbeds. He had earned his freedom, but the stockie that followed – a rarity on this length – went into the bag for supper. Half an hour later I was joined by the other angler. We reckoned we had caught a dozen between us, from a stretch thought by most to be pretty much below par.

The cuckoo was still calling in the chestnut as we left, his tones echoed by another somewhere across the valley.

᧙ 18 ᧙
Food for Thought

The mystery of the trout's so-called selectivity continues to exercise the minds of fly fishers as it has for centuries past. We know that fish sometimes feed on one species of insect to the exclusion of others which are present in similar numbers, but the species for which this apparent preference is shown may differ from one stretch of water to another, from day to day, even from one half-hour to the next. Despite constant debate over many decades, no satisfactory explanation for this intriguing aspect of trout behaviour has yet been advanced. For if, as has been suggested, it were based on taste, or the notion that, size for size, certain flies are of greater nutritional value, why would trout so regularly switch their attention from one species to another? When we find an answer to this question we will be able to mount an appropriate artificial with confidence, and for a good reason, rather than simply keep hoping that the law of averages will produce the desired result.

There can be little doubt that the trout's choice of natural fly is governed by one overriding consideration: availability. It is critical that trout gain more energy from their food then they expend in obtaining it. A number of important factors determine that, although several species are present, some of these, or just one, may be more easily secured.

Trout usually ignore pale watery duns (*B. bioculatus*) in favour of blue-winged olives (*E. ignita*). This is because the former tend to hatch very rapidly from the surface, yet the latter may struggle for a considerable time before freeing themselves from the nymphal shuck. Other ephemerids also display their own individual hatching characteristics and varying rates of eclosion, and these are further influenced by changing patterns of wind, rain, temperature and atmospheric pressure. All upwinged duns can take longer to emerge in cool or wet weather for example, so we often find trout rising eagerly in these

71

conditions. Likewise in warm, settled weather we may notice an abundance of reed smuts, spent spinners and land-bred insects about the river. Trout feed on these when the flies fall or are blown onto the water, yet to pursue them while they are dipping or gyrating above the surface is a largely unprofitable exercise.

Captive insects are commonly taken in preference to those which may escape at any moment. As many have observed, however, there are times when trout appear to behave in a less-than-logical fashion. Let us imagine that a strong cross-wind is blowing from the right bank. Although buffeted by the blast, more sedentary flies, such as the blue-winged olive, are likely to maintain their natural line of drift, whereas quick-hatching species like pale wateries, at the mercy of every gust, may be blown towards the left-hand margin where they become heavily concentrated on the surface, unable to make their speedy departure. The fish know an easy meal when they see one, but the perplexed angler now discovers that, although trout usually take BWO in preference to pale wateries, on this occasion the situation is reversed. Those 'sitting ducks' rising along the far bank refuse his BWO pattern again and again.

Climatic changes can occur throughout the day, each one causing subtle variations in the availability of individual insects. Once we realize this, and note the outcome, then accurate deductions may be made that will significantly reduce the element of trial and error. We may also see that, while the close representation of aquatic flies is an essential part of our sport, our skills at the vice are of little value unless we can also recognize the effects of such natural phenomena. Otherwise we may spend fruitless hours presenting the fish with beautiful imitations of insects which they are currently ignoring!

A further piece in this jigsaw is the density of the surface layer. At one fishery I know well, the main river runs deep and relatively slow, held back by a set of sluice-gates, while a parallel carrier stream flows unimpeded and is thus quicker and more broken in character. Although good hatches occur in the side stream, most of the flies emerge rapidly from the well-oxygenated water; even blue-winged olives may float only for a few seconds, while the pale wateries shoot into the air like *Polaris* missiles. The angler may notice few fish rising regularly on station, but a number will be moving laterally, bulging beneath the surface as they intercept ascending nymphs and those in the act of eclosion. On the main river trout feed in a very different manner, for here the flies often sail on for twenty yards or more before becoming airborne. As a variety of duns, spinners and other insects become trapped in the clinging film, the fish can simply suck them down at their leisure, displaying little partiality between species. Examinations of trout stomach contents have confirmed this. However, autopsies can be misleading when cited as evidence of discriminatory behaviour. True, we sometimes find only one species present in the gut – but is it not also true that on these occasions this was the only fly on the water, or the one more easily acquired, at the time?

Selectivity then, if we can call it that, is governed by the availability of particular species in a particular place at a particular time. But, if more food-forms are invariably present beneath the surface than on it, why do trout rise at all? Here we should consider the energy gain/loss equation in greater detail. On many days there are periods when free-swimming nymphs migrate *en masse* up to the surface layer and back, and from one weedbed to another. On such occasions trout will indeed feed on nymphs exclusively, for this is where, for the time being, their bread is buttered. But, equally, there are times when the nymphs remain at rest among the weed fronds or on the stream bed. Shrimps and snails may be similarly inaccessible, while water lice and other creatures lie hidden beneath stones or buried in silt and rotting vegetation. Trout may dash into weed beds from time to time in an attempt to dislodge food items, and they may root about on the bottom or in the margins, but they can expend a great deal of energy in the process. Indeed, mature fish usually remain inactive during these periods – which occur mostly in high summer. When rising, on the other hand, trout exert virtually no energy. They lie up in the water, aided by the swim bladder, and usually in a cushion where they can maintain station with little effort. A minute adjustment of the fins lifts the fish a few inches in the current to sup upon insects floating directly into a chosen feed-zone. Even when relatively few flies are on the surface, each represents a plus in terms of energy input, while a substantial hatch adds significantly to the trout's nutritional account.

As we marvel at the wondrous display of aquatic creatures and come to appreciate their dependence on a pristine environment, we know that each is in fact on the very knife-edge of existence. This is the survival game in earnest. The trout, ever striving to maintain condition, cannot afford to slip into that unstoppable downward spiral if it is to reproduce successfully and see another season.

ভ 19 ভ

The Wilton Diaries

In idle moments we may picture some limpid shallow on the Itchen, a majestic sweep of the middle Test, or the Kennet's sleek, mysterious depths. The Wiltshire Avon may spring to mind, or Plunket Greene's beloved Bourne. These rivers are renowned the world over, their hatches and catches recorded in fine books spanning the decades, their beauty captured forever by gifted painters and photographers. It may seem strange, then, that comparatively little is known of an unsung chalk stream which rises on the western slopes of Salisbury Plain, the quality of whose fishing has rivalled, even surpassed, that of the most famous trout streams.

It was in the spring of 1968, my first season on the Wylye, that I glanced through the diaries belonging to the Wilton Fly Fishing Club. At first I thought that the entries under 'weight' in the final column – 6 lb, 5 lb 2 oz, 4 lb 5 oz and so on – referred to the total catch taken by each member. Then, reeling slightly, I realized these were the weights of individual trout. Riveted to the page, I could hardly believe the evidence before me.

No takeable fish were introduced, then or since, yet I noted that one member, in four days fishing, had captured five trout with an average weight of 4 lb 10 oz. Another killed two averaging 4 lb 12 oz. Two consecutive days in 1953 produced a remarkable bag, the seven largest trout averaging over 5 lb apiece and the heaviest going to 7 lb 1 oz. In 1954 an angler recorded a brace with an average of 5 lb 6 oz; while in the four-day period of 27–30 May that year the twenty trout entered averaged 3 lb, and included fish scaling 6 lb 14 oz, 6 lb 5 oz, 4 lb 9 oz, 4 lb 7 oz and 4 lb 4 oz – wild trout every one. No wonder this water had been kept a closely guarded secret!

Few catches before 1950 are revealed, although a record exists of a Mr Haviland, one day in 1927, having taken five trout weighing a total of 15 lb, and on another occasion a fish of 6 lb 11 oz. The heaviest ever recorded appears to be that landed by Mr Carlton-Cross at South Newton in 1924 which scaled just over 7 lb 2 oz.

I heard stirring tales of epic battles from old members, such as C.B. Wrey, W.N. (Nick) Roughead, 'Winco' Everidge, Sir John Paskin and R.G. Longman (the publisher). All these grand fishers are gone now, and by the time I joined the Club the monster trout had mostly departed too. I managed to secure nineteen fish of two pounds or more in my first seven seasons, five of which topped three pounds, including two of 3 lb 5 oz, while my friend Chris White captured a fish weighing 4 lb 6 oz on a Mayfly in June 1980. In more recent times, Roger Mills has landed a trout of 5 lb 1 oz (taken on 11 June 1992) and two of 4 lb 4 oz.

Between 1950 and 1970, though, dramatic changes took place in the balance of fish stocks. Only 479 trout were recorded from 1950 to 1955 inclusive, around 80 per year, yet 1974–78 produced 2,378 trout, some 475 per season, and the average weight fell to under 1 lb. This was due in part to the removal of large numbers of coarse fish and grayling, and a ruthless onslaught on the pike. The survival rate among immature trout thus increased sharply to a point where the river was bulging with 10–14-in. fish, a few of which grew on to reach impressive proportions.

Moreover, in 1950 the Wilton Club had just fifteen members, who fished mostly in May and early June. By 1978 the membership had risen to around forty, fishing from April to October. The sport was magnificent throughout the 1970s, but by the mid-1980s we began to notice worrying signs. Wild trout were still being taken in some numbers, but it became clear that nature was no longer replenishing the stocks as hitherto, so that by the early 1990s the annual catch had fallen alarmingly. So had the Wylye herself, whose former swift and ample flows were dwindling fast.

Some blamed the drought – a significant factor, certainly, yet in the past the river had withstood such periods naturally, so great were her reserves in the aquifer. Now there was a more sinister development: borehole water abstraction. This had increased tenfold between 1970 and 1990 (Halcrow Report), causing the main river to fall steadily, and many sidestreams, winterbournes and other traditional spawning sites to decline or vanish completely. Silt had built up, gravels became impacted, and oxygen levels were markedly reduced. Fly life suffered greatly as a consequence.

It is to the Wilton Club's credit that it resisted the easy option of turning in sizeable trout. The members agreed that to create instant fishing here was unthinkable. Instead, a fry stocking policy was adopted in the early 1990s, and this has re-established a most satisfactory head of young trout, many now in the 1–2-lb bracket. As these breed, mingling with the original inhabitants, there is every reason to suppose that a totally self-regenerating stock will flourish once more.

Wisely, the Club has diverted the currents here and there in order to cleanse the river bed, created small weirs, and loosened gravels to encourage widespread spawning. In late 1993, after a year and more of high rainfall, the river looked in wonderful shape, with an abundant flow of clean water, healthy beds of ranunculus, increased fly hatches, and trout feeding boldly as good trout should. Those who have waited so patiently for a change of fortunes, fishing less frequently and returning most of their catch, may now receive their just reward. All appears set for a return to the fruitful days of 20–25 years ago.

Over a century has passed since the Wilton Fly Fishing Club came to the lower Wylye, having fished the Kennet (as the Hungerford Club) from 1878 to 1891. Forty-five rods now enjoy anytime access to some six miles of main stream and carriers. The length divides comfortably into twenty-four beats, for the purposes of recording catches and to ensure that members have plenty of lightly fished water at their disposal. In practice, fewer than half of the beats are likely to be occupied on any one day, even at the height of the mayfly period. Members receive six free guest tickets, for use after 10 June, and may share their rod with a friend at any time. The trout season runs from mid-April to mid-October, after which anglers can continue fishing for grayling, pike or coarse fish until 14 March.

Thanks largely to the enthusiasm of Club Secretary John McGill and the dedication of Norman Smith, the full-time keeper, this long stretch of the Wylye is maintained to a very high standard today and yet, happily, cannot be described as 'carpet-slipper' fishing. Habitat is considered the prime factor in the provision of wild sport. Along with sensitive weed control and healthy flow rates, this means cover, in the shape of trees, bushes and bankside vegetation which offer both shelter for the trout and a challenge to the stalking angler.

Whether or not the diaries ever bristle again with five- and six-pounders, I like to think this lovely river will come brimming through the meadows each season as of old, that upwinged duns will sail down in droves, and portly trout will continue to rise like gentlemen a hundred years from now.

⚙ 20 ⚙

The Height of the Season

To the dedicated fisherman the matter of arranging the annual holiday can be an awesome business. If he has a family, the chances are he will have to take most time off at a period when trout fishing is least productive, and the amount of time he allows for fishing depends largely upon his conscience and the understanding of his wife. While the rest of the family think about finding a place in the sun, the poor angler would probably be happier for the lack of it, and lucky is the man who is able to get off for a couple of weeks on his own at the time of his choice.

I suppose I knew from an early age that I was destined to be an angler, for in family affairs there has always been a restraining hand on my arm, as if in warning. Whether the sacrifice is worthwhile is a matter for each individual, but a look through my fishing diaries convinces me that at least there are compensations!

An analysis of my own results shows clearly that the two-week period ending around 10 June has been the most productive of the year where I operate on the chalk streams of Wiltshire, and that the second half of that period is usually the very height of the season. A further, and perhaps surprising fact is that sport has been entirely consistent, despite vastly differing conditions. Whether spring has arrived early or late, and whether there has been non-stop wind and rain, or a calm sunny spell, results have shown a remarkable similarity over the years.

To the angler, time is a vital factor to his enjoyment of the sport. If he has to be back for his dinner at a certain hour, or if he has to meet relatives or take his wife shopping, he cannot concentrate on the job in hand; he is forever looking at his watch, and, as the dreaded hour approaches, it is odds on that the trout will start rising as they have never risen before. Absolute freedom, and the time to concentrate his whole being to the sport, are most essential.

Thus it is that as I drive down to the river at the start of my holiday towards the end of May, it is as though the spirit had been released from some dark prison, and the heart is free. My landlady, in her cottage by the stream, is the most perfect hostess to a fisherman that can be imagined. The angler may drape his line all over the garden or clean out fish at the kitchen sink, and even the muddiest boots cause no comment; the table in the back room is littered with all the bits and pieces which are accumulated by a fly-tier over the years. This is indeed a home from home, in which the angler is always welcome, and even the cat sniffs appreciatively at your clothing as you pass. Best of all, perhaps, is that meal times are entirely flexible, varying month by month with the changing season. Mind you, I stay here many weekends as well, and have done so for a good six years, so I suppose I am now accepted as part of the scenery.

The weather of course, is sometimes so bad as to be almost unbelievable, and 1972 was worse than that. For the entire fortnight there was a howling wind, reaching gale force at times, blowing downstream. It was cold, and for much of the time rain fell in torrents. Even so, the period from 25 May to 10 June produced 53 trout, 26 of which were retained at an average weight of just over 1 lb 2 oz. Mayfly hatches were good on both Avon and Wylye, and there were some immense hatches of olives and iron blues. The harder the rain, and the stronger the wind, the better they seemed to hatch, and at times every fish in the river appeared to be feeding at the surface. A pity, I thought, that so few fishermen were to be seen, for surely we would hear fewer complaints about lack of fly if anglers did not fish only in those conditions most conducive to human comfort. The Avon gave me my first two-pounder, a fish of 2¼ lb which should have been heavier – and I had to land him pretty smartly, for a pike of some ten pounds followed the trout and snapped at him once or twice before I could get the fish into the net. The next took a Grey Wulff Mayfly pattern and was so surprised that he shot through two weedbeds at high speed. He appeared to be going to Salisbury, but eventually I managed to steady him up, whereupon he leaped three times into the air and then came to the net like a lamb.

Towards the end of my holiday I had one splendid day on a tributary of the Avon above Salisbury, when trout rose all day and everything went right. The first three fish were taken on the Grey Wulff, the best going to 2 lb exactly. This one was in a difficult lie, under some overhanging branches, and at first did not appear to me to be sizeable.

But Doug Newell, the well known bailiff and fly-tier, reckoned it would go to 2 lb – and how right he was! The next two trout were taken just before sunset on the Pale Evening Dun. The second gave me a terrific scrap, rushing about all over the river and spending as much time in the air as in the water. It turned out to be a rainbow of 1 lb 1 oz, which was a surprise, since we never stock them – it must have been introduced by some generous neighbour upstream.

I now had five good trout in the bag and wanted a big one to complete my limit. In the deep, slow-flowing pool ahead a very large fish was rising to sedges with that characteristic 'chop' of a heavy trout. The rise was small but the sound was unmistakable, and he was very close – barely a rod's length away as I stood knee-deep in the water at the edge of the pool. The fly fell right first cast, he took, and we fought a grim battle for half an hour in near darkness. The trout made its way downstream, as they always seem to do on this river, and the pull was so strong that I could do nothing but let him go. Fortunately, he did not go far, but again and again he bored down into the depths with relentless power, and I knew that if I simply kept a tight line and waited he would tire before I did. In fact I told him so. I talked to that fish as only one who knows he is alone dares to do, and when he was on the grass I saluted him, for he had given every last ounce of strength he had. He scaled 3¼ lb, and the holiday was complete.

The following season, 1973, the results were almost identical in unsettled conditions, in which some days were wet and some were fine. Wind and temperature varied from day to day, giving the complete mixture. Twenty-three trout were retained out of a total of fifty-five caught, two more than the year before. The average weight was the same, and the three best fish scaled between 2 lb and 2¾ lb, all taken between 5 and 10 June. This year the Mayfly did not account for many trout, which were taken mostly on Pale Evening Dun, Iron Blue and Sedge.

Between 25 May and 9 June, 1974, when the weather was mostly warm and sunny throughout, the figures were very similar, twenty-three trout again being retained out of sixty caught. For the third successive year the average weight was just over 1 lb 2 oz. Once more three over 2 lb were taken, going to between 2¼ lb and 3¼ lb, and this time two of them were caught on the Sedge, on 4 and 7 June, and the other on a Pheasant-tail Nymph on 26 May. Scales from the larger fish were sent to the biologist at the Wessex Water Authority and it was found to be about 4½ years old, which shows a remarkable growth rate. Indeed, when one considers that a 13-in. fish usually weighs about a pound after three years' growth, this one, at 19½ in. and 3¼ lb after 4½ years, shows the terrific feeding potential of some of our chalk rivers.

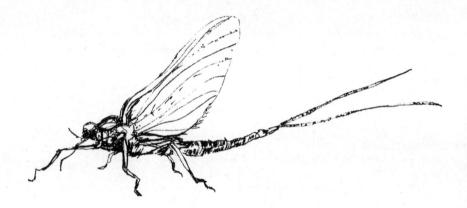

↵ 21 ↵

Mayfly Holiday

The sight of the first really big trout I spotted in 1980 made me stop dead in my tracks, scarcely daring to breathe. He was lying close in against the right bank some hundred yards above the cattle bridge at South Newton, and was certainly the heaviest trout I'd seen on the Wylye since 1970, when I spent three whole weekends after a fish in the 6–7 lb class, without result.

Although fished on an 'any-time' basis by a possible maximum of some six rods to the mile, this stream nevertheless produces such a head of native trout as to make stocking unnecessary. The average weight taken is just under the pound; a two-pounder is a real prize, and a fish of more than three pounds quite exceptional. Crayfish, shrimps and minnows abound, so that the very large trout seldom rise, except to mayfly, and occasionally to sedge or BWO on summer nights.

The hatches of mayfly were especially heavy last season, heavier than I have known in the fourteen years I've fished here. I make it my business to stay down by the river at this time, fishing every day for two to three weeks at the end of May and into June. Even so, the presence of a big trout soon becomes common knowledge amongst anglers, so I am not always able to select the spots I want, and a spirit of healthy competition prevails.

This monster, I determined, was going to be my fish, but conditions during the first three days I was after him were never quite right. Much of the time, even when a stream of succulent mayflies floated over his nose, he just lay there unmoved, and the visibility, although perfect on the rare occasions when the sun shone on the water, was not good enough to encourage me to use a nymph. I was determined not to fish the nymph 'blind', relying only on the possibility of leader-draw indication. No, if and when he took my fly, I wanted to know it, for I would need the odds well and truly in my favour.

Meantime, while waiting for my trout to come on the rise I spotted two or three other good fish moving. One, directly opposite my position, would rise in short bursts, taking perhaps half-a-dozen flies in quick succession, then resting for ten minutes or so before surface-feeding again. I tied on a fresh point and newly dressed fly and, as soon as the fish began rising, dropped it six inches in front of his nose. It dragged slightly across stream towards me. The fish pursued it and rose in determined fashion, but missed the fly. He looked very big. Perhaps I should try next time from the other bank.

From time to time I looked along the Union stream, a well-known haunt of big trout further down the valley. Between the two railway bridges two fish in the region of three pounds had taken up station, and downstream, below the lower arch, was a trout which made the tiny ring and audible smack of an exceptionally heavy fish.

Thus it was that my holiday was spent waiting for, and occasionally casting to, one or other of these big trout, and sometimes taking advantage of the more regular activity among smaller fish on somewhat shallower and swifter reaches further upstream. The first of the big fish with which I really got to grips was on a narrow part of the Union. He was a perpetual cruiser, a rare occurrence on this stream. When feeding on mayflies, he swam upstream and down at considerable speed, beneath a high bank which cut out reflected glare. I could see the trout clearly as he took nearly every fly which came within range, but timing the presentation was far from easy, for his beat covered some fifteen yards of water. On two occasions, however, I got my fly to land just right. On the first day, fishing off the high bank, the right, I thought I had timed the strike perfectly, but after a short run and some furious slashing at the surface, the trout got off. Next day, kneeling to cast from the left bank, I hooked the fish again. This time he shot so high into the air that he was actually above my head as I knelt, and I can vividly recall looking up at the fish as he seemed to hang there for several seconds, only some five yards from me, before plunging back into some reeds growing in mid-stream. The trout burrowed into the tough vegetation until he rid himself of the hook, and I was left to reel in a single broken reed-stem.

I saw no sign of the other three-pounder on this stretch, but some days later the one below the railway bridge was feeding well on surface mayfly. I could not see him clearly, but was aware of a huge shape appearing slowly beneath my fly, and the gradual whitening as his jaws opened. He looked a colossal trout – possibly of a size regularly caught here back in the early 1950s, between 5 and 6 lb – but my fresh 4-lb nylon point should be adequate. There was barely any surface disturbance, but one moment the fly was there, floating high, and the next it was gone. There were no fireworks, no savage leap, not even a run. Just a solid jar as if I had hooked a tree-trunk, a porpoise roll from the trout, and then '*ping*'. The trout departed, and the line drooped sadly from the rod.

As recorded before in these pages, 10 June has always proved an especially lucky date for me, so when that day dawned I was ready to do battle with the giants which had thus far evaded capture. Between 3.30 and 5.30p.m. the mayflies hatched in huge numbers, and trout rose all over the river in the most abandoned way: at either side of me as I waded in the stream, a yard or two behind me, even under my rod-point. There was so much activity that I thrashed water in all directions, unable through sheer excitement to settle down and stalk selectively. In any case, John Hunt and Geoff Lee had occupied 'hunter's water' on the Union stream, while Chris White was at my South Newton haunt with another rod who had gone off after borrowing Chris's landing net.

I fished below Great Wishford, on a reach which in previous seasons had yielded heavy fish, although I had spotted none so far this year. One day in the 1979 mayfly season, from a catch of seven trout taken in a two-hour session, I had kept four over the pound, the two best going to 2 lb 10 oz and 2 lb. Today, although things were apparently more promising, I could manage only two takeable fish, both just under the pound.

It was late in the afternoon when I saw Chris running across the field towards me. Something sensational was up. Either the guest had fallen in the river, I thought, or, worse still, he'd caught one of 'my' fish! (Mind you, I had taken one of his back in 1974 which weighed 3 lb 5 oz, so I owed him one.) Sure enough, when we reached the club-room, there was the big trout which had risen opposite me while I was waiting for my original monster above the cattle bridge – the fish which had missed my dragging fly. Looking down at him now, noting his colour and proportions, it dawned upon me that this was my original monster. Clearly, the spot where I had seen him lying unmoved was his resting place, and when feeding he had taken up a position across the river, near the far bank. At 4 lb 6 oz, this was the largest trout to be caught here in the past 24 years – and Chris had landed him without his net!

I was back at the cottage, collapsed over a cup of tea, when Geoff and John joined me. John had caught one of the Union three-pounders – not the one I'd hooked – and Geoff carried a trout of about two pounds. The other Union fish, the high-jumper, was killed later by Peter Starks, at 3 lb 6 oz. Of the great trout below the railway, the 'tree-trunk' in which I had snapped my 4-lb nylon, there had been no sign, nor was there again that season.

Yes, 10 June is a lucky date all right – for some! But I'm not complaining. My holiday yielded me 61 trout (35 of which were kept), two grayling and one dace, all save one on Mayfly. My friends (well, they *were* friends) got nearly every big fish I'd marked down. Just let them wait, though; this year, it is going to be a different story.

22

A Week with Vincent Marinaro

An American accent is unmistakable to the British ear, especially when it competes with the incessant thud of a juke box. 'Say, what is this,' demanded the vibrant tones, 'some kinda honkey-tonk?' The voice was that of Vincent C. Marinaro, on his first and last trip to England's chalk streams in May 1976.

His plans had gone badly awry, though. Vince was not a happy man, and I could see his point. First, his host, who had supposedly arranged for Vince and himself to visit a number of prime waters, decided he couldn't make it; and, no, guests were not allowed to fish unaccompanied. Second, he discovered that the George Hotel in Winchester, where F.M. Halford often ministered to his disciples, was now an office block, and furthermore all accommodation in the city appeared to be booked. Also he knew nobody in southern England who, on the cancellation of his fishing, could secure access to any half-suitable bit of water at such short notice.

This looked a bleak prospect, but Roy Darlington, with whom I shared two fine Itchen fisheries, eventually found a hotel in Southgate Street which had a small third floor room in an annexe across the road. There was no lift, no bar, no room service, and Vince would have to cross over to the main building for his meals – and to enjoy the music! As to fishing, Roy and I would fix him up somehow, even though May was our busiest season.

I was elected as fishing guide, which suited me fine. Not only did I want to see how Vince would fare in testing chalk-stream conditions, I also wished to know the man behind that somewhat daunting exterior. Was he really embittered, or sardonic, as he has since been portrayed by many, even those who never met him? I, too, have seen photographs in which the down-turned mouth, the hint of a frown, might suggest a certain rancour. But it soon became clear that Vince's demeanour was that of one who cared deeply for all that is best in our sport, who could not bring himself to accept any sort of decline in standards – ethical, moral or environmental. To me, the picture of Vince on the rear jacket cover of his *In the Ring of the Rise* says it all: concern for nature, devotion to his rivers, and a love of wild trout. That facial expression captures but one emotion, compassion, and this is how I believe posterity will judge him.

Our week together was not without incident, humour, and an element of farce. On a broad shallow of the Itchen below Winchester, a good trout had taken up residence on the far side of a surface weed-raft. I'd tried for this free-riser many times and was keen to prove that our trout can be as tiresome as any on the Letort. But Vince made me take first shot, watching closely as with a cross-stream cast I succeeded only in dragging the fly over the fish's nose time and again. 'It's all a matter of angles' said Vince, moving several paces downstream. Waiting for the next rise, he placed his line on top of the weed bar, first arresting its forward travel to put an elegant upstream curve in the leader. The fly bobbed naturally down the ripple, disappearing in a gentle ring, and the rod arched as a vigorous trout sped towards the far bank.

As Vince played his fish, a small oriental gentleman approached us. He came here every year, and although I had charge of this fishery I never knew who he was or where he came from, for he spoke no recognizable tongue. But there was much bowing and smiling, and he was such a pleasant fellow I had not the heart to question his presence on private water. As Vince was about to kill the trout – because he thought I would wish it, for he took few of his fish – the little man looked skyward and commenced a strange chanting to some unknown deity (I had heard of sacred cows, but this was something new). Seeing his evident distress, Vince unhooked the trout and quickly slipped it back to save further embarrassment.

Downriver, we found a fish sipping tight against the bowl of a large willow on the far bank, its branches hanging down into the water for many yards in either direction. This was an impossible situation, compounded by a swift flow in midstream which would cause the line to belly almost at once and the fly to drag far short of its target. Here I was to witness a preview of Vince's amazing Puddle Cast, illustrated in the aforementioned book, which was due out that autumn. This delivery is well known today, but at the time I could hardly believe my eyes as the fly, perched on the slower current, sailed on, and on, and on into the deepening gloom beneath the tree. It was about an inch from the fish when the line finally straightened, there was a half-boil, and the fly skimmed sharply away across the surface.

Next day Vince and I drove over to Stockbridge on the Test. As we came down the hill into this tiny one-time coaching town he exclaimed, clearly disappointed, 'This is Stockbridge?' I believe he'd thought it would look more like Dallas or some such place. Having taken some shots of the famous Grosvenor Hotel we motored down to Houghton Mill where Marryat, Francis and Halford had enjoyed such happy times. Just above the road bridge, on the Bossington beat, we met head keeper Mick Lunn trying to teach one of his fishermen how to catch a trout. This gentleman had been a member of the prestigious Houghton Club for seven years, and this was his first ever day on the water! We watched his line fall in a tangled heap about three yards out. A three-pound trout rose slowly from the depths, picked the fly out from a mass of nylon, and hooked itself firmly in the side of the jaw. We wondered later whether this man ever fished again – perhaps he thought it was all too easy.

Back on the Itchen at Avington, close to Lord Grey's old water, I had brought Vince to see the monster rainbow trout reared by the late Sam Holland. By selective breeding and heavy pellet-feeding Sam could produce record-breaking fish weighing up to twenty pounds. Vince was not impressed; before we got out of the car he growled 'This is a pig farm', and he kept muttering 'disgusting' and 'you can't treat fish this way' as we walked around the ponds. Then I noticed Sam approaching. He had a fiery temper and I feared the worst. Quick as a flash I got between them, talking fast and loud enough to drown Vince's remarks, before shepherding him back into the car and away. He cooled off by the time we got back to town, congratulating me warmly for having averted a tricky international incident.

The Abbotts Barton fishery above Winchester was meat and drink to Vince. G.E.M. Skues had fished here for 56 seasons, along with many whose names are now legendary. This is hunters' water, par excellence, said by William Senior and others to be the most challenging in the south. Vince revelled in it, stalking his prey like a cat among the reeds. He fished slowly and methodically, with the utmost stealth, spotting and creeping up to each in turn. Rapid, punchy delivery was not his style; nor did he cast until he was confident the odds were in his favour. I marvelled at his accurate, featherlike presentation, the line settling gently with just the correct amount of slack.

Vince did not speak a lot unless he had something to say, and then it was worth listening. I'd describe him as analytical, studious even, yet with an inner contentment sometimes lacking in those of a more excitable nature. I took no note of his captures but somehow they didn't seem important. It was doing the job right that counted. As I drove down Southgate Street after dropping him off, I looked back at the slightly stooped figure ambling away into the distance. I knew then that this would be my last glimpse of Vincent Marinaro, one of the most cultured, innovative fishermen of our time.

23

Chalk Streams on a Shoestring

Those who are keen to fish the chalk streams, but who, because of what they have read about high costs and 'exclusiveness', have never made more than tentative enquiry, may be heartened by my own experiences in 1984 when, because of my resignation from a long-established and quite expensive fly-fishing club, I was forced to seek my trout elsewhere, and on a slender shoestring at that.

I was fortunate in that, since I live by a river, I had some local knowledge. I knew that the landlord of the local pub, on payment of a small sum, would allow me, as he does others, to fish the hundred yards or so alongside his lawn, well-patronized of a summer evening by lads and lasses from the village and the occasional coach party. For a similar fee, I enjoyed access to 150 yards of a tiny winterbourne which joins the main river a couple of miles up the valley. Further upstream again, I was given leave to fish on about half a mile of main stream and carrier, along with a dozen other local anglers who sometimes compete for space with the inhabitants of the village and their children and dogs (most of whom, it seems, love to walk the banks and gather by the adjoining hatchpool). My only 'perks', if you like, were free membership of the local angling club, whose stocked lengths I fished very little, and four or five guest tickets on other waters. In total, my fishing cost some £20 for the year, plus a trout licence, and there was no restriction on any of these waters as to when I could fish.

To the casual observer, the concrete-flanked stretch of the Avon in Salisbury's central car-park, at the back of a supermarket and along by the public library, might present somewhat limited prospects for the serious fly fisherman. Yet, as I drove over the exit bridge one morning during the mayfly, the spreading rings of three or four good trout were spotted against the brickwork on the far bank. I had to take a friend home to South Newton, but within the hour I was back, crouched on the tarmac of the public footpath, preparing to address these city-dwellers who had doubtless never seen an artificial mayfly.

A few lads were fishing with the inevitable float-fishing gear – I don't think they had ever seen artificial mayflies either – and they stood with mouths agape as the fly, cocked merrily, floated over each trout in turn. The first fish wolfed it readily, but I mistimed the strike and something weighing about two pounds plunged into the depths. Number two was well hooked, but shot into a thick weedbed and shed the fly. Then I was fast into a lively fish which dashed downriver and jumped three times clear of the water, much to the delight of motorists, office staff at windows opposite and sundry passers-by. This one was netted, and so was number four, which I had to drag over and through dense weed-growth with the rod bent almost double. A showman like Plunkett-Greene would have revelled in such an occasion, but it was too much for me; I departed with my brace of pounders, making a mental note to return late of an evening, when I could creep about unnoticed.

The sedge fly was on when next I fished here, causing trout to slash and boil in all directions. I could cover ten rising trout without moving from one spot – along the shallow margin ahead, out in midstream, and beneath the bushes on the far bank. It was just a matter of casting out, giving the fly a short twitch and bang, they came like gentlemen. Three times more I returned, and on each occasion had breathtaking sport with these native trout, although I rose and missed many, and lost some beauties. I remember thinking that if this stretch were out in open country instead of in the heart of the city, it would command a huge rent – but then, perhaps, it would be stocked with 'easy' trout, and the wild fish would be gone. How lucky I was to know the water in its natural, balanced state, albeit in a most unnatural setting!

The 'fun pool' as it has become known, and the stretch of main Wylye and parallel carrier above, are so full of native trout and grayling that you can scarcely take a step anywhere close to the banks without seeing the furrows of departing fish. Yet, if you keep your head down and wait for a few minutes, they sidle back to their lies and resume feeding. This water was the mainstay of my fishing activities, as most evenings in summer and occasional afternoons when I could get time off would find me somewhere on that length, either kneeling beside the shallow side-stream, in the wood half-way up the main, or wading the thin water up by the duck-pond at the top end.

Despite the almost constant presence of humans and other creatures in and about the water, sport here was quite amazing. You could bet that wherever you cast you were covering a fish, and – always provided it had not been scuttled by you or someone else or his dog, or a cow or water-fowl – the chances of getting it were good. I seldom had a blank, and when I could choose my time so as to be able to fish in comparative peace for an hour or two, I enjoyed some wonderful fishing with six or eight trout to record in the diary, although most were returned to the water. Dry fly fared better than nymph, for fish were usually on the rise somewhere, and reflected surface light made for difficult nymphing conditions. I ended the season with 82 trout caught on this water alone, and 52 grayling, up to the end of October.

Near Amesbury a short piece of classic Avon fishing occupied my attention on a number of summer evenings. Deep and mysterious, with a steady flow and good hatches of fly, this reach contains a head of pike and numerous coarse fish, so that the trout are few but heavy. Most evenings when I went there two or three trout would be rising like clockwork, with that characteristic sip of a large fish. I met only one other fisherman here who, like me, would creep out as the sun was setting. He was a soul-mate (though I never knew his name), for as anglers our approach and our attitudes to the game appeared identical. Seldom have I fished in such harmony with another rod.

We knew that each could rely upon the other not to spoil the water, to address each of these big native fish with the utmost respect, and at the least sign that a trout was becoming suspicious to crawl away from the bank and move on. It is that kind of water, where no stocking is done, only the most cautious hunter stands a chance, and if you get one fish you have done well. My score here was just four trout, but one was a beautiful two-pounder. My unknown friend fished the length more than I, and his score was certainly better, though numbers meant little to him. It is rarely that you meet another angler with whom you feel this kind of affinity for natural things. Knowledge and experience are of no matter, but to have your very roots in nature is to be possessed of uncommon understanding.

I did get other two-pounders; one from a carrier stream off the recreation ground in Wilton, one from the Chilhampton Farm length of the Wilton Club water, and one of 2 lb 8 oz from the Wylye above Steeple Langford Church. The pub water yielded only half-a-dozen trout up to 1 lb 5 oz, but the little winterbourne, so shallow for much of the season as to be barely fishable, produced twenty fat trout to 1 lb 7 oz and 34 grayling, the two best scaling 1 lb 6 oz apiece.

My catch for the season was 207 trout, all but eight taken on dry fly, 154 grayling (to October) and five dace, from waters which many a fee-paying rod would consider pretty much below par. Only 24 of my trout were other than pure native, four of them rainbows.

I love exploring such less-sophisticated places, and in seasons past, in 'no-man's land' beneath motorway bridges, along the ancient city walls, or in little-known tributaries and side-streams in the chalk country, I have had the sort of fishing you dream about. To me, at any rate, though difficult, and sometimes exasperating, this is real fishing for nature's own fish – poles apart from the artificial substitute which man creates and for which you can pay fifteen or twenty times as much, for perhaps one day per week. All you pay for on exclusive waters is more space – not, as many imagine, more fish.

✐ 24 ✐

The Darlington Years

It is fitting perhaps that Winchester, with its academic and literary traditions, should have been at the forefront of early dry-fly and nymph fishing development. A veritable Who's Who of the angling world gathered here, including Irwin Cox, joint proprietor of *The Field*; four of its most revered angling editors in Francis Francis, William Senior, C.H. Cook and H.T. Sheringham; G.S. Marryat (universally acclaimed prince of fly fishers), and legendary contributors such as F.M. Halford, Major Carlisle, G.E.M. Skues and H.S. Hall. Skues' magical writings are so etched upon the imagination that we can picture every spinney, each bend and tussock and 'wink under water', even if we have never visited his beloved Abbotts Barton stretch. What is not fully recorded is its more recent history, and in particular the role of another great man of the Itchen, Roy Darlington, whose firm resolve and selfless dedication over more than two decades have snatched this famous fishery from the very jaws of extinction.

Many chalk streams suffered decline between 1939 and 1945. Anglers and keepers went off to war, water plants remained uncut or were stripped out by insensitive hands, and pike and coarse fish multiplied. Abbotts Barton, whose intricate network of carriers flow through quaking marshland, required more attention than most to guard against massive encroachment. But the main river was dredged during this period, causing it to become deeper and narrower than hitherto, and making insufficient water available to feed the numerous side streams, some of which were reduced to reed-choked, silt-laden ditches.

The Piscatorial Society fished the length for fourteen years until 1971, after which it was rented by a small syndicate. John Goddard's moving account of a day he spent here in 1973, taken from *The Way of a Man with a Trout* by Donald Overfield, says it all: 'I have never been so horrified or upset in my life when I observed the apparent rape

93

of the fishery.' He caught the one fish he found rising but 'gently removing the hook I slid the trout back to freedom, as I honestly felt at the time I was probably looking at one of the last trout to be taken from this fishery.'

Few could have foreseen the dramatic changes that would occur during the next twenty years. Roy had heard the lease was available. 'I've often thought I must have been mad,' he recalls, 'but this was Abbotts Barton, one of the most historic trout waters in the world. How could I let it fade into obscurity?' Roy brought his family down from the Midlands to Yate, near Bristol, having arranged a transfer with his firm, Philips. I remember knocking at his door on many a morning in 1975, 'Got to get to work', he would mutter repeatedly as he stumbled about at the crack of dawn, half asleep, searching for his spectacles.

The situation appeared desperate at the start. Roy and Ron, his brother, had to pay the rent, find money for much-needed materials and introduce a stock of trout – and hope to goodness that some fisherman would buy a day ticket, or better still a season rod. The rest was graft – unremitting, back-breaking toil: removing vast accumulations of silt, digging out deep-rooted reed mace, cutting river weeds and hacking back the jungle of bankside vegetation. Soon Roy had a small group of helpers, each working strictly to his instructions. We were fit, able as a team to wield Ron's hefty de-silting scoop, and always ready for a laugh when one of us fell into a bog or, as in my case, had to jump into an icy river to avoid a bucking horse.

Little by little, as the water improved, so the paying rods arrived, and the bank balance began to look healthier. Roy and I were able to secure a lease on the Manor fishery just south of Winchester, where Halford had worked on *The Modern Development of the Dry Fly*. And we employed a part time keeper, Andy Vaughan, a man with the strength of many. New stews were constructed, footbridges repaired or replaced, and a fine fishing hut erected. An enlarged hatchway was completed to divert water from the main Itchen into the Five Hatches carrier, which in turn feeds the Junction and Park Stream beats below. A further stretch at Pudding Farm was added to the fishery. By now, Abbotts Barton had regained some of its past reputation, and we were privileged to welcome many well-known anglers here, including Conrad Voss Bark, Brian Clarke, Donald Overfield and John Goddard, and from overseas Vincent Marinaro, Datus Proper, Preben Torp Jacobsen and Raymond Rocher.

The future appeared rosy, but in 1980 Roy suffered a set-back. Mrs

Iris Whitfield, the owner, sold much of her land and fishing to the Hampshire and Isle of Wight Naturalists' Trust. Long negotiations ensued over the terms of the lease, the number of rods to be granted access, and the nature of work that was to be carried out. At this point Roy gave up his tenancy, and the Abbotts Barton Club was formed. With a committee of seven making the decisions, Roy found the day-to-day management of the water increasingly difficult. 'I seriously considered packing it all in,' he told me. Happily, some fourteen years on, the situation has been resolved. In late 1993 the club was disbanded, and Roy once more has charge of the fishery, together with his friend and co-lessee Stewart Newell.

Abbotts Barton will never be quite as Skues knew it from 1883 to 1938. Some of his favourite haunts were lost when Winchester Council acquired the lower meadow towards the city – McCaskie's Corner, Red Hole and the length known as Swift Lake ('being neither swift nor a lake') among them. But the best of the fishing survives: over three miles in total, including Duck's Nest Spinney, the Barton Carrier, Five Hatches and Jenny's Creek, which Skues called the Highland Burn, and most of the main stream, where the old man's ashes were scattered in 1949. (We erected a fitting memorial here in August 1980.) The 'ugly modern factories' to the east, referred to in Goddard's piece, are barely noticeable to anglers of today. Nearly a quarter of a century has elapsed, the screen of trees is fully grown, and the scars have healed. The river and its side-streams have matured too. Little sign of Roy's early restoration work remains.

The fishery no longer supports a large stock of wild trout, but Roy maintains a sensible balance. Fry, yearlings and 1½–2½ lb target fish are introduced to supplement the natural stock: fish that are inclined to peg away, sometimes for the entire day, as they feed on an assortment of emerging nymphs, reed smuts, upwinged flies and spinners. Hatches of mayfly (*E. danica*) have reappeared after an absence of some seventy years, while the evening rise to small spurwings, pale evening duns and blue winged olives can be a sheer delight.

William Senior described this stretch as the most challenging in the south, a view echoed by connoisseurs of today. Above all perhaps, it is just such a glorious spot to be. 'It's a lovely place to meet old friends,' says Roy. 'We reminisce over a glass or two, watch the sun go down over the meadows, and maybe have a cast now and again. Isn't that what fishing is all about?'

Abbotts Barton is champagne water indeed.

ক০ 25 ৩৩
Mental Block

My friend Ron Darlington had an astonishing encounter on a Midlands river, which seems to confirm the view once expressed by Skues that 'the average angler is made of ivory from the ears up'. Ron had been fishing side by side with a number of anglers whose across-and-down, wet-fly style was proving entirely fruitless. Trout were rising all around them, so he fished with a dry fly and caught fish after fish, much to the surprise of the locals.

When he suggested that they might consider changing to the dry fly, so as to enjoy similar success, one retorted: 'That's all very well, but we don't fish that way up here, mate!'

PART TWO

'Only an idle little stream,
Where amber waters softly gleam,
Where I may wade through woodland shade.
And cast the fly, and loaf and dream.'

Dr Henry Van Dyke

✍ 26 ✍

A Latticed Bridge

While the name of G.E.M. Skues is forever linked with the Abbotts Barton water at Winchester, it is interesting to recall that some of his most significant observations were made after he had given up his rod on the Itchen and moved to a peaceful Wiltshire valley where he was to fish out his final years. Indeed, although Skues fished this intimate and utterly charming little stream for seven years, while living at the Nadder Vale Hotel (now a private residence) between 1940 and 1948, it is a curious fact that comparatively few of his disciples have paid his last haunts a visit, nor I suspect do many even know their where-abouts.

Mind you, these are not the kind of classic chalk-stream reaches depicted in old volumes, with wide waters flowing bank-high like polished glass, and chocolate-box cottages that peep between weeping willows fringing the crystal stream. Nor do you see shiny, expensive motor cars parked inside the gateways while their occupants disport themselves about cosy fishing huts, clad in the latest angling garb. The members of the club here, which I have just joined, seem more inclined to fish in old gardening clothes or ancient, well-patched sports coats. They dress as Skues himself might have dressed, which is fitting in a place so steeped in fishing tradition. An Orvis badge, a Garcia sticker, even one of the more gaudy, multi-pocketed waistcoats, would strike a discordant note I feel, bringing you suddenly back into the 1990s. Most of us join clubs like this to escape from the present – or at any rate old codgers like me, who were brought up on wild trout, size 15 hooks and silk lines, rather than stew ponds, braided leaders and nymphs that go 'plop'.

Wherever you go on this little-known stream you come across famous landmarks: places of which you have read in *Angling Letters* or *The Way of a Man with a Trout* but may never have seen. On my first day here I stumbled upon an iron latticed bridge which spans the river down by the garden of the hotel, and spied a trout lying on the bottom an easy stone's throw upstream. I was sorely tempted to do as Skues had done, and see how many pebbles the fish would take, but, as a new boy, I thought it best to hold my hand. I looked towards the stone buttress to my left in case a two-pounder should be in position. I could see exactly how Skues would have cast to that trout, using a wonderful new American material called nylon, and shared his consternation as the fish shot beneath the bridge, sawing his leader back and forth along the wire. He had been amazed by the strength and resilience of the substance, and lost no time in telling the angling world about it.

And of course I examined the cobwebs minutely. There were *Caenis* present, with the shiny black thorax, as Skues had discovered in 1939, but no sign this day of CP (*C. pennulatum*) which he had named large blue-winged pale watery, now known as the large spur-wing. I did, however, recall one delightful passage from a letter to C.A.N. Wauton: 'He [M.E. Mosely] thinks that anglers should be satisfied to let CP dun pass as BWO but that will not do. The pattern which kills when BWO is on is NBG in a hatch of CP.' Always a great one for his abbreviations was old Skues!

It seems that throughout his eight years as a resident at the Nadder Vale Hotel, Skues went to the latticed bridge almost daily, and for the three years he fished this water (before he lost his rod here and took fishing on the Bemerton length further downstream) he was in the habit of putting up and taking down his rod here. Many an hour he must have leaned with his arms on the parapet gazing into the stream, dreaming no doubt of his past life and wondering how long he could go on fishing. I have little doubt that it was here that he looked upon the little river for the last time, and said farewell to his beloved chalk streams forever.

Today, this two-and-a-half-mile stretch of the Nadder is fished lightly, and with care I think, and some respect. I often make the latticed bridge my starting point, and I put up and take down my rod here too while searching for rising trout towards the shallow by the hotel garden. The stream benefits from surface run-off water – unlike the Wylye, which joins it below Wilton and whose flows dwindle alarmingly in these days of borehole abstraction. Here, innumerable stickles and pools over a relatively steep gradient ensure that healthy flows are maintained in drought years. Trout have plenty of shelter in well oxygenated water as the stream winds this way and that in a series of tight bends, overhung by heavy clumps of hawthorn whose pink and white blossom is a picture at mayfly time.

The size of the trout might not satisfy those who operate on crack waters, but most are pure natives, nut-brown with few red spots, delicate fins and wide, pointed tails. Most weigh between 11 oz and 1 lb 6 oz, but I caught one old warrior here which went to 2 lb 4 oz. Trout are numerous, the fish sometimes rising only a yard or two apart during a heavy hatch. But you are inclined to fish sparingly nonetheless, knowing that man could so easily ruin the fishing by turning in too many stockies. To date, of some sixty trout captured, ten have been stock fish. These have come home for supper, but most of the wild fish have been returned.

As I approach the angler's final stage, in which the future becomes increasingly uncertain and the past slips more sharply into focus, I have time to savour my secret little stream, to marvel at nature's ability to produce, despite man's inexorable advance, and to thrill at the sight of the kingfisher and the sip of the trout as he takes the floating dun or spinner. In 1949 Skues' ashes were scattered close to a favourite spinney on the eastern bank of the Itchen by his old friend Mullins, but I sometimes wonder whether in spirit he lingers still by a certain iron latticed bridge nestling peacefully in the shelter of the Nadder valley below Ugford Farm.

ఌ 27 ઌ

Duty Calls

As usual, my holiday had been a rapturous period of tranquil reverie and joyous ineptitude, but today I hoped to secure a modest dish, if only to complete my 'fish round' in the village. One of the great pleasures of our sport is the opportunity it affords to distribute our catch, but so far this season I had neglected my duties.

An angler with such a mission does not need distractions, yet the scene as I approached our short stretch of the Itchen was quite breathtaking. Monkey flowers filled the disused carrier stream, encouraging me to linger with the camera, while the meadows beyond were a blaze of pink and blue Speedwell and Forget-me-not with here and there a delicate Marsh Orchid standing proud in the morning sunshine. I tore myself away, only to encounter a gregarious psychiatrist friend, who admits to being more disturbed than most of his patients, searching through his fly boxes. (He carries at least a dozen of these in two fishing bags, each containing about fifty patterns, and wastes a lot of time worrying about which one to tie on.) I told him that I'd been wasting time too, talking to the flowers, and he turned sharply to ask if they had started answering back. By the time we had taken coffee from his flask, and talked of the weather, the prospects of a rise, his dog, his wife and my financial straits, over an hour had passed.

At length we went our separate ways, I to a deep part of the river where four sizeable trout had been feeding well two days before. Sure enough, although no duns were visible on the water, all were rising in business-like fashion, two under my bank and two in midstream. The two bankers lay in fixed stations, sipping away like clockwork, but those in the middle were moving this way and that, making bow-waves and occasionally thrusting their nebs clear of the surface. I had met this phenomenon before, and the memory-bank served me well. Diagnosing reed smuts at the margin and near-surface nymphs over

102

the weed beds further out, I tackled the two nearer fish first. I seldom attempt to imitate the tiny smuts, finding that trout usually accept a size 16 Black Gnat readily enough, but I failed to remember that they barely open their mouths when taking these little flies, and struck each rise too soon, missing both.

But another trout had started rising two yards ahead. This time I held my hand and saw the rod stoop to the weight of a good fish, which seemed intent on making his way across river to warn my two active friends in midstream. I had to halt his progress, so lowered the rod to the horizontal and swept him downstream as hard as I dared. The fish sped beneath the vegetation some yards below, where I let him remain as I moved down the margin, reeling in loose line as I went. Soon I was immediately above his bolthole, in full control of the tackle and with my net at the ready. Tightening up, I saw him boil on the surface, but soon he was thrashing in the net, all 2 lb 2 oz of him.

Those in mid-river were still at it, so the Skues-style nymph was dispatched on its deceitful errand. The lower trout furrowed sideways towards it; I struck, but felt nothing. His movements had ceased, so I crept towards the fish above. This time there was no mistaking the leader-draw, and a moment later a short, silvery trout leaped a good yard into the air, coming down smack on his flank. Winded perhaps, the fish came to the net without fuss, measuring fifteen inches for his 1 lb 9 oz.

By now, I was surrounded by a herd of playful bullocks. The ritual was that they would tiptoe forward to nudge me in the back, until I kicked up my heel behind me, at which they would scamper off in delight; as soon as I turned to more urgent matters, up they would come again to continue the game. So I decided to move off, have lunch and drive over to the Wylye, where I was to meet a friend that evening. It was only mid-afternoon, so I looked in at Durnford, on the Avon, where I took the last Salisbury Club disk left, that for beat 15, and drove up to the stone bridge at the bottom of that reach. The two members on the beats below told me they had been out all day and not seen a single fish. They cast a most elegant line, and both kept on pitching to nothing in particular as we chatted.

Moving on to my beat however, I noticed two trout lying out above the bridge, each well on the feed. I do not cast as beautiful a line as some, but here was a situation in which sensible watercraft might prove the more critical factor. These fish are approached almost daily, so it is the sight of an angler, his ever-waving rod and the snaking line, which causes them to go down. I lengthened my leader to eleven feet by adding a three-foot point of fine nylon and, keeping well down among the grasses, wafted the Black Gnat to alight some two feet ahead of the nearer trout. He tilted slowly in the water, sipped, and plunged violently as the rod bent in homage before the meshes received his 21 oz. The further trout behaved just as the first had done, except that I had to bully him out of a weedbed, and he, too, scaled 1 lb 5 oz. The brace had been spotted, hooked and landed within the space of fifteen minutes.

I had hoped I could depart without meeting the other members, for, no matter how humble, I would be dubbed an expert or something worse, but they were approaching the bridge and saw my two trout. They were most interested in what fly pattern I had used. I wanted to suggest to them that by standing on the bank and casting all day they were denying themselves the chance of sport, but any such advice would have been unwelcome in the circumstances. In any case, fishermen have to learn such things for themselves, although some never do, of course.

After taking refreshment in the Swan at Stoford, my friend and I sallied forth for the evening rise on the Wylye, upstream of Great Wishford. By 8p.m. a good rise was in progress, but experience had taught me that it is usually the grayling which begin feeding before sundown here. Later, in twilight conditions, the river sometimes boils as both trout and grayling are on the go. But if you wait later still, the grayling go to bed, and only the trout, including the heavyweights, will rise in earnest. Leaving my favourite pool until last light I fished up the shallows, having changed to a Pheasant-tail spinner, and caught several well conditioned grayling of between 1 and 1¼ lb. Compared with trout, grayling can be very difficult to unhook, having gristly mouths in which the barb becomes firmly embedded. If they cannot be freed simply, while still underwater, I am inclined to take them, since they are not as robust as trout and many which are returned fail to survive.

It was approaching 10p.m. before the trout began their evening meal. The massed concentration of sherry spinners had fallen on the water, and I was amazed at the number of wild trout rising. We often get a false picture of trout populations (always tending to underestimate), but now the river was alive; sad, I thought, that most fishermen go home long before the real action begins. As often happens, however, I failed to take full advantage of the opportunity. One trout, rising just a yard or so to my right, jumped so high he nearly landed in my wader-top. I twitched him free. Another, moving well under the reeds on the far bank, tore downriver, leaped three times and came off. But upstream, hard against my bank, I secured two beauties, one of which stripped out most of my line as he headed in vain for the sanctuary of an old hatchway.

In near darkness, the barn owl ghosted silently over his hunting ground as the two of us stalked our respective quarry. Soon, by the glimmer of my torch, I weighed the two trout, and reckoned I could call it a day. Six trout, taken from three different rivers and averaging 1 lb 7 oz, plus five firm grayling, would make a good supper for a number of elderly folk and others along the valley.

ఆ 28 ఴ

Spiritual Prostitution?

'The days when Frederick Maurice Halford bestrode the fly-fishing world like a giant with none to say him "nay" are no more.' We can surely detect a sigh of relief in these words from G.E.M. Skues, for now it was time to charge that surgical nib and make his final incision, establishing once and for all the legitimacy of the nymph as an effective and wholly sporting supplement to the dry fly on chalk streams.

That Skues miscalculated the level of resistance among his contemporaries is apparent not only from the growing impatience displayed in some of his later works, but by the fact that at the time of his death in 1949 most southern fishermen still viewed the matter of sub-surface fishing with some misgivings. The valuable contributions of Frank Sawyer and Oliver Kite in the 1950s and 1960s added further weight to the discussion, while numerous writers have since developed patterns and techniques which have taken our thinking further, and deeper, than Skues himself would perhaps have considered prudent.

His method was essentially a logical extension of dry-fly fishing, in which close imitations of emerging or near-surface ephemerids were offered to individual trout feeding on natural insects at that level. Sawyer's method was to present a weighted, general purpose nymph to fish feeding at some depth, including those which Skues' patterns were never designed to reach. There can be no doubt Skues was fully aware that trout take nymphs in mid-water and close to the stream bed, but he chose to overlook the obvious possibilities of weighted artificials and any kind of impressionistic patterns, fearful perhaps that these would represent the thin end of a very divisive wedge. What unbridled excesses might follow?

Had his technique remained the only form of nymph fishing devised, we can say with some confidence that it would by now have gained widespread acceptance. Latterly, however, the issue has become so clouded by the gradual intrusion of shrimp patterns, damsel nymphs, goldheads and heavy lures that a process which might otherwise have continued to evolve naturally has been halted by those who sought radical change. Indeed it has been reversed to a point where many fishermen have now rejected the nymph completely.

Whether or not we feel it is over-restrictive, the fact remains that no chalk-stream fishery I know permits the use of artificial nymphs without explicit qualification. Some fish the dry fly exclusively, some only dry fly and emergent, in-film nymphs, while others elect to use nymphs only after midsummer. Restrictions on hook sizes or the use of lead or copper wire in the dressing usually apply too. Even on the Itchen length fished by Skues for 56 years some ninety-five per cent of the trout taken today are caught on dry flies – this despite imitative nymph fishing being allowed all season.

Such has been the reaction, as I see it, to the spread towards the chalk streams of flies and fishing methods best suited to still waters and some rain-fed rivers that many are now seeking a clear definition of what a nymph actually is. Kite, writing in 1966, was in no doubt.

> The term Nymph is often loosely applied, but to the nymph fisherman its meaning is altogether more precise. Several kinds of winged insects are of importance to the fly-fisher, but one, and one only, concerns the nymph fisherman: this is the order of aquatic upwinged flies or *Ephemeroptera* . . . to these insects alone, at a certain specific and recognisable stage of their development, is the term Nymph applicable. When the larva approaches maturity, the wing cases begin to form on its dorsal thorax and become readily apparent to the observer. It is at this stage that the larva is properly termed a nymph.

However, he excluded the mayfly (*E. danica*) nymph from his fly box, writing in *Nymph Fishing in Practice* (1964) 'it would be spiritual prostitution for me to put on a nymph on a no. 5 hook and use this to butcher trout with.'

❧ 29 ❧
Follow My Leader

My friends tell me they can detect the takes of nymphing fish simply by watching for leader-draw, yet I estimate that I miss a large majority of opportunities while fishing for unseen trout, especially at depths of more than a few inches. Of course, it depends to some extent on the type of water we are fishing – whether it is a slow glide, a rippling shallow, or somewhere in between – and also on the mood of the fish: they may grab the nymph determinedly on one occasion and sip in the fly so gently on another. Just occasionally I have a succession of unmistakable pulls that leave me in no doubt, but by and large I reckon I fail to spot any indication in about nine cases out of ten.

Discussing this with a colleague who maintained that his average rate of take detections was vastly higher than this (in fact he insisted he hardly ever missed one), we decided to put the matter to the test, on a smooth and relatively swift-flowing stream whose surface was broken here and there by swaying fronds of ranunculus. Our initial vantage point was close to a disused chalk-pit where the road runs high above the river, enabling the observer to spot every fish lying out. Light conditions were perfect, and we could see seven trout hovering near the weed beds, along with a shoal of a dozen or so grayling in a pocket below. We selected a Pheasant-tail nymph, weighted to fish at or a little above the trouts' level, a depth of between one and two feet. Leaving me to watch from above, my friend was soon wading quietly up the margin towards the group of grayling, but unable to see them from his position.

Pitched well ahead of the shoal, the little nymph trotted down unhindered until it was judged to be just in front of the leading fish. Lifting the fly fractionally brought an instant response, the leader drew sharply forward, and the first grayling was on. A slack line and barbless hook enabled the fish to shake the fly free. The performance was repeated three more times, each take clearly marked by a pronounced draw of the leader. So far, my friend had proved his point, but what about the trout?

The grayling dispersed, moving away down river as the angler approached the weed beds. The first delivery was a yard off target – understandably since he was casting 'blind'. Despite this, the trout came across current, sidled up to the nymph and sucked it in. With a shake of the head the trout ejected the fly and disappeared beneath the nearest water plant; the fisherman remained impassive, quite unaware of what had occurred. With guidance from above, the next chuck landed the nymph within inches of trout number two. He rose quickly, taking the fly and spitting it out again in one clean movement. Again, no reaction from the fisherman, who had seen nothing.

The next trout was lying in a quiet cushion of slack water immediately above a weed patch; if ever there was a spot where some draw would be seen, surely it was here. Placing the fly four feet upstream of the trout, so as to minimize the effect of any ripples which might distort his vision, the angler waited for that eternal three seconds of free drift, poised in eager anticipation. The nymph trundled past the fish, which then swung round and took the fly sideways-on. It turned back upstream, released the deceitful lure and regained its original position. But once more the fisherman was able to discern no indication, nor was he when a 'too accurate' shot put the nymph right into the mouth of a 1¼-pounder, which simply opened its jaws to eject the fly while remaining on station.

So the final score was 4–0 to the angler while grayling fishing, and 0–4 against when trout were the intended quarry – an interesting exercise from which we may or may not draw some useful conclusion.

৩ 30 ৩

Kentish Glory

A chance encounter with two London-based fishermen brought back memories of another meeting twenty years before, when I too had enjoyed some outstanding sport on the Kentish Stour, a stream they had recently visited. I had been introduced by Timothy Benn to a man I had heard much about, David S. Martin, whose carefully planned strategy of planting out fry and yearlings over a number of seasons had ensured that a well graded stock of trout was maintained throughout, with a fine new generation of mature fish coming on to sizeable proportions each year. Naturally, such excellent trout fishing close to the metropolis meant that access to the club's water was difficult to obtain, so I was determined to make the most of the day I had been so kindly offered.

On 8 July 1977 Tim put me on the broad, shallowish beat immediately above Shalmsford Bridge, one mile to the east of Chilham, while he went off downstream. To my delight I noticed a dozen or more trout moving this way and that among the bright patches of ranunculus and rising now and again to the occasional dun. Some fish appeared to be feeding almost exclusively on near-surface nymphs while others were inclined to pursue the fleeting olives and pale wateries. As ever, I would have to meet each challenge as it was presented, with no preconceived notions as to which of my patterns, if any, the trout would accept. And yet at this stage of the season my eye was well in, and I felt confident as the Itchen Olive settled a foot or so ahead of the nearest riser. The fish looked, decided against, and then turned to follow the fly a couple of yards downstream towards me, taking it before I had gathered in the loose line. I tried striking but, with coils of line everywhere, made no contact, and the trout just swam into a weedbed with a puzzled expression on his face.

Another fish was feeding really well a yard further across the stream, but he wanted nothing to do with my Itchen Olive, despite continuing to push and bulge at the surface in a seemingly suicidal manner; the fly must have passed over the trout's nose at least twenty times. This caused me to question the worth of a pattern that had proved so popular in Hampshire, but rather than change it for another, I decided to bite off the hackle, spit on it and pitch once more to my insatiable friend. He had it at once, and before I could say 'supper time' he was off on a journey I shall never forget, rushing and leaping his way down river. In a split-second the fish had torn through a dense weedbed and gone to ground under the far bank, while the line had somehow wrapped itself around my right ankle. I found I was unable to wade beyond midstream, and got a bootful for trying. Then the trout deserted his sanctuary and legged it at high speed towards Canterbury. He may well have got there for all I know, since all I had on the end when I reeled in was a very unhappy looking fly – what was left of it.

Somewhat dejected, I addressed the next trout, which was rising in a sheltered pocket above a mass of surface weed. This one took the Itchen Olive right away – a smaller version this time – and again I had a scrap and a half among the vegetation before sliding the fish along the top of the weed-raft, a piece of ranunculus neatly draped over his eyes. At 1 lb 7 oz and fifteen inches long, the trout was spot on Sturdy's Scale and soon nestled in my bag, along with two large dock leaves. Then I secured two more beauties of similar size, each tearing line from the reel in the most alarming fashion. I was unsure of the club's rules about how many I should take, so these were released by removing the hook with thumb and forefinger while the fish were still under water.

The hatch was nearly over by now, but wading slowly up the shallows I was able to hook and return four smaller trout on my sawn-off Olive before Tim joined me for lunch (bread and brie as I recall), and we fell to chatting of this and that and snoozing the afternoon away. He had taken a fish of 2 lb 14 oz (I had suspected when he left me earlier that he had an appointment with a known adversary), and what a magnificent trout it was. I suspected, too, that I was being 'sized up', and sure enough in due course I was invited to write a little book for beginners, *How to Start Trout Fishing*, which Tim's firm Ernest Benn Ltd published in 1980.

A storm was brewing in the west as we made our way upstream to East Stour farm for the evening. The clouds were approaching fast and the wind was getting up – so much so that I doubted whether there would be much of a rise. Tim, sportsman that he is, insisted that I fish for the few risers we did spot, and in about half an hour I had returned three mighty scrappers up to 1 lb 4 oz on the dry Itchen Olive. At last light we found a trout rising in the dark tunnel beneath an overhanging bush which my companion reckoned would be a good 'un. I experienced some difficulty in getting the fly to the correct spot, and when I did the Olive was refused. Tim diagnosed sedges. How right he was, for at the second chuck the rod hooped over as a solid fish dived deep. Fortunately he did not go far but simply bored down and down into his bolthole, eventually tiring himself and coming to the net after a fight lasting some five minutes. This made up my brace for the day, 1 lb 12 oz and 1 lb 7 oz, with a further nine trout to 1 lb 8 oz returned. I have seldom known trout quite so strong and determined as these, before or since, a tribute to David Martin's thoughtful approach to river management.

But what of the present? How did the river seem to my young friends who fished there in 1997? They told me it had suffered from low flows in the past five years or so, as have many others. I was delighted to learn, though, that the stocking policy remains largely the same, that the descendants of those grand trout of the 1970s strip line and fight like fury, and that sensitive hands still tend this lovely stretch of the Kentish Stour. I understand too that the Chilham Mill water, comprising an excellent length of the main stream and parallel carrier, together with a stocked stillwater, is now accessible on a day permit from the Mid-Kent Water Company.

❧ 31 ❧

Treasures Beyond Price

As some of us anxiously review our financial position in the light of 'slimdown' or a crumbling welfare state, it may be interesting to consider how one particular angling hobo managed to enjoy quality fishing in 1994 despite somewhat impoverished circumstances. Given that I fish four days or part-days a week, and that my trout-fishing budget cannot now exceed around £350 p.a., including transport costs, I must ensure that I pay no more than £2 per day on average for access to trout waters. This lets out stillwaters for a start, which doesn't bother me unduly, but what about the southern chalk streams, and the moorland rivers I love to visit?

Fortunately I run an old diesel car, and have a tent which I use on trips to Dartmoor and Exmoor. Fishing can be very inexpensive here, catch limits are more than sufficient to meet my culinary needs, and nature's fruit and veg may often be gathered by the wayside. Even allowing for any pitch fees, I live as cheaply on the moors as I would back home, and the sport can range from the superb to the hilarious around campsites at holiday time. I recall catching four trout one afternoon in a pool occupied by a number of bathers, the slippery stones causing me to take the plunge more than once, and landing a further seven fish soon after their departure. My neighbours and I enjoyed a hearty meal that night (they supplied wine, mushrooms and apple pie), and even the leaping of the sea trout just yards away failed to rouse me to fresh endeavours.

The diary reveals that I also fished 69 days on a total of 11 different chalkstreams last season. Seven of these outings were at the invitation of friends, the remaining 62 days being spent on the ten miles or so of the upper Avon, Wylye, Bourne and Nadder managed by my local angling club (£84 p.a. for anytime access), on a six-hundred-yard stretch of the Ebble, or on odd bits of untenanted water I've sussed

113

out near superstores, factories, public parks and the like. Some of my most enjoyable fishing was on these last waters, not least because they are largely unkeepered and unstocked, and thus often provide ideal conditions for wild trout.

One downtown beat is the home of Chipper the cat, whose insistence that you catch fish is quite touching. Chipper doesn't know the meaning of polite enquiry and, as a serious hunter, finds the concept of catch and release distinctly unpalatable. He sticks like glue as he rubs and stretches round your calves, head butts your knees as if trying to upend you in the river, and mews so pitifully you feel positively guilty if you blank. Many a time I've flailed away into the darkness to secure a quarter-pound grayling for this persistent critter. Once I hooked a two-pound trout and tried to pretend I hadn't caught it, slipping it quickly back in the hope that he'd not noticed – of course he had, and the look of reproach haunts me still.

My total catch on the chalk streams between 15 April and 15 September (after which I concentrate on the grayling) was a modest 129 trout, of which eighty per cent were native fish, while my adventures in Devon produced 78 wild trout in 20 days' fishing. I reckon my 89 outings cost under £1.70 on average in fishing fees, my fuel (over and above normal consumption) about £140, and my rod licence and items of tackle £30, giving a total of £320 in all over this 22-week period.

I've read a good deal about wealth, privilege and elitism, often by those writers who portray the least attractive tip of the chalk-stream spectrum. Sure, you can pay £150 for a day's high-rise stockie bashing, or book a pampered stretch for corporate entertainment with banqueting, guiding, etc., included. You may even meet a Duke or an Earl and catch five-pounders from his lawn. But, believe me, this kind of commercialism has nothing in common with those sensitively managed fisheries where the great majority of anglers operate, most of whom have no more spare cash than the next person.

So, if you find yourself in the Nadder valley one evening and notice a dim light glowing in the humble weatherboard structure nearby, you may spot a lone figure bent over a single ring as he fries a trout for his supper. This is a lifelong southern fisherman who, like many of his fellows, hardly projects the popular image which those from other areas have come to expect. As the outside world becomes ever more vain and acquisitive, so his priorities have focused increasingly on the simple messages that nature whispers to those who care to listen.

‹∘ 32 ∘›

The Golden Hours

The likelihood of our arrival at the riverside coinciding with a spectacular rise of trout may seem remote, yet periods of intense feeding activity occur on most days as midsummer approaches. The trick is to know when, during a possible 16–18 hours, such an exciting scenario is in prospect. The fact is that many of us, for whatever reason, fail to take advantage of the wonderful opportunities on offer at this season.

I well remember the retired gent with a camper van who used to park by the river for much of the summer. He never seemed to be fishing, even though I sometimes arrived before 10a.m. and often didn't leave until long past my supper time. But a delicious aroma of frying trout would come wafting across the car park of a morning, while the record book fairly bristled with his entries. I even entertained uncharitable thoughts as to his methods, but one day I plucked up the courage to ask him how he did it. 'Well, these trout become mighty wary in the daytime when anglers are about,' he answered affably, 'so I fish before they arrive, and again after they've all gone home. It depends on the weather of course, but in these warm conditions that's when the trout rise best anyway.'

This really made me think. After all, I'd been coming up with all sorts of excuses to get off work so as not to miss out on the alleged hatch, yet here was a man who caught most of his fish at a time when I could have made it comfortably. It figured that, since many of our trout topped 1½ lb, and since they appeared lethargic, jittery or ultra-selective in the heat of the day, they must feed like mad at some other time in order to maintain condition. What I had not realized was that natural insects were present in sufficient abundance outside 'normal' fishing hours to bring on a general rise.

During the seasons which followed I ventured forth at daybreak, at nightfall, even in the early hours of the morning (on a stretch lit by street lamps), and on enough occasions to form some fairly positive conclusions. I was relieved to discover that night fishing appeared largely unproductive – although I've occasionally caught brownies while sea-trout fishing elsewhere – nor was there much point in going out in the pale glow of a summer dawn, delightful though this was in other respects. But as I lingered, I soon found that a few trout would begin to rise quietly just as the first rays of the sun touched the water surface. In settled weather this happened so regularly that I decided to investigate more fully.

None of my books made any mention of early-morning fishing, yet as the sun slowly ascended so the rise of trout became stronger. There were relatively few duns to be seen at this hour (and those mostly aborted 'left-overs' from the previous evening), but a variety of spinners floated on or just beneath the surface, including small spurwings, medium olives and BWO (sherry) spinners – and, interestingly, pale evening spinners, which are said by some authorities to be rarely seen on the water. My variations on the standard Pheasant-tail worked a treat, and for the last species I used palest orange tying silk instead of the normal red.

As the sun rose in the sky, sedges began to scuttle about on wooden or stone structures, encouraging me to bounce a few appropriate artificials off bridges and the like, which often resulted in a welcome 'splosh'. But this post-sun-up sport, lasting up to two hours or so, is usually a more delicate, sipping affair in which trout can become so preoccupied that some of their natural caution may be lacking.

From around mid-June hatches of broadwings (*Caenis*) become progressively heavier, continuing until well into August. These tiny ephemerids have a predominantly cream body, two rather stubby broad wings and three tails. It is worth going out at sunrise on a warm, still morning just to witness the amazing spectacle of hundreds of duns hopping and skipping on the surface, of flies transposing everywhere, including on your clothing, while a massed concentration of soaring spinners sways this way and that on the gentle air, like a giant ivory curtain. The trout sometimes project their nebs above the surface while pursuing the quick-hatching duns, but they feed in a more dainty, yet rapid, clockwork fashion when the spinners are floating down. A useful pattern which I use to represent either stage is constructed as follows:

GM Broadwing

Hook:	16–20
Tying silk:	Light brown
Tail:	Four or five cream cock fibres
Body:	Cream-coloured stripped quill
Thorax:	Exposed tying silk
Hackle:	Cream cock, wound well down the hook shank.

Some twelve hours later the rods are gathering for the evening rise, the timing of which is likely to vary, depending upon which species of insect are present. On rivers where small spurwings hatch in good numbers, for example, the activity may begin an hour or so before sunset, while a fall of spinners, some of which come to the water quite early, will often trigger a general rise at this time. Pale evening duns sometimes put in an appearance before sunset, while reed smuts may be on the menu too. Where blue-winged olives and sedges are the principal diet, though, the timetable may be quite different.

Those who are unfamiliar with the water may decide to pack up when all is quiet and the sun has sunk below the hill, perhaps little realizing that a serious rise of trout is imminent. My home river is a case in point. Here there is sometimes a half-hearted rise only, or no movement at all, until 15–20 minutes after the rim of the sun has disappeared, when the surface can suddenly come alive with hatching duns and the rings of feeding trout. The air becomes thick with BWO spinners, especially around weirs and hatchways, and, although the angler may have just 30–40 minutes fishing, they can provide the most exhilarating sport imaginable.

Accurate presentation is all-important now, since the fish need not move more than an inch off line in order to take their fill. As the light fades, position yourself so as to look directly into the afterglow, whose reflection on the surface will enable you to spot rise forms and the whereabouts of your fly for perhaps ten minutes longer than would otherwise be the case. Concealment is much less important in the near darkness, indeed you may see or hear trout gulping down the flies right under your rod. Dap for them – or, if you've changed up to a heavier line with a short leader, you can make mini roll-casts – but make sure the fly keeps floating well or you could be missing takes. This is electrifying stuff, but we have to be clinical and super-efficient if we are to make the most of it: trout of a pound or less can be landed inside fifteen seconds; then it's a quick squeeze in the amadou pad and the fly is passing over the next fish.

Some of the largest trout in the river are likely to be rising now, but watch out for the moment they switch their attention to sedge flies. Look for the scurrying wake on the surface, and listen for the splashy takes. This is your last chance, for in five or ten minutes the rise may be over.

Then the river sleeps, and the angler plods home across the meadow. These are the golden moments we remember all our days. But if we had just followed the crowd who fish from mid-morning until sunset, what sport we might have missed!

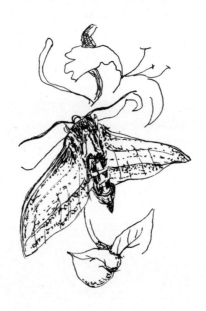

~ 33 ~

An Evening in Summer

When the may blossom fades, and the alder and dog rose flower in the hedgerow, our trout rivers take on a very different character. The excitement of the mayfly is over, the water at noonday has lost much of its sparkle, and the small upwinged duns which encourage trout to rise so freely in the daytime are fewer in number. The occasional fish may yet be found rising, perhaps beneath the footbridge or in the shade of an overhanging bush, but for me this is the time to savour that most magical period of all, when hatches of evening fly are at their height and the air becomes alive with radiant spinners dancing ecstatically towards the climax of their brief airborne existence.

If we have driven thirty miles or more, perhaps straight from work, it can be some time before we are fully attuned to the life of the river. It is a mistake, I feel, to begin casting too soon, maybe even using the same fly that we finished fishing with last trip and without checking the leader for any weakness. Keen though we are, it may be better to sit quietly for a while, allowing the sounds and sights of the waterside to enter our soul. Now we might change our point nylon and test other blood knots, see that the meshes of our folding net fall free of the metal rim, treat a couple of flies with floatant and ensure that their eyes are clear of varnish. Later, in the hectic moments of last light, we may be glad that we did these things.

Watching the water has a calming effect, and when we are calm and relaxed we fish better. As we watch, the river will reveal her secrets, giving us an inspiration that no amount of studying the contents of our fly-box can bring. Rivers vary widely in the kind of evening sport they offer, and the season and general climatic conditions will have a bearing too, but on many of the streams I fish between mid-June and late August, given settled weather, we may expect to see small spurwings and pale evening duns hatching from about an hour before sunset. Some small spinners will be on the water too, and there may be reed smuts or black gnats.

During this pre-sunset period, blue winged olive spinners (sherries) will be gathering and beginning to surge forward in a seemingly endless procession. This upstream migration may continue for a distance of a mile or more until the insects reach their egg-laying site, nature's way of compensating for the inevitable downstream drift of the current. (Blue-winged olives have difficulty ridding themselves of the shuck as they emerge and often travel much further downstream than other insects as a consequence; also their eggs can be swept for long distances on the stream, since they are laid in the fastest water.) They visit the same small areas of heavily broken water night after night, season after season. Here they dance in frenzied concert, gyrating in massed concentration, yet never in my experience coming to grief in collisions. The merest touch of another insect, or a leaf or grass stem causes them to shy away instantly as they guard their precious bundle. Almost simultaneously, some time after the sun has gone down, they release their egg-balls to disperse among the gravels. The spent flies die upon the stream, and, even as they twitch in final spasm, freshly hatched duns, the product of last year's nuptials, sail proudly alongside in newness of life.

The trout are poised up in the water, sipping down the spinners and the duns with rhythmic abandon. This offers a golden opportunity to the angler who can judge which are the largest fish and is then able to deliver the fly with pinpoint accuracy.

Even as we arrive at the river sedge flies are dancing their wild evening jig just above the surface. Their numbers are incalculable as they dart this way and that, dipping onto the stream and causing little rings to appear all over, as if it were raining. An immature trout, maybe an immature angler too, will become excited at the presence of such a vast amount of fly life – the little fish leaping out of the water and the fisherman casting with enthusiasm in his direction. The truth is, however, that a Sedge pattern seldom brings a positive result at this time. Better to leave the artificial in the fly box until last light – often so late that the rise appears to be over for the night. It is now that the sedge flies emerge, and the trout begin to feed upon them in earnest. You hear a splash out in the darkness, then another, and then a boil, most of the activity occurring in faster-flowing stretches. You peer into what is left of the afterglow and spot the rise forms. For ten minutes or so you cast repeatedly, now floating the fly over a fish, now twitching it, both on and under the surface.

You catch one, or maybe you do not. Either way you are a million miles from city streets, the polluted air, the raucous din, the crush of humanity jostling to earn a crust. You have been back with your ancestors; stalking, hunting as they did in the mists of time. You write it up in the fishing diary, and you relive that evening when you are old – or maybe your grandchildren will read it some decades from now, when you are fishing in another place.

꩜ 34 ꩜

BWO Mysteries

If there is one fly which has brought me more magical fishing moments than any other it is the blue-winged olive (*E. ignita*). A number of intriguing questions about its way of life remain unanswered, and its behaviour may even appear to be somewhat eccentric. I believe, though, certain unique safeguards have evolved in the case of the BWO which ensure that it is the greatest survivor of all our upwinged flies. While the iron blue, medium olive, pale evening dun, small dark olive and the spurwings have suffered decline in recent years, (indeed one or two have virtually disappeared from some rivers), the blue-winged olive has remained a constant standby, appearing in much the same density as hitherto.

The BWO seldom, if ever, emerges in the strongest sunlight. Hatches may occur in the daytime during autumn, winter and spring, when temperatures are relatively low, but the main concentrations appear between mid-June and mid-August, some ten or fifteen minutes after sunset. This would suggest that the outer skin of the nymph case is particularly susceptible to hardening or drying out, a theory reinforced by the fact that this species experiences greater difficulty than most in freeing itself from the nymphal shuck. Even in cool conditions, the insects may struggle wildly for several yards on the surface before eclosion, often losing one or more of their three tails in the process.

The nymphs are robust creatures, certainly, but I believe the species' continued survival depends as much upon its choice of habitat as on its hardy nature. Night after night and year after year, the female flies (sherry spinners) select the same areas of tumbling water for egg-laying, favouring spots such as weirs, hatchpools and the like, where the fast currents have cleansed the river bed for some distance downstream. It is known that the larvae of some flies perish as a result of grazing areas of silt where contaminants have built up, but the majority of immature blue-winged olives feed among stones and vegetation in quicker-flowing, well oxygenated stretches. As many have observed, it is from these more turbulent reaches that the heavier hatches commonly occur.

Another fascinating characteristic of the female BWO, which does not apply so markedly in other species, is that of flying in massed procession upstream on summer evenings. I have watched other flies, including mayflies (*E. danica*), join the throng for a short while, as if caught up in the carnival atmosphere, but blue-winged olives will often travel for a mile or more to reach one of their traditional egg-laying sites before nightfall. Early on, while there is light, their journey may be quite leisurely, but as darkness approaches they surge upstream faster, lest they should fail to arrive at their final destination. In calm conditions, the main body of insects usually fly a few feet above the angler's head, where only the most observant may notice them, but a breeze will cause them to fly some two or three yards closer to the water. During half a gale I have watched this pageant take place within inches of the surface.

The reason they migrate in this way is clearly in order to compensate for the downstream movement of the current, which would otherwise bring about their eventual extinction. As to why they journey so far upriver while others do not, we may conclude that a longer downstream drift of the egg-balls in quick water, together with the prolonged period spent on the water in the dun stage, means that in its spinner stage the BWO needs to travel further upstream than other species to reach its egg-laying areas.

The only other explanation, it seems to me, is that the blue-winged olive may have evolved over a longer period, and has thus adapted its lifestyle to cope more successfully with changes of habitat. Doubtless the other species are in the process of developing similar safeguards. Man seldom plans more than a century ahead, if that, but this is a mere pinprick of time in evolutionary terms.

༄ 35 ༄

Sunset Specials

Deceiving our quarry with close representations of the natural insects upon which they feed is surely the essence of fly-fishing for trout, yet one thing I've learned the hard way is that designing lifelike imitations, although satisfying in itself, is only half the battle in terms of meeting the challenge before us. For consistent success it is also helpful (indeed critical in some cases) to become familiar with the life cycle and individual characteristics of the species in question.

I recall one evening after midsummer when the importance of such knowledge – or rather my lack of it – was brought home to me most forcibly. I had noticed hundreds of small dark olive spinners congregating on the wall of an old cart bridge. Marching in procession like soldier ants, just above the water-line, they followed a crevice which led down to their egg-laying site on the stonework beneath the surface. I could see them bobbing up again when their task was completed, but failed to realize that, instead of breaking the surface film most of them drifted away a fraction of an inch under water. The trout downstream of the bridge were rising with enthusiasm, but what I considered an almost perfect copy of the natural fly, presented with passable aplomb, continued to sail over fish after fish with monotonous regularity. It was only when I studied the water closely and saw no flies floating on the surface that I twigged. Wetting my dry fly thoroughly, I pitched it to a persistent riser with a minimum of false-casting and landed my fish just before the activity ceased.

The lull was only temporary. A mass of sherry spinners had been flying purposefully upstream for some time with their green egg-balls at the ready, and I was fully prepared with my Pheasant-tail mounted on the point. Again, I should have examined the water more carefully, for neither sherry spinners nor the duns of the blue-winged olive had yet appeared. Instead, when I finally woke up to the situation, I found that a hatch of pale duns was in progress. These were small spurwings. I changed to my Itchen Olive, designed some years ago when I fished that lovely river, and managed to secure a wild trout of over a pound.

By now, the sun had gone over the hill, the small spurwings had vanished, and the fish started to take the BWO in earnest. The dun and spinner stages of this species are commonly on the water simultaneously, the former sometimes struggling vigorously to free themselves from the nymphal shuck while the latter float on the surface quite inert. Some trout will pursue the hatching duns, making a distinctive rise form that Skues described as a kidney-shaped whorl; some quietly sip down the lifeless spinners; and others may feed on either stage impartially.

A precise imitation of each of the two stages is not crucial in my experience, but two points are worth remembering. First, when trout appear to favour the dun, imparting a fractional movement via the rod (the tiniest drag of just an inch or less) can work wonders. Second, when the flies are thick on the surface, as often occurs just after the main spinner fall in areas downstream of broken water, pinpoint accuracy of presentation can be vital. Now the trout may simply rise in one spot without the slightest deviation, taking as many as twenty or thirty flies a minute as they enjoy a period that represents the most significant 'plus' in terms of energy gain available to them at this season.

On this occasion I caught no further trout, largely because I was unable to judge the whereabouts of my fly in the failing light. Since then I have employed more hackle turns at BWO time than are normally necessary, which aids presentation, and also improves my ability to detect the take and time the strike accordingly.

The use of imitative patterns in which we have confidence, and which have proved to be effective, is undoubtedly a major factor in our success, but equally important is the often overlooked matter of where, when and how we fish them. My own favourite dressings for evening fishing during July and the first half of August are given below. They have served the test of time on a wide variety of rain-fed and spring-fed streams alike.

Itchen Olive. A most effective dry fly when small spurwings are hatching. It may be used to represent a number of other species simply by changing tying silks. This pattern is featured in *Fifty Favourite Dry Flies* by Donald Overfield and *To Rise a Trout* by John Roberts.

Hook size: 14
Silk: Primrose
Whisks: Four or five stiff grey fibres
Body: Mid-grey seal's fur, lightly dubbed
Rib: Tying silk
Hackle: Three or four turns of light grey cock hackle.

Wet Pheasant Tail. This is a very successful pattern when presented to trout taking the submerged spinner of the small dark olive.

Hook size: 16
Silk: Medium red
Whisks: Three or four light grey/brown hen fibres
Body: Two cock pheasant tail herls
Rib: Tying silk, optional
Hackle: Two turns of rusty dun, soft in fibre

Dry Pheasant Tail (variation). Similar to the traditional dressing, using quality grey cock hackle and whisks.

To represent the blue-winged olive (sherry) spinner:

Hook size: 14
Silk: Medium red
Whisks: Five or six stiff grey fibres, 15mm long
Body: Three cock pheasant tail herls
Rib: Tying silk, optional
Hackle: Five or six turns of mid to light grey cock, long in fibre

To represent the blue-winged olive dun. Dressing as above, substituting hot orange tying silk.

ॐ 36 ॐ

Dawn Patrol

Early morning mist clung to the dark water as the little craft moved quietly across the lake. Not a breath of wind touched the surface, no ring of rising trout, and no bird had yet stirred to herald the dawn. Only the muffled sound of the oars and the gentle swish from the bow betrayed the presence of the two anglers slowly approaching their destination.

The operation had been meticulously planned, with the feeding pattern of the great trout studied from the cliff-top above and the angles of drift and presentation noted in detail. The fingers of white cloud began slowly to disperse as the first glimmerings of a new day revealed the mighty rock-face looming before the boat. The anchor, lowered by hand, inevitably created some disturbance, but now it was time to produce the flask and wait silently for an hour, perhaps more, until the sun's rays reached the lower rocks where the insects had gathered after last evening's hatch.

The two fishermen had watched this little drama before, from their hidden vantage point in the scrub high above. The sedge flies would scamper over the boulders in the early sunlight, oft-times falling into the water where they jinked and gyrated and turned somersaults in their efforts to become airborne again. The remnants of last night's spinner fall would be trapped in the surface too, along with sundry midges, beetles and the like, all concentrated into the bay and lapping along the ledges where trout lay waiting for their first meal of the day.

Full of expectancy, the pair watched the sun's slow ascent, its rays reaching down ever further from one outcrop to the next. A trout nosed the surface, but it was too soon to cast. Better to wait until the fish had locked into their feeding pattern. Now they were cruising along the food lane at a good pace; later, as more insects became avail-

127

able, their movements would be regular, less hurried, more predictable.

Five minutes, ten minutes passed. First a moth, then two sedges struggled in the water, then a large black insect they couldn't identify. Several rise forms broke the surface: some mere dimples, others violent slashes which made the blood race.

The first angler lengthened line, casting so as to allow the Sedge pattern to fall gently from the rock. The head-and-tail rise cautioned him to delay his strike before setting the barb securely home. He had identified the likely boltholes during the reconnaissance – one beneath the rock-shelf, where a cut leader was a real possibility, the other a submerged tree-trunk trapped against the cliff forty yards away. The fish was a big one, a five- or six-pounder, with all the power of a really wild trout. It sped beneath the boulders like a shot, but the angler was ready. With rod bent almost double he battled the trout into open water and then, knowing what would happen next, let the reel sing as it darted towards the submerged log, bringing side-strain to bear only when the backing began to show, diverting the fish at the last moment. Perplexed, the great trout swam towards the boat, but the fisherman had anticipated this, too. His tackle was sound, his nylon of sensible strength. The net was already held submerged by his companion. They did not lift the fish aboard, but eased the hook free and watched their beaten quarry glide slowly back into the depths.

The feat was repeated, almost exactly, and the second angler released his trout. What an unforgettable brace – more than ten pounds the pair! In silence the fishermen rowed back to base, each lost in his own thoughts, while the remaining trout rose in peace. With the incident recorded in detail in their fishing diaries a golden memory lives on as if it were yesterday, against the day when two old friends can only dream of past adventures.

Thomas Hardy country. Dorset's major chalkstream, the Frome above
Dorchester

Graham Swanson fishing a carrier of the Itchen near Winchester

below
A jewel of the Wiltshire downlands. May blossom-time on the River Ebble above Bishopstone Church

Gordon Mackie fishing the River Nadder in Wiltshire, one of Salisbury and
District Angling Club's many trout waters

Grayling time.
November on the Heale
Water of the Avon at
Middle Woodford above
Salisbury

A tricky cast among beds of water buttercup. The Ebble near Coombe Bisset

The author hooks a good trout below Barford St Martin on the Nadder

Prime habitat.
High summer on the Itchen at
Abbots Worthy, Hampshire

The tumbling Hoar Oak Water
at Watersmeet, Exmoor National
Park

Moorland grandeur.
Upper Teign FA water near
Fingle Bridge

below
Cherry Brook, a tributary of the
West Dart in the heart of
Dartmoor National Park

The author wades a wooded stretch of the River Teign below Chagford in Devon

Cream of the year.
The upper Barle near
Withypool on Exmoor

The sheltered valley of the East Lyn in North Devon

✑ 37 ↻

The Record Trout

One of the strangest angling incidents ever related to me featured my good friend Raymond Rocher, who regularly visits these shores in late summer to stalk our famous rivers. I had put him in touch with Roy Darlington, who holds a lease on Skues' beloved Itchen length to the north of Winchester, and thus it was that Raymond found himself beside the Barton carrier on the morning in question. Laying siege to a big trout feeding in the crystal depths just above an old hatchway, he succeeded in hooking the fish and moved smartly up the margin in order to gain control of his lively opponent. To his surprise and alarm, however, the trout was not the only lively creature to have taken up residence at that spot; as Raymond played his trout from the bank top, he discovered he was walking on a wasp's nest. First one or two buzzed around his head, then half a dozen, and before he knew it the best part of the swarm had joined in the attack. His fish was far from played out, so he could not net it before running for cover. He had no alternative but to drop his rod beside the stream and beat an instant retreat.

The terrain between the main Itchen and the Barton carrier is not conducive to rapid acceleration, however. It is composed of spongy grasses and reed beds intersected by disused ditches and runnels which once formed part of the old water-meadow system. In short, wasps can fly a good deal faster here than a man can run, so there was no chance of escape. Raymond had been stung a number of times during the chase, and eventually he stumbled and fell headlong to the ground, where his infuriated pursuers took their full and fearful revenge.

In a state of semi-consciousness, my friend called for help, but his cries went unanswered. At length, however, when Raymond was so weak he was almost ready to give up the ghost, another angler heard a faint sound among the vegetation and found our distressed victim. It was clear that Raymond needed urgent treatment, so the fisherman helped him to his feet, escorted him back to the car and drove straight to the Winchester Hospital. However, the queue in the casualty department was such that there was a long wait, during which Raymond could only sit there in angling garb and suffer his agonies in silence. Some two hours elapsed before the ministering angels had done their stuff, and Raymond still felt groggy in the extreme, wanting only to return to his hotel bedroom for a much-needed sleep. His companion, who had remained with him all the while, drove him back to the fishery to collect his gear.

Walking the half-mile to the scene of his adventures was a painful and laborious process. Raymond approached the spot rather more carefully this time, picked up his rod and began to reel in loose line. As he did so he felt resistance. Suddenly the rod came alive as a large trout rushed out into midstream. Not wishing a repeat performance, my friend bustled his fish away from the danger zone and brought it quickly downstream towards the stone hatchway, netting it out from there.

Raymond weighed and measured his trout, and with an unsteady hand entered it in the record. The archives of the club reveal to future generations that this was the heaviest fish taken that season, at well over 4 lb, but few of those who marvel at its dimensions will recall the singular manner of its catching.

✌ 38 ✍

Salmon are 'Keeper's Perks'

When I was invited to tell the story of my 'fish of a lifetime' I turned the diary pages back to 8 July 1972. I had already captured five wild trout of over two pounds that season (the largest 3 lb 5 oz), any one of which might have qualified, yet my tale features a salmon that weighed more than all of these put together.

The incident occurred less than two miles south-east of Stonehenge, at one of those huge Avon hatchpools. When I arrived the salmon lay close to the surface, immediately above the centre pillar, having leaped the near-vertical race through one of the two open hatches. Looking upstream from the hatchway bridge, the left-hand of the five gates was open, the next two were closed, the fourth was open, and the right-hand gate was closed. Above the hatches the surface level of the deep millhead was about two feet below the concrete sill which forms the bank, and behind me roared the pool itself, into which the water descended at least six feet from the millhead.

I knew of course that I had virtually no chance of landing this fish even if I were to hook it, but no fisherman worthy of the name – with or without permission to fish for salmon, licence or no licence (and I had neither) – would have turned down such an opportunity. My first attempt was at about 2p.m. The fish took my small nymph, went down the near (left-hand) gate and came unstuck – inevitably, my 8½-ft fibreglass rod, No. 5 line and size 16 hook attached to 3-lb nylon were clearly inadequate. I went off to catch a trout instead, returning at 4.30p.m., by which time my salmon was back in his original lie above the hatches.

This time I determined to take reasonable precautions. Replacing the thinner part of my leader with a length of 10-lb nylon and tying on a silver-bodied fly of the Polystickle variety that had last seen water at Blagdon a year or two earlier, I proceeded to dibble this in front of the

131

fish. The fly jigged invitingly as it passed to one side or the other, touched the fish's nose, or danced along the flank. I must have presented the artificial fifty times without response when suddenly the salmon moved sideways and took in a most purposeful manner. Pausing until the fish had the fly well in his mouth, I tightened hard and awaited developments, glancing at my watch as I did so. I did not have long to wait for the fireworks.

The salmon shook its head once or twice and then, realizing it was still tethered, decided on a speedy departure. Once again it turned tail and shot down the left-hand gate. It went careering around the pool below me, jumping twice high into the air and wrapping my line neatly around a weedbed. Then there was a mighty splash in the mill-head above. At first I thought it must be another fish, or maybe a large bird had dived in, but line began to strip from my reel and a colossal thrashing ensued some twenty-five yards upstream. So the salmon had leaped back up the race, this time going through the other open gate (the fourth).

My line, impeded by the weed growth and now halfway around the hatch gates, had ceased to run freely, and this acted as a brake on the fish, which then back-pedalled until it settled once more in front of the hatches. We had reached something of a stalemate, and for a while I pondered the best course of action. Clearly I had to get this fish down the fourth gate again if I were to have any hope of playing him properly. I unclipped the landing net and prodded at the salmon to make him turn down the hatch to his right. The fish turned left, ducked under the net and scooted through the near gate for the second time!

This had to be the point at which we would part company, for the line was stuck solid, completely encircling the hatches. The salmon, also helpless as long as the hook held, swayed to and fro in the centre of the racing water six feet below. Something had to give, and I had a dreadful feeling I knew what it would be. But I wasn't done yet, even though I had abandoned my tackle on the bridge and the fish was out of reach. I considered tearing a branch from a nearby bush, but the line was under immense pressure from the current, as taut as a bowstring, and any attempt to hand-line the fish could spell disaster.

Then I twigged. My car was parked a hundred yards away across the field, and in the boot lay my spare rod and line. Was it just possible. . . ? I covered that hundred yards in something approaching world record time, in waders. Having threaded line No. 2 onto rod No. 2 I inched my way along the sloping sill which skirts the pool and managed to touch the line to which my fish was attached, then to hold it. Gingerly I eased it towards me, groped in my pocket for my nail-clippers, and cut the line. I now had two lines – one, attached to the spare rod, in my left hand, and one with a double-figure salmon on the end in my right – the spare rod was tucked under my arm, and I was teetering above that swirling hatchpool.

Never, ever, can it have taken so long to tie a simple knot, and all the time one kick from the fish would have seen the last of him – and of me too, very likely. After a nightmare of twisted fingers and thumbs, though, the job was done. At last I was able to move back from the brink and play the salmon off the reel with my second rod down to the shallow pool-tail. The fish had little fight left now. He buried his head in the weedbed, a great tail waved invitingly above the surface, and I heaved my fresh-run prize ashore, collapsing on the bank beside him. The battle had lasted one hour exactly.

Back at the keeper's cottage, Mike Cridge measured the salmon at 34½ in., while the scales recorded a weight of 13 lb 8 oz. Mike insisted I take a cut from near the tail. Generous of him, I thought, for he tells me that in these parts salmon are always reckoned to be 'keeper's perks'.

ᥰᥱ 39 ᥱᥳ

A Humble Brook

I'm assured there are those lurking in the bushes who are not of the modernist school. Perhaps, like me, you know little about trout culture, leader systems or micro-fibbets, while the prospect of donning eye-catching apparel just to strut the southern catwalks catching and releasing stockies may not seem particularly attractive. But then, as I say, some of us are light-years behind the times.

You would be hard pressed to maintain a stylish profile on Graham's little stream anyway. Here you wrestle with clawing thorns, sink in boggy margins, and curse because you have no backcast. You switch, roll and shoot the fly anyhow through gaps in the foliage to unbelievably difficult lies. The only way you can cover the trout is to crawl on your belly, or kneel in the river with water trickling into your waders, as the fish rises not three yards distant. You think the trout must surely take fright as you raise the rod tip, unship the fly, and slowly draw back the catapult. Then 'ping', out goes the fly, and you pray that it lands where it should. Most times it doesn't, so you try again, but by now the trout has departed.

I suppose I've caught less than a dozen fish here over the years, but this time things looked very promising. Olives were hatching, trout were rising well, and there was a nimble feel in the air. First however, we would sit awhile in Graham's aged Bedford camper drinking tea, discussing the usual sad topics like farming practices, water resources, angling editors and the state of our bank balances. We had to be back at Search Farm by 3p.m., and were expected to provide fish for supper. I had taken the precaution of securing a brace the previous day, from a 'free' stretch near home, but there were a total of four to feed. So we wandered across the meadow at 12.15p.m., Graham going down to the mill and leaving me to fish the top hundred yards or so.

So many trouty pockets and corners exist here that the temptation is to hurry on to the next. But today I felt lazy. I just wanted to savour the delicious scent of water mint and listen to the drone of bees among the willow-herb. Two young horses munched appreciatively to my rear, a large dragonfly settled on a nearby reed stem, and the kingfisher 'pipped' as he darted upriver. A trout rose within a few feet of my position. Up he came again, but I missed him, feeling just the merest touch. I resumed my reverie, and a blue-winged olive perched trustingly on the sleeve of my sports coat.

Above the murmur of the stream I detected a faint 'kiss', repeated every ten seconds or so, and tracked it down to a tiny bay beneath a bunch of yellow monkey flowers opposite. This trout moved two feet out into the current to take my dun pattern, plunged and boiled at the surface, and eventually came tumbling into the net as a lone mallard started heavenward in a shower of droplets.

At the bend twenty yards upstream a clockwork riser was at work, above a bright starwort bed, but he went down as I approached. Then, as I was about to creep forward to another likely pool, a brown shape rose slowly just a rod's length ahead. My fly settled gently three inches from his nose. The fish turned, followed and finally sucked in the artificial so quietly that no ring appeared on the surface. I couldn't give him an inch, but the hook and the leader knots held, the fly coming free only when the trout was safely in the meshes.

It was 1.20p.m. when I returned to the camper for more tea, and to write up a modest catch in Graham's log. Although trout were still feeding steadily, I felt that one more cast would break the spell, overfill the cup, and cloud a perfect day. What was so memorable about it? Well, the setting I suppose, and the timelessness of it all, and the fact that some of our trendy ideals haven't reached this valley yet.

ఁ 40 ఔ
Nymphing Subtleties

It seems only yesterday that I caught my first trout on a weighted nymph, fished specifically to a visible fish lying just upstream of an old stone bridge over the Box Brook near Bath. Until then – it was late summer 1964 – I had employed only the dry fly and traditional wet fly methods on this rain-fed stream, little realizing that waters of a broken or less than crystal character could be fished successfully using an exciting new technique developed on the upper Avon in Wiltshire. The chalk streams seemed a world away, yet I was soon to discover that the specialized art described by Sawyer and Kite has a wider application than many appreciate, on a variety of rivers and stillwaters throughout the country. Indeed, as levels fall and water plants flourish at this season, stalking and hunting visible trout is often the most rewarding option.

One of the major advantages of sight fishing is that we reduce the element of chuck-and-chance virtually to zero. We cast less frequently, to targeted trout, and spook fewer fish as a result. The importance of locating the trout before they detect our presence cannot be over-emphasized. Slow, deliberate movements, concealment and underwater observation are vital considerations, along with the ability to present the fly accurately, delicately, and at the correct depth, while ensuring that neither the rod, nor line nor fly frighten our quarry. If this sounds demanding, we should remember that trout are wary, unforgiving creatures, so we cannot do the job half right and expect results; failure in any one of these areas is likely to ruin our opportunity. I should know, for since that initial success I've made more mistakes than most, but we learn the hard way in this game.

The ability to spot trout at depths ranging from a few inches to several feet is a matter of training the eyes to penetrate the surface layer, and then scanning every detail possible within a chosen area.

136

This is much more difficult in reflected light conditions than it is where surface glare is cut out by bankside vegetation. Trees, bushes and reedbeds provide 'zones of visibility', yet the light shining off more open water can create a dazzle effect, allowing only limited vision even when wearing Polaroids. The nature of the stream bed can be a critical factor too. Silt and algal growths limit our ability to spot fish, yet a patch of clear gravel may reveal the whereabouts of trout which might otherwise have gone unnoticed.

Some anglers walk slowly along the margin in an upright position in order to obtain maximum visibility over a wide area; this certainly enables them to cover a stretch more quickly. However, many prefer to choose concealed vantage points, close to 'trouty' lies, where they can concentrate fully on an area of limited extent. Fewer fish are disturbed this way, while the behaviour of each can be carefully noted before a cast is made. If no trout can be seen, a slight movement of the head – maybe of just a foot or two – brings a fresh panorama into view. We spot a shadow here, the rhythm of a beating tail there, or the outline of a fish previously hidden by a rock or a weed frond.

Having located a feeding trout, some important questions need to be considered. How can we catch it, bearing in mind that the fish is alert, the water is clear, and a bright sun beams from a cloudless sky? Surely he will shoot off as soon as we raise the rod? First, we should resist the temptation to start pitching at once. Let's just watch, and try to calm the nerves. How deep is he lying? Is he moving some distance laterally as he takes passing nymphs? Is he more inclined to take those to his left, or his right? If the fish is lying in mid-water, at a depth of two or three feet, we will need to deliver the fly well ahead of his lie – how far ahead will depend on the pace of the current, the weight of the artificial fly and the diameter of the leader point.

This means we may have to pitch the fly six feet or more upstream of the trout when using 3-lb nylon and a fly tied on a size 14–16 hook. If we have some nymphs constructed with lead, rather than copper wire, a shorter drift may be possible. Of course, if the trout are prepared to rise in the water the matter of fishing at the correct depth becomes less important, but often they continue to feed only at their current level. It is usually a mistake to present a nymph that is far larger than the natural ephemerids (14–16) simply to obtain greater depth, since the sudden appearance of a bulky shrimp or caddis among a procession of diminutive nymphs may well cause alarm. Such patterns are more appropriate when fished close to the stream bed.

In most conditions, I find a horizontal cast is less likely to spook trout than the standard overhead delivery. This also allows us to put a bend or crook in the line so as to avoid shadowing fish. For most of my nymphing work I like a rod with a fast tip action which will set the hook instantly, a high-floating line, and a leader of around 9–10 ft steeply tapered down to a 3–4-lb point.

Detecting the take is simple enough when trout are plainly visible. We see the fish turn or surge forward, the mouth opens and we tighten just as it closes. Don't delay the strike, as some do when fishing a dry fly, for a nymphing trout often ejects the fly in the merest split second. Where hooking fish becomes tricky is when they are only barely visible, or when the trout moves a foot or so from a visible position into a ripple or an area of reflected light; we feel sure he is about to take, but we lose sight of the fish at the critical moment. We may see leader-draw, or an underwater wink, but equally we may not. My advice is 'if in doubt, strike'; if you wait for some indication you will very likely be too late.

Variable light conditions can work to our advantage, however. If we spot an indistinct shape in a position where the odds of seeing the take are remote, we can sometimes encourage the fish to move into our 'zone of visibility' by casting deliberately to one side, where we want our fish to be! I've had trout move up to six feet on occasion, and once saw a friend bring a fish halfway across the river, which was around twenty feet wide at that point.

Positive 'inducement' is sometimes necessary, especially if we expect trout to travel such distances. We place the nymph far enough ahead of the desired taking area to allow it to sink at least to the depth at which the fish is lying. Then, when we judge that the fly has drifted close enough for the trout to see it, we give the nymph pronounced lift by raising the rod tip. This sharp movement is not strictly imitative, but is done to make the fish notice it, in the hope that he will come across to investigate. If he does, revert to free drift or very minor movement of the fly, for a trout will often follow an unnaturally active artificial without taking, just as it will when a fly is too large or of strange appearance. Having said this, a trout's reaction can vary markedly depending upon whether it is wild, naturalized or recently introduced. But in general, for fish feeding regularly on station, I would advise fishing the nymph inert in the first instance, then, if necessary, apply slight inducement to lift the fly just an inch or so, and change to some kind of shock tactics only when all else has failed.

When trout are cruising it is tempting to pursue them up and down the river, or around the margin of a stillwater, now and then lengthening line as they recede into the distance. But this is one reason that fish become so jittery on popular waters. Of course, we cannot prevent other anglers from making trout harder to approach, but those who select a piece of water where visibility is good and wait for fish to enter that area very often record the better catch. Trout are accustomed to our antics, and become wary of them, so the fisherman who keeps his head down and casts only when an opportunity arises can catch them off guard. Indeed, the fact that he remains hidden may mean there are more unsuspecting trout in his area than elsewhere. Reflected light can be more of a problem on lakes than on rivers, so any patch of paler sand, gravel or chalk is a bonus in terms of visibility. You can induce trout to move over this zone as previously described, or even pop a nymph there in anticipation, lifting it gently whenever a fish comes into view.

ꕥ 41 ꕥ
Calculating Fly Density

The wind howled in the treetops, and the rain lashed the dark surface of the stream. It was cold and thoroughly miserable, and there was nowhere I could take shelter. Yet I was rooted to the spot, almost unable to believe the evidence before me.

It was 9 September 1976, just after the long hot spell that year had broken, and what I was witnessing was the biggest hatch of upwinged duns I have ever seen. Iron blues and medium olives, blue-winged olives, pale wateries and spurwings, as if they had been waiting all summer to emerge, floated down in dozens, hundreds, thousands, millions! How could I possibly convey an accurate impression of this hatch when describing the spectacle to my friends? What should I write in the diary, a big hatch, a very big hatch, a massive hatch? Such phrases would be meaningless.

The only way to record numbers of fly is to count them, and then and there I formed the habit of doing just that, even though it can only be a rough-and-ready guide. There were between twenty and twenty-five insects to the square foot of water surface, not just down one side but right across the river – which at this point was some fifteen yards wide and flowing at a rate of about two feet per second – and the hatch continued at this level for at least half an hour. I counted only the flies sitting on the water, taking no account of those flying off. Even allowing a substantial ten per cent margin of error, a reasonable estimate of the total number of floating duns which passed me on that occasion would be in excess of three million – and in that thirty minutes not one fish rose.

I have witnessed several hatches of mixed species numbering ten or twelve to the square foot over somewhat shorter periods, and a big showing of large olives one April day, before I started estimating this way, which in my recollection must have numbered fifteen to twenty per square foot at its height and lasting twenty or thirty minutes.

Mayflies (*E. danica*) tend to be localized, appearing more strongly on one reach than another, along the margin, or in one or two favourite bends, depending upon the distribution of the silt-dwelling nymphs. Numbers may not be as great as we first imagine. Up to half a dozen mayflies to the square foot is not uncommon in my experience, but they often appear in flurries which then die down again, or are concentrated into certain areas where the wind has blown them towards one bank.

As to spinners, certainly those of the blue-winged olive (sherry spinners) can be counted with a fair degree of accuracy as they fly in procession upriver on a summer night. Sometimes mayfly spinners will join the throng, as I saw on one extraordinary evening this season. Female mayflies had been flying overhead for some time, but when none appeared spent upon the surface or could be seen dipping, I walked up to the bridge to investigate. Looking up into the darkening sky above, I counted some twenty-five pass me every ten seconds over a period of ten minutes or so, along with sherry spinners in such quantity that they outnumbered the mayflies by at least fifteen to one. A rough calculation would suggest that some 1,500 mayfly spinners and over 22,000 sherries passed me in those ten minutes alone, and that in a year when mayflies have appeared to be very sparse compared with other recent seasons. We should not forget, however, that in a dry spell mayflies can become airborne almost at once, which may give a false picture of the actual numbers hatching. Few of us, of course, ever see more than a tiny proportion of the blue-winged olives that emerge.

Such immense quantities of fly are almost inconceivable. But they do illustrate the extent to which nature will over-produce to allow for the enormous natural wastage that occurs. Whether she can cope also with the increased destruction wrought by man, and for how long, is another matter.

৩ 42 ৩

Echoes from an Ancient Valley

The pages of my diary usually come alive as the first tints of autumn appear in southern valleys. Nature bustles with activity now, sensing that urgent tasks must be completed before this generation of species can be laid to rest, and many birds and fishes have important journeys ahead. I had an important journey in late 1991 – a fishing trip to distant parts – so I was determined to savour every magical moment of an English back-end season. My butterfly records included thirty Small Tortoiseshells on the buddleia on 4 September, as many as twelve Commas on a single bramble bush on 22 September, and excursions to a nearby tract of unspoiled downland to photograph the Chalkhill Blue, Adonis Blue and the rare Silver-spotted Skipper. On my final day on the Nadder I was accompanied by a flock of some 120 goldfinches chattering excitedly prior to their departure.

Looking back over the past few months I felt a great sense of joy, and some sadness too. The little hillock where the lambs had played King of the Castle so happily in May was deserted now. I recalled how foolish my quiet words had seemed as I urged them to enjoy every minute of every day, for they would be so few. And the cygnets, less endearing now, had taken it in turns to ride on father's back on those lazy days of June. Another winter would have to turn to another spring before I would see the yellow flag and the marsh marigold again, and the dog rose and the alder in high summer. Every fisherman knows that feeling of nostalgia as autumn approaches, yet he knows that he has more to be thankful for than those who never experience our secret delights.

It is curious how little is known of the Nadder, even though it is believed that this was once the mightiest of all the Wessex rivers. It may indeed have continued to the east in prehistoric times, past what is now Salisbury to join the sea at Southampton, with the Wylye, the

Avon and the Test as its main tributaries. Certainly the immense width of the valley and the contours of the surrounding chalk downs suggest that this was so. But that was before the Avon carved her majestic channel southward and took the waters of the Nadder and Wylye with her towards Christchurch, leaving the Test and Itchen to feed the existing Solent estuary. Either way, the Nadder is a relatively small, intimate stream today, a little narrower perhaps than its sister the Wylye below Steeple Langford.

Most authorities tell us that the derivation of the Nadder's name is lost forever in antiquity, although Camden suggests it is because 'it creepeth with crooked windings like an adder.' My own theory is that she was originally christened the Madder, being more liable to brown spate than other chalk streams. Strictly speaking, this is a semi-chalk stream, for, while in the lower reaches the river receives water from her own springs and benefits from pure chalk-fed tributaries such as the Fonthill and Teffont brooks, the upper waters rise out of greensands, and are more acid. Thus the river runs clear for much of the season, but rises and becomes discoloured after heavy rainfall.

Years ago I was told by an old farmer's wife: 'When the stream runs brown 'tis because the Moonrakers is about.' Legend has it that these curious folk prowl the Wiltshire countryside at dead of night when the moon is high, oft-times raking the river's depths with their pitchforks, while sensible villagers remain locked behind their cottage doors. It seems this story began when a group of robbers, disturbed while trying to recover their booty from the moonlit pool, offered the excuse: 'Cor love 'y sir, can't you see we'm trying to take out that big shiny cheese lying there in the water.'

The valley echoes with ancient folklore, and on the river's banks Sir Philip Sidney received a lock of Queen Elizabeth's hair, given with her 'owne faire hands', while Spenser, Shakespeare and George Herbert each drew inspiration from these soothing waters.

Of greater interest to fishermen perhaps is that the great G.E.M. Skues settled by the Nadder to fish out his final six seasons between 1940 and 1948. Here he found many river flies, including CP (the large spurwing), in the cobwebs of the iron latticed bridge, scoured the adjacent meadows in search of soldier beetles and tested a new American material called nylon on a two-pound trout that sawed his leader back and forth along the wire beneath the bridge. Skues was inclined to complain to friends about his lack of sport, yet in 1941 he secured three trout of 2 lb 9 oz, and six of between 2 lb 2 oz and 2 lb 6 oz, while in 1939 his bag included fish of 3 lb 3 oz and 2 lb 2 oz taken from the same hatchpool. The larger trout, despite Skues' wishes that it be given to a local farmer, had already been sold in Salisbury for 5s 6d!

Few wild fish reach such proportions now. All the same, the brisk current, deep pockets and clean gravels ensure a healthy stock is maintained. The aquatic larder is more than sufficient, and overhanging trees and bushes abound, providing both cover and a further food source. Many trout lie in inaccessible spots, but sometimes, with luck and a little courage, a speculative shot between the branches will bring a handsome reward.

Other stretches glide gently through untilled pastures and offer sport of a more classic nature beneath the open skies: exciting sport in which the fisherman marks his rising trout, stalks quietly through the reeds and watches in tense expectation as his dry fly approaches the widening ring. Then everything seems to happen at once – the sip, the boil of a one-and-a-half pounder bucking furiously as the net is slipped from the belt. Such individual incidents tend to merge into a delightful whole, but the diary records a number of similar encounters here during the season, and my best trout was a grand old warrior of 2 lb 4 oz.

I cherish my bit of the Nadder today as another man might savour his garden. I potter, appreciating the glorious sights and sounds of the valley, and I watch spellbound as the surface becomes speckled with upwinged duns, and the spinners shimmer in untold thousands around the latticed bridge at sunset. I never cease to marvel at nature's ability to produce – indeed overproduce, compensating as she does for so much wastage. Given half a chance, or a fraction of one, nature will always come back fighting, again and again, as long as man does not close her eyes completely with his tarmac and chemicals and borehole pumps. It is as though she is biding her time, so that when we finally understand the error of our ways, or bring about our own destruction, she will return triumphant in all her glory.

∽ 43 ∾

Back-end Adventures

The final weeks of the 1992 season found me on seven different rivers and a spring-fed stillwater, allowing ample opportunity to stalk brown trout, rainbows and grayling, all of which are in fine fighting condition as the first tints of autumn appear.

My day on the Ebble at Bishopstone was something of a sentimental journey, because some years ago this stretch had been rented by a long-lost friend, Tony Earle, a grand old Wiltshireman who would rather lean on a gate and yarn than fish. This we did together on many an occasion (I recall his words near the end, 'I'll still be about you know. You'll see me creeping along that bank of a summer's evening.') But I could only fish from 11a.m. until 2p.m. this day, catching two small trout and losing another before spying a large group of grayling feeding on the shallows up in the orchard, near a charming old dovecot.

They were in clear water about two feet deep so a stealthy head-down approach was vital. I changed my leader to 2½-lb breaking strain, knotted on a small Pheasant-tail nymph and watched for signs of unease among the fish. They continued to feed boldly, so I pitched the fly ahead of them, lifting the rod-tip fractionally as it neared the shoal. Three or four grayling shot at the nymph at once and I tightened into a silvery beauty of close on a pound. Strangely, the remainder appeared quite undisturbed – you get days like that, sometimes – and in the next half-hour five more came to net, the largest a handsome fish weighing 1 lb 6 oz.

My rod at Holbury Lakes in Hampshire gave me access to a length of the river Dun, three miles from its confluence with the Test below Mottisfont. On a dark, showery day when the flies were buffeted against the far bank by a lively breeze, I spotted three or four wild trout rising, along with some small rainbows, and it was one of the latter which took my CDC Red Spinner, sent by my French pal Raymond Rocher. This fish proved remarkably strong for his weight, just 12 oz, as did the leaping, pink-shot pounder that followed.

Over on the lakes I tied on a weighted nymph in the hope that I might encounter one of the beautiful 'blue' rainbows which are introduced here. Having no luck in Willow or Long Lakes, I tried the Pond, fishing close to the little flower-decked island. At the third cast my leader eased forward, and a hard-fighting trout went rocketing into deeper water. Winding in furiously, I managed to coax the fish towards my bank, only for him to tear line from the reel once more. After two further runs the trout came to the net, still full of energy. Sure enough this was a 'blue' weighing 2 lb 3 oz, a bar of bright bluish silver with barely a trace of pink, and the fins and sharply pointed tail as perfectly formed as any pure native.

The Nadder above Wilton can be highly challenging, often inviting the use of unorthodox tactics. Tight corners abound, with overhanging trees and bushes whose branches grow down into the water. One such was the home of an especially difficult trout which rose with the merest dimple against the far bank, under a semi-submerged hawthorn, quite unapproachable with a conventional cast. The only way appeared to be by casting across and down, but a lot of slack line would be needed to allow the fly a yard of free drift down the trout's heavily protected channel, and the trees denied any kind of overhead, loose delivery. I could shoot a tight-looped horizontal cast through the gap, just, but instead of floating the three feet the fly would drag almost at once.

Clearly, I would have to execute a punch-shot, so that the line would bounce back on recoil, and then, with luck, the resulting slack would enable the fly to float unhindered for the required distance. Sometimes you have to risk everything in one seemingly crazy attempt, but on this occasion the ploy worked, and the fly bobbed down on the current into the trout's lair. There was a tiny suck, a boil at the surface, and soon I was battling with a vigorous trout, my line hitched up in all directions among the foliage. I had to bring the fish upstream, applying considerable sidestrain, but somehow the line untangled and I was able to haul him away from the snags. At 13¼ inches and weighing 1 lb 5 oz this was one of the finest wild trout I've ever seen.

Next day I was on the Test, upstream of Wherwell Priory. There is no way I could afford a day here, but a kind friend had sent me over to fish his vacant beat. It had been my impression on previous visits to this lovely river that the trout population is composed almost entirely of stew fish, yet I have long questioned the oft-repeated notion that the spawning grounds are unable to produce an adequate head of fish, maintaining rather that heavy stocking crowds out the native trout giving them little chance to become established. Either way, the first six fish I hooked were all wild, from 11 to 13 inches – the one I kept scaling a remarkable 1 lb 1 oz at just under twelve inches. About 4 p.m. the larger stockies began to rise, three averaging over 2 lb coming to my Olive in quick succession, plus three fine grayling.

The trout on the Wylye and Avon were becoming ripe with spawn towards the back end, but each river provided wonderful sport, with grayling up to 1¼ lb, mostly taken in the quicker gravel runs on small palmered dry flies and bumble patterns. But I like to round off the season with a brace of trout for supper if I can, and last year it was the little Bourne at Hurdcot which allowed me to enjoy this simple delight. The first of these was a 'banker' I had tried on previous occasions without success; today he was lying further towards midstream, directly in front of a big starwort bed, poking his neb out of the water as he rose to blue-winged olive duns. My Olive pattern makes no attempt to differentiate between the various species, but he took like a good 'un just the same, a wild beauty of 10½ inches.

In a slow-flowing cushion of water near the far bank another likely candidate was supping away quietly, but the brisk flow close to my bank suggested instant drag. After many a disaster I had learned that this problem can sometimes be overcome by extending both rod and arm well forward so that the line settles beyond the faster current. In this case I was able to place the line some ten feet out, well clear of the race, and had the satisfaction of watching my fly sail naturally over the trout before it disappeared in the next rise form. This fish was a little larger than the first, but the two sizzled comfortably side by side in my frying pan along with a slice of bacon, a few mushrooms and a knob of butter – a grand finale to be sure.

ഛ 44 ഛ

Grayling on the Shallows

The sight of a broad shallow alive with feeding fish is enough to quicken the pulse of any keen angler. It was mid-November on the Wiltshire Avon, not far from Amesbury, on a bright morning after a hard overnight frost. Experience has taught me that the grayling shoal up in deep water in such conditions, but as temperatures rise they often move onto the gravels to feed during the middle part of the day. With luck, I should have at least three hours fishing, allowing plenty of time to plan a thoughtful, unhurried approach.

Watching from the bank, I could see grayling lifting and turning right across the width of the shallow, in water between one and three feet deep. The few large olives that appeared, and the occasional blue-winged olive and sedge fly, were taken with a swift, gliding rise, while shadowy forms ghosted this way and that over the stream bed. Light conditions were most favourable when I looked across river towards a stand of willows on the far bank. Elsewhere, surface glare rendered the grayling virtually invisible – yet as I waded across I must be especially careful not to disturb these unseen fish.

Grayling will sometimes continue feeding happily despite the fisherman's presence, but in sunny conditions over thin water it is usually a different story. It would be best to cast infrequently I felt, holding loose line in my hand until I sensed the fish were totally confident. A single cast should tell me all I needed to know; the grayling would either take boldly, display the jitters, or remain impassive.

My entry drove a small group of fish down river, an early indication of what kind of day this might prove to be. Heron-like wading was a must. After several minutes I was five yards out, and here I paused to study the river bed as thoroughly as visibility allowed. In total I estimated there were over a hundred fish within casting range of my chosen route, and the nearest were in a shallow depression behind a weed bed some five yards distant.

As the small Red Sedge alighted I saw the grayling duck sharply, and realized what I had done wrong. While my shadow and that of the rod had fallen well clear of the fish, the line was passing immediately above their heads. After waiting a few minutes I side-cast again, this time checking the line as it extended, causing the leader to settle in a gentle upstream curve with the fly bobbing nicely down the desired food-lane. There was no reaction, save what I thought was a quick glance from one of the half-pounders. To offer the same fly a third time might be unwise, so I tied on a Pheasant-tail nymph, pitching it two yards further upstream, now employing an overhead cast to place the line ahead of the danger zone. When I judged the nymph to be a foot or so short of the leading fish, I raised the rod-tip fractionally and prepared myself for a lightning take. Sure enough, there was a sudden dart, a quick strike, and a lively grayling spiralled away downstream. Wading after the fish, I guided him towards the bank and netted him out before he could make other plans; a bar of gunmetal silver, with a rich purple tinge along the back and a trace of gold beneath the flank.

At 1 lb 5 oz, this was the largest fish in the pocket. The remainder might be difficult to tempt now, so I skirted below their position and crept along the gravel towards a group of a dozen grayling occupying an area of three square yards in stickly water, little more than a foot deep. The broken surface might cause me to miss the sight of a take under water, so I attached my favourite dry fly – a beautiful French creation that has no name but represents the blue-winged olive well enough. Here I faced another problem, for the two larger grayling were flanked by several fish of ½–¾ lb, four of which hovered rather too close to me for comfort. I had the option of trying to catch all four – an unlikely event, which in any case would create much disturbance – or removing them by some other means. Moving the rod point very slowly over the lie, from an upstream direction, I shepherded them quietly down river. This is a perilous business, but I was lucky and the path was now clear.

I saw the first big grayling rise from the bottom, but I managed to hold my hand, setting the hook firm and sure. The second rose and looked, sank, then turned and came again, taking the fly with a kind of back-pedalling corkscrew motion. Even large grayling seldom strip line from the reel, unless they get into fast water; they seldom go into weedbeds either, and only one in fifty will leap in the air. The fish usually swim downstream, where they lie across the current with their huge dorsal fin erect. They are dogged fighters but become confused if you guide them into slack water; here you can often sweep them quickly into the net in a single movement. These two were beauties, going to 1 lb 10 oz and 1 lb 9 oz, and I was still less than halfway across the shallow.

In midstream I discovered a four-foot scour in the river bed which I had not noticed from the bank. Around twenty grayling were in residence, one of which looked close on 2½ pounds. He lay at the back of the shoal, so I could not present the fly without smaller fish seeing it first. At this depth, a weighted Grayling Bug was called for, pitched to the head of the pool. I was able to watch three fish eject the fly before my big friend drifted slowly sideways, opened his mouth and was on. He was already in his bolthole, so made no move to depart but instead bored strongly this way and that, shaking his head furiously. All I had to do was keep a tight line, shifting the strain from one direction to another. When he tired, it was a simple matter to approach the pool from below and slide him into the net. But, like so many grayling that appear to be well over two pounds, this one went a fraction less on the scale.

It may be that I had passed up an opportunity to take a sackful this day, for I finished around 2.30p.m. with only half the water covered and grayling continuing to feed in earnest. But the excitement of spotting and stalking the larger fish had brought satisfaction enough, and the cup may so easily run over. And it was good to know that most of the fish had remained blissfully unaware of my presence and would offer me further thrilling days in the winter months to come.

⨌ 45 ⨌
Grayling, Pride of Autumn

Few rivers offer such a wealth of autumn and winter fishing as those which flow southward from the chalk downlands of Salisbury Plain. While headwater streams and tributaries are noted for their wild trout, and the main Hampshire Avon for its salmon, sea trout and coarse fishing, in most middle and upper reaches it is that mysterious and delectable fish the grayling which predominates.

Some anglers join clubs on the Upper Avon and Wylye just for the grayling, having fished elsewhere all summer – for, unlike rain-fed northern and western rivers, these spring-fed chalk-streams remain fishable throughout much of the winter. They are less liable to flooding and discoloration, so that the fish are often visible in the water and will feed well from October to March, even in severe weather conditions.

Certain fisheries allow downstream wet fly or trotting with coarse tackle after mid-October, yet traditional dry-fly and upstream-nymph methods usually bring the best results through to Christmas and beyond, provided the rivers remain clear and at reasonably low levels. Contrary to popular belief, the larger grayling are usually caught on fly, rather than worm or maggot. Our local coarse-fishing match, at which the top weight may be 30–35 lb, seldom produces a two-pound grayling, while of the fifteen or so over this weight I have seen in the past ten years, only three were taken on coarse-fishing gear. The two heaviest grayling from this area in recent times, each over three pounds, were caught on fly from a small tributary stream. You will hear tales of fish in excess of four pounds having been seen, but we should remember that grayling sometimes look much larger in the water than they actually are. In any case, it is best to believe stories of huge fish – any fish – only when they are on the scales.

Having fished mostly for trout during the past six months, it takes a little while to adapt and begin to 'think like a grayling'. Fortunately, the tackle need not be changed, only the tactics. A finer leader point may be required, for grayling can be extremely gut-shy, especially on hard-fished waters, and a wider variety of fly patterns may be necessary. Grayling are not generally selective as to which natural species they will take, but you may well find they will accept a certain artificial greedily one moment and refuse it the next. You very often get half a dozen rises to one pattern, and maybe land a fish or two, and then find they show no further interest in it. But change to a completely different fly, and up they come as eager as ever. Size can be most important; for grayling it often pays to use one or two hook sizes smaller than you do for trout.

Provided you do not frighten the fish badly, in which case they may depart *en masse*, you can rise them again and again until you either catch them or they stop feeding. They can be alarmed by the continual falling of a fly line, or by its shadow, so a longer leader may be needed. And frequent resting, say for periods of five minutes in every fifteen, will pay dividends. It is good policy to alter your casting position quite often, too, so that the fly is presented from different angles, and to fish it at varying levels – in-film, submerged and high-and-dry. Variety is the key to successful grayling fishing.

The sight of an angler on the bank will not usually cause grayling to cease feeding, provided the fisherman does not move suddenly. After standing perfectly still for a few minutes, I sometimes find grayling lying within two yards of my position, but if I try to cast, or dap, they quickly swim away, although not necessarily very far. They behave just like sheep when seriously disturbed, gathering together in tight shoals, but the fish will only rush off to another part of the river if you really scare them by clumsy wading or by repeated waving of the rod above their heads.

Grayling are more difficult to hook than trout, I find. The strike should be as fast as you can make it, for we lose more fish because we tighten too late than because we are too quick. A hard strike is no bad thing, as long as your leader point will stand it; otherwise the barb may fail to penetrate the gristly tissue around the mouth. When you strike quickly but feel nothing, it may not be because you have missed the fish, rather that the fish has missed your fly. Grayling usually rise from some depth, turning slightly side-on to take, so that any miscalculation, or any last-second movement of the fly on the current may cause the fish to rise marginally off line. Take heart, for you will notice that grayling miss many of the natural flies too.

While you can fight a trout very firmly, even bully it into the net (indeed there is much to be said for this as a general policy), grayling should be played most carefully. If you try to drag them towards you they almost invariably move downriver and into fast water if they can. There the fish lie across the current with fins erect so as to offer the maximum resistance. Hauling a large grayling upstream is asking for trouble, and you have no alternative but to follow him downriver. If you tighten hard he may be away downstream again, and off you go in pursuit once more.

I find the best ploy, provided I am certain the fish is well hooked, is to slacken off strain at once. Play him gently, keeping the line straight but not taut. Then you 'persuade' the fish with slow, delicate rod handling towards a landing position you have marked some yards downstream. Lead him quietly, without hustle, and he will follow quite meekly; try to pull him and he will get downstream first and pull *you*! It is unlikely that a grayling will go to weed, and it very seldom leaps from the water. The fish usually tires quite quickly, and then you can bring it to the net with a sideways sweep of the rod. But beware! Any hesitation now and you may find the grayling has a kick or two left in him.

I well remember the sad day I lost one of my heaviest grayling. The fish was played out, so I thought, lying motionless in the net which I had placed on a high bank, well back from the lip, while I clambered out of the stream. When I was halfway up the bank, hanging on to a less-than-secure tuft of grass, I watched helplessly as the grayling flipped four times, finally toppling over the edge and away into the depths, having left the hook embedded in the meshes!

'Lady of the stream' is an apt name for the grayling. She can be fickle, contrary, sometimes downright obstinate. Yet she is playful, shy and will never display ill humour. Pander to her mood, treat her fondly, patiently, and she will respond by giving the most exhilarating sport imaginable.

✑ 46 ✑

Chasing Shadows

That grayling are liberally distributed in some areas yet comparatively localized or absent elsewhere may be largely attributed to the widely differing geological conditions existing in these islands. The source, alkalinity, temperature and flow rate of a particular river, and the resulting composition of the stream bed, have a marked bearing not only on the degree of proliferation, but also the feeding habits, nomadic tendencies and shoaling behaviour of the species, and hence the methods we employ in bringing about her capture.

I am fortunate enough to live near what I consider to be two of the world's finest grayling rivers, certainly if sheer density of fish and sustained surface activity are the criteria. These are the upper Avon and the Wylye in Wiltshire, where the natural stability of the environment ensures that extensive stretches to the north of Salisbury contain stocks to gladden the hearts of a growing band of grayling enthusiasts. While some of us continue to fish in much the same way as we do for trout, however, the grayling specialist will have made certain mental adjustments come October, and perfected a variety of skills to meet a very different challenge.

The season in these parts may be divided into two distinct phases, coming before and after mid-November. Before this the fish are widely distributed in loose shoals about the river, favouring shallow depressions in the stream bed, pockets formed by weedbeds or other obstructions, and deeper pools scoured out by the currents. Here, providing the water remains relatively clear, they tend to feed at or near the surface for much of the day and early evening, so finding the fish usually presents no problem. Even as we approach them, grayling will often remain on station, so long as we move slowly and as close to river level as possible and make use of any background cover.

The major challenge on these streams in early autumn (which may not apply to the same extent elsewhere), is discovering how we can cast without spooking a creature which is so ultra-sensitive to the rod, the line or a shadow suddenly appearing overhead. It is true that on some days the grayling will continue to feed after a dozen or more presentations, plus the playing and landing of one or two near neighbours. On many others, though, and especially on club and day-ticket waters, they will flinch, duck or scatter at the first or second chuck, even though we are using a long, fine leader point and casting with the utmost delicacy.

The answer to this lies in the angle of delivery. If we can present the fly across or downstream on a longish drift for example, we may avoid creating such a reaction. Likewise, if false casts are made overland or downstream of the fish, and the line is then placed to one side as in a crook or curve cast, our object may be achieved. Windblown reed stems or branches can effectively disguise the presence of a fly line, while approaching a shoal 'out of the sun' (on the principle used by wartime fighter pilots) may well give us an advantage, always provided that 'shadowing' fish can be avoided.

Frequent changes of fly are often necessary, since free-rising grayling quickly become suspicious if the same pattern passes over them more than three or four times. Offer them something completely different, from a size 12 Sedge to a Black Gnat on size 18–20, an Olive dun to a Coch-y-Bonddu. Each new fly is likely to arouse fresh curiosity; if they refuse to take, try twitching it fractionally, or allow it to fish in-film or just under the surface. Remember that we should place the fly a foot or two further ahead of a rising grayling than we normally would of a trout in a similar position. And don't delay the strike, which should be quick, positive, but never violent.

Contrary to popular belief, highly coloured or flashy artificials are seldom successful at this early stage in the season. Indeed I have found they frighten fish more often than not. Imitative dressings are best when grayling are really on the go. Time enough to consider the need for inducement with attractor patterns when the fish feed mostly sub-surface as the year advances.

Sometime around Guy Fawkes day the grayling cease rising so consistently, preferring instead to feed below mid-water. Some will have migrated into the deeper pools, while others remain in shallow areas but have become difficult to locate. Even in bright weather you may be unable to spot the fish themselves, yet their shadows are some-times plainly visible on lighter portions of the stream bed. Either way, fish all likely pockets with a weighted nymph or grayling bug, watching intently for that tell-tale draw or slight hesitation on the leader.

As soon as the first hard frosts arrive most of the grayling move into the deepest parts of the river, which in ideal conditions will have a well-oxygenated flow at the head and areas of quieter water close by. Additional cover in the shape of overhanging trees, a high wall or a substantial reed bed usually attracts the heavier concentrations of fish, which can number in excess of a hundred packed tightly together within the space of a few square yards. Fish such areas thoroughly with a heavily weighted nymph, delivered with sufficient slack to enable it to sink freely. I find it often pays to fish the fly inert, paying particular attention to eddies at the very edge of quicker water, while a sighter attached to the critical part of the leader certainly helps in detecting takes. If you catch a grayling, maybe just a quarter pounder, then keep fishing that pool, exploring various areas and at different depths. Where there are one or two there are almost sure to be lots more, from pinks measuring a few inches to grandads of 1½–2 lb.

As to gaining access, some of the best and least expensive fishing is controlled by Salisbury and District AC. While some club beats are available on a day ticket I would strongly recommend taking out full membership, since this will allow access to some six miles of their more productive grayling stretches at any time, without booking, and also a season's trout fishing! Annual subscriptions cost £105, including the registration fee, which if you come several times a year can reduce your outlay to negligible proportions.

Alternatively, if you can manage only an occasional visit, I would mention two especially attractive day-ticket fisheries. The first of these, Avonsprings at Durrington, owns one mile of the upper Avon, once keepered by Frank Sawyer, where permits are available through to mid-March at £20 per day. The second, Langford Fisheries at Steeple Langford, has two lengths of the middle Wylye, one classic meadow fishing and the other a well-wooded section. Each runs to half a mile, and rods are available at £15 per day, also until mid-March.

✧ 47 ✧

Winter Quarters

Despite her contrasting patterns of behaviour from region to region, grayling share a number of common characteristics at this season, including a voracious appetite, catholic tastes and, above all perhaps, boundless curiosity. While rivers remain reasonably stable, this gamesome disposition can provide truly remarkable fly fishing through to the New Year and beyond, yet it is a bold angler who will make positive predictions as to when such exciting sport will occur.

It commonly happens that a stretch of water which proved highly productive on one occasion contains relatively few fish the next. Any slight changes in water level, flow rate or temperature can cause shoals to migrate from one holding area to another, while lengths regularly occupied since July or August may be completely devoid of grayling come November. We may be certain, however, that the lower the temperature falls the deeper the grayling will choose to lie; and, conversely, as temperatures rise, so a number of the fish may seek out shallower runs in which to feed, before retiring once more as it becomes colder towards evening.

Grayling tend to congregate in or near the same holding pools year after year, massing closer and closer to their 'winter quarters' as the season advances. Local enquiry often proves invaluable, or the water may be clear enough for you to locate the fish by sight. Failing that, note the positions of any rise forms carefully, for one or two of the smaller fish are likely to give the game away, even in the bleakest conditions.

Make trial casts at varying depths, using both imitative nymphs and shrimp patterns, and also patterns with a 'flash', such as goldheads or those that have a silver or gold rib and brightly coloured tag. Hook size can be very important, for the fish often prefer smaller artificials rather than those 'juicy' morsels which we may imagine will be more attractive. Of course, in order to achieve depths of several feet with flies dressed on 12–14 hooks it is usually necessary to build up the body with lead (as opposed to copper wire), and to employ a long, fine tippet of adequate strength, (bearing in mind that additional wear will occur at the eye knot). I find that some ultra-fine 'super strength' nylons are prone to bruising, and now prefer 3–4 lb standard Drennan for most of my grayling fishing.

Provided an appropriate pattern is fished at or near the level at which grayling are feeding, and in a natural manner, immediate takes are very likely to result. The snag is that we are often unaware of them. Fish after fish may accept our artificial, but in so subtle a manner as to give no indication that they have done so. We feel no touch, and notice no draw or twitch on the leader butt. Indeed, many have discovered on lifting the line for another cast that a grayling is on, even though the shoal was plainly visible and no fish appeared to move towards the fly.

In the absence of any firm evidence, I can only offer my unsupported hypothesis as to how this strange phenomenon occurs. I believe it likely that grayling, in common with some other species, have the ability to 'draw in' food items from a considerable distance. I have witnessed the amusing spectacle of tench in a stew pond sucking in pellets from fully eighteen inches away, just as the surprised trout were about to engulf them. Grayling, whose low-slung mouth and protruding upper lip are clearly well adapted to 'hoovering' among stones and gravels on the stream bed, doubtless absorb mid-water nymphs using a similar mechanism, in which water is drawn sharply through the gills.

While there are occasions when grayling take nymphs in a very positive manner, which leaves us in little doubt as to when to set the hook, there are others when it pays to develop a 'built-in' strike with every cast. At these times I now adopt the following procedure:

1   Deliver the nymph on free drift well upstream of the shoal, so that it sinks to the desired level.

2   When the nymph is nearing the fish, draw the fly slowly, for about one foot only, on a tight line.

3   Impart instant, rapid acceleration, which in effect acts as both strike or back-cast leading into the next delivery. Without false-casting, this tightly controlled sink-draw-strike motion becomes a highly efficient technique for covering many fish in a short time. It is generally a mistake to strip the fly at speed before the strike, for, while grayling are attracted by the minor inducement in step 2, any unnat-

ural movement of the artificial at this stage can prove counter-productive.

Play each fish downstream and away from the main body of the shoal, and avoid 'skylining' yourself if possible. When alarmed, grayling may mill about for a short time, but will usually settle and resume feeding within five minutes, unless seriously frightened. I often fish two or three holding pools in rotation, resting them after any considerable disturbance, or simply when takes become fewer. We can learn much from the coarse fisherman: his low-level position among the reeds, his slow, deliberate movements and his concentrated attention on what is likely to be happening below the surface.

Considering that grayling seldom dash into weedbeds or leap clear of the water in as determined a manner as trout, it may seem strange that a higher proportion are frequently lost during the fight or come unstuck at the net. This is because grayling have tougher, more gristly mouth parts. The hook either tends to lack penetration beyond the barb, or it fixes so firmly in the jaw that the fish can be damaged as we struggle to remove it. Either way, I would strongly recommend the use of barbless hooks, whether or not we intend to return the fish, since the ratio of hooked grayling to those landed will improve dramatically, as long as the angler allows no slack line to occur while playing his fish.

The mysterious ways of this most valuable species are only partly understood, yet as our appreciation of its sporting qualities continues to grow we can be confident that our knowledge will increase as the seasons come and go. One thing is certain, I shall be out there come rain or frost, trying to uncover her secrets for as long as I am spared.

৩ 48 ৩

The Grayling Factor

The introduction of grayling to southern chalk streams during the nineteenth century sparked off a widespread and sometimes heated debate that continues to this day. Many questioned the wisdom of such ventures, for it was thought the grayling's voracious appetite (for ephemerids and trout ova in particular), astonishing reproductive rate and sheer persistence in taking over prime lies were hardly conducive to the well-being of the principal quarry. A massive imbalance often resulted, to the inevitable detriment of trout-fishing interests. It was discovered, too, that once grayling were established, the clock could not be turned back.

Within four years of a modest stocking exercise on the Kennet in 1879 large numbers had spread from the Hungerford shallows down to Newbury and nets were removing them in their hundreds, several weighing between 2 and 3½ lb. *The Field* reported 'in the Test, where grayling were formerly unknown, they have been introduced with marvellous success ... they have increased and thriven amazingly' (24 March 1883) and H.T. Sheringham observed in *Elements of Angling* (1908) 'it is a common complaint that, introduced to a trout stream, it increases so rapidly that the original inhabitants get crowded out of both home and cupboard.'

G.E.M. Skues, who fished the Itchen for 56 years declared 'He is vermin there and should be exterminated if it were possible', and Frank Sawyer of the upper Avon refers to grayling as interlopers saying 'I have often cursed whoever introduced them.' Bags of over forty were commonplace, and I well remember Doug Newell, the Wiltshire bailiff, staggering beneath the weight of sixty Wylye grayling as he entered the Swan at Stoford one lunchtime. Club rules often stipulated that all grayling be killed, in or out of season, and some fisheries removed up to eight or ten thousand each year with nets and electro-fishing gear.

Few denied that grayling offer exciting fishing at times, but the view that they were a pest and must be ruthlessly controlled was pretty well universal in the south. That such opinions were held by chalk-stream fishermen, and seldom by those who operated in the north and west was understandable, since Wessex rivers provide the most ideal habitats: pure spring water, constant low temperatures, relatively stable flows, and an abundant food supply. While grayling thrive successfully in many areas, no waters in the UK are so well suited to their needs, nor do the fish rise so consistently to surface fly, or grow so large and numerous, as in those of central southern counties. Here, trout fishing has long reigned supreme. The very exuberance and sporting nature of the grayling has been her undoing.

In recent years, however, a distinct change in attitude has begun to develop. People are asking why, when these rivers offer such outstanding sport with the grayling, should Thymallus be treated so. She is after all a native game fish, ultra-selective on occasion, guileful in play, aesthetically pleasing to the eye and a culinary delight when in season. Yet she is removed by the thousand, culled even while spawning, to be replaced in many cases by stew-fed trout that are flabby and misshapen, sometimes quite grotesque. Can such management practices be justified?

Perhaps not, but there is a world of difference between the somewhat insensitive policies adopted by certain put-and-take fisheries, and the prudent strategy of those wishing to preserve or create wild trout and grayling fishing of true quality. If the increase of grayling is such as to prevent the existence of an adequate native trout population – one that will both ensure a healthy return to anglers and leave a majority for natural regeneration – then steps must be taken to reduce their numbers. The same may apply to waters that (perhaps because of a scarcity of suitable breeding grounds), are unable to produce enough trout, and are therefore topped up with fry or yearlings to provide sport in future years.

Of course extreme views will always be heard in the wings – both from trendy catch-and-release advocates and from the chuck-'em-in-the-hedge brigade. Perhaps we should not be unduly influenced by current thinking overseas, where there may be little similarity between the conditions and species under discussion, nor by the inflexible views of the anti-grayling lobby. The chalk streams give us the opportunity to enjoy the best of both worlds, provided we maintain sensibly balanced stocks. To do this we should consider a number of factors which are sometimes overlooked or may not be generally known.

It is estimated that chalk-stream trout lay between one and two thousand eggs, while grayling shed some three to five thousand. To achieve a high survival rate among their progeny, trout prefer to spawn in small spring-water tributaries, of the type that have declined in recent years, whereas grayling breed successfully over a wide range of habitat where flows, cover and oxygen levels are not so critical. Trout dig out carefully constructed redds, while those of grayling can be relatively superficial. Trout pair off while spawning, but a hen grayling may be attended by several males. Trout eat the eggs of grayling, and vice versa, but trout lay in mid-winter, when food is scarce and grayling are feeding up towards spawning. Grayling spawn around late March and early April when aquatic food forms for trout are more plentiful. Unlike grayling, trout are essentially loners and therefore require more space. Trout take up individual lies where they can feed in peace, but grayling are opportunists, forever seeking to infiltrate the trout's hard-won territory. Trout are aggressive, repeatedly chasing away the grayling, and can suffer considerable energy loss as a result.

Where grayling are left unchecked, there can be no doubt which species is the loser. We may conclude that back-end netting or electro-fishing is therefore essential on most well managed chalk-streams, the fish being transferred to waters elsewhere, but that removing them while spawning is neither necessary nor desirable. Our aim is to cause a marked depletion of stocks in the short term, allowing trout much-needed respite at spawning time, and enabling them to feed largely unhindered during the early months of the trout-fisher's year. Grayling are a nomadic, invasive species, well able to regroup after temporary setback. Given suitable water conditions they will always return, gamesome as ever, come the fall.

Grayling Catches 1969–1995
(August–November)

The period from August to November inclusive is the most productive for grayling on the rivers I fish, yet my diaries reveal that the final four weeks or so, traditionally considered as 'grayling month' have actually proved the least fruitful. It is true that the grayling provides sport throughout the year, and that some delight in the added challenge of fishing in deepest winter, but if we are looking for sheer opportunity, with hour upon hour of surface or near surface activity, then this autumn season is the most exciting of all.

In considering the following breakdown of my results, taken in periods of three years over a 27-year span, readers may find that the general pattern compares closely with their own, for the records show the extent to which grayling populations can be influenced by extremes of weather and by changing habitat conditions. It is a matter of regret perhaps that so few grayling fishermen – indeed none that I recall – have published details of their catches down the years.

	1969/71	1972/74	1975/77	1978/80	1981/83	1984/86	1987/89	1990/92	1993/95	Total
August	159	106	54	19	133	27	16	15	6	535
September	120	168	34	87	56	24	25	59	45	618
October	231	197	51	67	180	55	57	21	80	939
November	149	122	10	0	85	2	6	12	9	395
Heaviest	1 lb 14	1 lb 12	2 lb 1	1 lb 15	2 lb 2	1 lb 11	1 lb 15	1 lb 8	1 lb 8	
grayling	1 lb 10	1 lb 8	2 lb 1	1 lb 13	1 lb 13	1 lb 0	1 lb 15	1 lb 8	1 lb 0	

Of the eighteen larger grayling recorded, eleven were caught during October and two in November. The heaviest, at 2 lb 2½ oz, was taken from a Wylye tributary in August 1981, while a bigger one of 2 lb 7 oz (not listed here) was caught out of season on the Test at Newton Stacey in May 1986.

October has certainly proved to be the best grayling month, for me at any rate, with August and September pretty consistent and November more erratic. We may account for this by the fact that, by and large, weather and water conditions have remained relatively stable during the late summer months, whereas in November they can fluctuate considerably. Freezing temperatures drive grayling into deep shoaling areas and, as winter rains cause the water to become discoloured, the fish cease to feed so consistently.

The most important factor, however, appears to have been a gradual diminution in water supplies. The figures illustrate the effects of drought combined with borehole water abstraction during and after 1975/6 and again from the mid-1980s, a situation that has become increasingly worrying through the 1990s. Lacking the depth, flow rate, oxygen content and food supply of former years, some rivers can no longer support the big stocks of grayling that flourished hitherto.

There can be little doubt that grayling will return in large numbers if and when natural spring water supplies are restored, but the question of how this will be achieved as demands upon the resource increase is one which is exercising the minds of many grayling enthusiasts as we approach a new millennium.

PART THREE

And hoary frosts do hang from every bough,
where freshest leaves of Summer late did grow
John Dennys, 1613

ᘒ 50 ᘒ

Fisherman's Torment

Social gatherings can be terrifying at the best of times, but a recent party in the village was a positive nightmare. As I cowered at the back of the crowd, trying my hardest to look like a pot-plant, I noticed that my hostess had her beady eye on me.

'Ah, there you are Gordon,' she boomed across the room, bringing the conversation to an abrupt halt. 'You've been very quiet. Now we hear you are a fisherman. *Do* tell us all about angling.'

'W-well,' I stammered into the deathly hush, 'Um, it's like this you see . . . I go down to the river and . . .'. I shuffled my feet, wiped my palms on the seat of my trousers, and stared at the floor.

The Major came to the rescue. 'I admire you chaps, really do. So patient, sitting in rows all day under your umbrellas.'

'And fishermen look so sweet, don't they?' piped his wife. 'With those bright feathers in their hats.'

'Well, you see . . .', my voice sounded rather distant 'there are different kinds of fishing actually. I . . .'.

One of the local dog-walkers, whose daily route I knew well because that's where I often sit, made his contribution, 'I don't know how you can handle those beastly maggots, and as for taking the hook out of a fish's mouth! It's all too messy for me.'

I was a bit flushed by now. 'Well, as a matter of fact I don't really . . .'.

'And what about the beer you blokes drink?' says the radio buff, whose music had driven me from the water on several occasions. 'Is it true you each get through a crate a day?'

'Well personally . . .', I blurted, before being interrupted again. This time it was by the gardening fanatic; he considers himself the number one conservationist in the area, spending most of the year spraying weedkillers and insecticides over his plot. 'I think it's cruel to catch fish myself. We should allow all God's little creatures to thrive without any interference from man.'

'That's right' agreed the farmer, having just grubbed out a hedgerow and ploughed up the last remaining tract of downland.

I was quivering like a jelly, and close to boiling point. 'I really can't see that . . .'.

But the canoeist wanted his say. 'All rivers are navigable by right according to the treaty drawn up by King Harold in AD 985,' he announced.

Someone else butts in. 'Rivers are the rightful home of the swans, geese and moorhens, not people.'

'Right,' said another voice. 'Anglers just create litter. They're unsociable beggars who have no respect for the countryside. They should be banned.'

'B—but . . .' I choked, purple of countenance and frothing at the mouth. The vicar looked at his watch.

'Goodness, is that the time? I must fly.'

'Golly, I must be off too.'

'And me.'

By now I was gibbering with outraged frustration. Perspiration poured from my brow, my hair stood out in all directions, and the eyes blazed like burning coals as the guests departed.

'Fools! Hypocrites!' I screamed after them as they faded into the night. 'Can't you see I go fishing to get away from blinkered idiots like you. I'd rather speak to my maggots and flies any day. They understand me, and they talk more sense than you lot. Half-wits, morons, nincompoops. . . !'

Silently a vehicle drew up and two men approached, their white coats gleaming in the light from the hallway. As they stretched out their hands an alarm bell clamoured at my side, and I awoke in a cold sweat. It was 1 June, the mayfly was on, and I had an appointment with a three-pound trout under Street's bridge.

ᑲᐧᐧᐃ 51 ᕆᐧ

Where Life Begins

Young Jimmy had yet to experience the annual migration of which his grandfather Silas told such stirring tales. He had romped among the stones with his brothers and sisters, learning to guard his own little territory, and sampled the delights of his first mayfly season. Now, as he approached maturity, a new sense of adventure welled within him, for this year he, too, would make that epic journey, following the instincts passed down from his ancient forebears.

Jimmy didn't fully understand the reproductive processes, nor the significance of words like habitat in the matter of procreation. All he knew was that he should 'follow his nose', pick up the scent of the purest water, and keep to that course until he reached the golden gravels that had featured in the stories of old Silas. He could just picture the sparkling shallows full of clean water from the springs, and the bright weedbeds swaying this way and that in the glancing currents.

When late autumn arrived, Jimmy felt a strange compulsion to leave his home and begin moving upriver. Ever watchful, he dodged the large cock fish that hovered in his path, avoided the pike lying motionless in slack water, and stayed well out of range of the purposeful, stalking heron. On and on he travelled, beneath wooden footbridges, through the old stone sluices and up tumbling cascades, bent only on answering that urgent call known to each new generation of trout.

The river had seen dramatic changes since fish life first came here. Wayward marshland had been drained, new channels created a head of water to turn the great mill-wheels, navigable canals had been formed, and an intricate network of irrigation streams straddled the low-lying meadows. There had been years of drought and years of flood; years of plenty when trout had multiplied, years of heavy predation, of tar pollution, and other years when coarse fish had encroached in their thousands. Yet always, over countless centuries, there had been the reassuring voice of that little bourne bubbling forth from the ground, whose water was as crystal, cleansed of all impurities. No matter what minor disasters befell fish populations of old, those unfailing springs had ensured the survival of the species.

As he felt the push of sweet water, Jimmy knew he must press on up the small gully to his right. Silas had told him he would see some impatient or weaker trout spawning in the main river, an exercise which might yield a poor return. For maximum survival among his offspring, he was determined to seek out those shining gravels he had dreamed of in his youth.

Nature had prepared a pristine nursery area, with a plentiful supply of oxygen, sufficient cover among the plant growths, and a delicious rush of cold water to soothe Jimmy's tired muscles. His mate had scoured out her nest. Their flanks touched as open-mouthed with ecstasy, the pair shed their precious seed among the loose stones. Jimmy felt this was the greatest moment in his short life, as if it had been the very purpose of it all.

Old Silas has been gone these twenty years, while Jimmy himself died soon after his first spawning. Their descendants know that same joyous urge to follow the hint of pure water towards its source. Even now they search for those magical gravel beds, which, as legend has it, once caused the parent river so to teem with native trout that the pickings of pike and heron and angler had no noticeable effect upon their numbers.

Adult fish still pass on the folk-tale to their young. One day soon, they promise, fresh water will come brimming forth once more from the constant springs just as it did when Silas and Jimmy explored the valley where life begins.

ᑌ᙭ 52 ᖇᐤ

Loafer's Luck

I've been called many things, but never a workaholic. In my daily life I'm inclined to shamble about, musing absent-mindedly on this or that, and find even washing the car or going to the supermarket a major chore. By the river 'I sits and thinks, or sometimes I just sits', happy to be there, watching the spinners dance and the trout making rings across the surface. If I stir myself sufficiently to put up my rod and pull on my waders, I may cast a line now and again – or maybe not. When I meet a kindred spirit we will often lean on a gate yarning the evening away until all the flies have sailed by and the rise is long gone. Then homealong, with the diary for company, where I write up another lovely fishing day, record the sighting of a bird or flower or a hatch of duns, dreaming of the scents and sounds of the waterside and of magical outings yet to come.

The idiot box in the corner of my tiny abode holds few attractions now. It is forever urging me to rouse myself, to buy a new wonder product, or keep fit, vote for some specious politician, or make a note of that forthcoming action-packed drama. No longer a soothing companion, it has become strident, competitive, piercing my consciousness with unwelcome messages. To find real contentment I must turn again to my fishing books, to the diaries or scribbling pad, or return to familiar haunts where peace and tranquillity are the natural order of things.

Strangely enough, while I am no more skilful than other anglers, and less so than many, I regularly catch my share of trout – indeed more than most. I deserve no credit whatever for this; it is in no sense a boast, simply a fact. And I believe I know the reason: one best illustrated perhaps by a day I spent some years ago with a friend we will call Malcolm.

The stretch we shared was about half a mile long and contained a fine head of naturally-spawned trout, plus a few stocked fish which, though unwelcome here, tend to drift down from a water upstream. I knew Malcolm was a hard-working and dedicated fisherman, keen to succeed, so suggested he move on ahead. I loafed about a hundred yards or so behind, admiring his agility and the wonderful accuracy and delicacy with which he presented his exquisite artificials.

Malcolm's casting repertoire was immense. With switches, rolls and double-hauls, delivered while standing, walking, crouching or wading, he could cover every part of the stream, even dark corners beneath the overhanging willow. He had fished most of the beat before I made a cast, pitching my fly at short range from a position among the tall grasses. While much of Malcolm's fishing had been to distant rises near the far bank, I had noticed four trout feeding quietly almost under my rod; and the fact that they were so close made for the simplest of chucks, without any drag problems, and in each case an easy, well-timed strike.

It was clear to me that Malcolm, whose enthusiastic approach work and determined casting had caused most of his fish to go down pronto, would have to be something of a magician to catch one; yet I, in my extreme idleness, had needed no great expertise to secure a leash of wild trout without undue exertion.

By the end of our day Malcolm was close to exhaustion, having bagged two stockies and a grayling. At a rough estimate I would reckon he had made over a hundred casts to one of mine, yet my total catch was some four times greater, albeit that several were returned. Malcolm's words remain with me to this day, 'I think fly fishing is all about identifying and overcoming problems, and what a challenge the trout presented today! Perhaps I would have taken more if I'd elected to fish the lower end, where you were.'

I was too lethargic to think up a suitable reply – but there was really no answer to this comment anyway.

ᴄᴏ 53 ᴏ̃ᴠ
Media Hype

'Is this what our sport has come to?' asked Mark, holding up a fishing journal whose front cover depicted an angler, dressed like a Christmas tree, playing a dead rainbow. 'No wonder right-thinking fishermen are so concerned about upholding decent standards.'

'Magazines are in the business of promoting fishing as a leisure activity,' I protested. 'They have to attract readers.'

'But they could do it in a more ethical manner,' Mark insisted. 'These modern writers are such blatant self-publicists – always wearing funny garb just to be noticed. Their material is published not for its value, but because they represent some kind of role-model for those seeking an identity.'

'It's the same in all sports,' I argued. 'People want to read what the personalities have to say, and beginners need someone to copy.'

'All right,' Mark agreed, 'but let it be somebody we can admire, for their experience, their knowledge and insight, rather than their quirky phrases and gaudy appearance. What sort of fishermen will our youngsters turn out to be?'

'Modern ones,' I answered, 'with up-to-date ideas. If you had your way we'd still be wearing plus-fours and sitting on shooting-sticks reading poetry!'

'I wouldn't go that far,' said Mark, 'but what's so wrong about tradition? Fly fishing has its very roots in the past. The ways of trout and the insects they eat haven't altered in centuries. Why should we want to change it?'

'The sport may be the same fundamentally,' I countered, 'but our know-how has advanced no end. We have vastly improved tackle and equipment now. We've created thousands more fisheries where everyone has a chance of catching fish, and successful new fly patterns are being designed all the time.'

173

'But that's my point,' Mark retorted, 'we're no longer concerned about the quality of our sport, only quantity: how to kill more fish and bigger fish. These come-lately experts seek to belittle our great traditions, portray the sport as some kind of theme-park recreation, and advise the use of flies and techniques that would make our grandfathers turn in their graves.'

'Why shouldn't anglers try to create more lifelike patterns?' I asked him.

'Nothing wrong with that at all,' Mark conceded, 'but I see no point in discarding tried and trusted artificials just for the sake of change. Writers are obsessed with "newness", yet traditional dressings like Greenwell's Glory, Gold-ribbed Hare's Ear, Pheasant Tail and Lunn's Particular are better imitations of the natural flies than most modern concoctions.'

'Surely the angling press are only reflecting current attitudes?' I suggested.

'No they're not,' Mark answered, 'they're creating them. Look at these stories about a 22-pounder causing traffic chaos at Long Springs, a triple-limit of 15 trout totalling 60 lb from Somebury, and this wonder-fly the Distressed Bog Beetle taking three seven-pounders in successive casts from a famous Hampshire river (and by the way you can get day tickets or arrange "corporate entertainment"). They are just raising the level of greed and expectation among otherwise caring people, and exploiting living creatures for their own rotten ends.'

'So what can we do about it?' I queried, accepting there was some truth in what he said. 'Tell newsagents they mustn't sell them? It's a free country you know, and anglers can read what they want. Anyway, you bought that one didn't you?'

'Not any more,' Mark vowed. 'I picked it up on impulse, but now I've seen some of the ghastly pictures and read the pseudo-intellectual claptrap, I'll consign it to the bin where it belongs. At least we can still exercise a degree of choice, thank goodness.

'Yes, it's each to his own,' said I. 'But, don't forget, the *Sun* always outsells the *Independent*.'

'Now there's a thought,' Mark replied. 'I'd rather see the beautiful creations on Page Three than these overdressed posers anyhow. Maybe we should have a word with the editor.'

Ever the naturalist, old Mark.

ᥫ 54 ᥫ

Cuthbert's Last Stand

Cuthbert had become an impressive specimen. Born in the river some six years back, a mixture of the right genes and luck – for he was one of the first to hatch out – had given him a head start, so that he quickly outgrew most of the young trout of his generation. He had seen many of his brethren gobbled up by larger trout, or by the perch or king-fisher, but somehow Cuthbert's reflexes, his instant awareness, and his speed off the mark had always allowed him that split-second advantage over his fellows.

The predators that Cuthbert was most wary of were the heron, whose stealthy approach was difficult to detect, and the pike, which sidled up alongside him looking so innocent and friendly, and yet, as he had seen, would snap up an unsuspecting trout in a flash. Cuthbert had developed the habit of dropping downstream frequently to chase away any fish encroaching on his beat, and while doing so he kept a constant watch for his long-legged foe. As for the pike, he had learned to recognize the restless signs and knew when to make himself scarce.

Cuthbert had the greatest respect for these natural enemies and remained ever vigilant. But those shadowy figures, the anglers, with their waving sticks and long lines which fell on the water, were another matter. They were not predators in the strict sense, killing for food, but were nevertheless capable of removing large numbers of his colleagues on occasion. Some were released, but others he never saw again.

He felt no sorrow. If they were unable to see anglers standing on the bank and took their lifeless lures of fur and feather, they had it coming. As it was, the majority of those caught were the 'newcomers' anyway, those silly creatures which the same shadowy figures introduced in their hundreds. The anglers relied on luck and the law of averages: cover enough water, cast repeatedly, and you should catch fish.

Cuthbert viewed the whole business with some disdain. The newcomers were stupid and so, he thought, were the anglers he could spot so easily.

Thus it was that as the years passed Cuthbert grew big, bold and confident. But in his eighth season, although his shoulders were as heavy as ever, his food intake became insufficient to maintain his lower body in prime condition, and those excursions in defence of his territory began to tire him more quickly. In June he rose to the mayflies as usual, preferring to wait until no shadowy figure was about. Today, having scanned the horizon, he fed with abandon, trying to make up the few ounces he had lost.

But through the grass and reeds there stalked an angler. Like a cat he paused, crept forward, and paused again, knowing Cuthbert's movements well. For two years he had watched and waited. Never once had the great trout seen him, although on two or three occasions the fish had inspected an unusually lifelike pattern which had settled gently on the surface above him and drifted on the current just as the naturals did.

Like the heron, this angler froze for long periods; like the pike, his sly movements were almost imperceptible. His head did not appear in the fish's field of vision, his rod was held low, and his cast was a horizontal one. The fine leader curved slightly upstream, the breeze caused the fly's wings to quiver invitingly above the water, and Cuthbert opened and closed his cavernous jaws. Quickly the fish plunged away towards the weedbeds, shaking his head, but too late.

The fisherman had lain awake many a night, planning each move, anticipating every conceivable run his old friend could make, and when he was on the bank he felt a poignant mixture of elation and sorrow. The trout knew that his compassionate adversary, in the knowledge that Cuthbert was past his best, would spare him the pain and indignity of a lingering death. For here was a true angler and a sportsman – one in a thousand perhaps – for whom Cuthbert felt the same kind of respect he had shown to those predators in the wild.

ᄭᓂ 55 ᠺᘉ
What's It All About?

'It's all very well these blokes writing about world-famous rivers,' I observed, 'but how many of us get to fish them? Joe Bloggs and his mates – that's ninety per cent of ordinary anglers – have to make do with second rate sport.'

'Nonsense,' countered Wally, 'fishing is just as rewarding on lesser known waters, often more so. I'm as happy on my local brook as on the Test or the Tay. Fishing is fishing, wherever you are.'

'But you don't catch thirty-pound salmon or ten-pound trout in your brook, do you?' I asked. 'Hardly,' Wally answered. 'But who needs to? It's all a matter of priorities. Look, people driven by ambitions of wealth often own big houses and drive expensive cars. These are symbols of their success, just as having a rod on the middle Test and catching ten-pounders is simply down to how much money you've got and how you want to spend it. Good luck to them, but my priorities are different.'

'That sounds like sour grapes,' I said.

'Far from it,' Wally insisted. 'If you are rich enough, you can buy success, or the illusion of it. Let's be honest, there's a stretch not far from here where so many tame trout are put in that my old granny would be a success too, if she wanted to pay the silly prices. What money can't buy is the ability to fit into the natural world, or the skill and fieldcraft necessary to hunt down wild creatures. We've had people on this brook who have never troubled to learn the correct techniques. They look totally out of place, and quite unable to cope.'

'Maybe that's just lack of experience,' I wondered.

'No. The fact is they are so accustomed to obtaining everything on demand, including their fish, that, when confronted by a real challenge, they discover something they can't have, no matter how many zeros they write on the cheque. Some get very angry, but let's hope the experience has taught them to be humbler men.'

'So are you saying that the poorer an angler is, the better fisherman he is likely to be?' I asked.

'Well it figures doesn't it? Waters that hold large stocks of big fish are inevitably more costly, and results can be obtained more easily. But is the easiest fishing necessarily the best – or does our level of pleasure and satisfaction increase according to the degree of challenge?'

'So you maintain that lesser-known waters actually offer better sport than the more famous ones?' I suggested.

'It's down to what we think fishing is all about,' said Wally. 'I know a fellow who has just caught his hundredth ten-pound trout from a rather expensive ticket water. What pleasure does he now derive from hooking two-pounders? But to the chap on the brook a hard won two-pounder represents the prize of a lifetime. The big fish expert must be positively bored with fishing by now, yet the other is brimming with youthful enthusiasm because he has hurdles yet to climb and goals to achieve.'

'But when your son is old enough, surely you'll want him to catch fish right away, and so retain his keenness,' I enquired.

'No way,' Wally answered. 'If he's going to be an angler he'll earn his fish. If he has to crawl in the mud to keep out of sight, and gets scratched by thorns and takes three months to get a trout, I'll be a happy man. When he comes home with that first tiddler and fries it for his tea I shall know I have a real angler on my hands – one whose grounding will ensure that fishing is a life-long passion, rather than a trivial exercise governed by the great god money. The true riches are to be found in the angler's soul, not his wallet.'

✂ 56 ✃
Fishy Business

John Crouch got up to answer the phone. 'Keeper's Cottage, Crouch speaking.' It was Mr Wilson-Stacey, businessman, one of the rods.

'Ah Crouch, there you are. Now, look here, I have a guest with me today, Sir Basil Ormsby-Geech, you know – very influential man. We'll be fishing until 6p.m., then discussing a major contract. He's a hopeless angler, but I'd like him to catch a big trout – should help negotiations along, if you follow my drift. Have you a fish marked down?'

'Nothing much in the river, sir, but there's a nine-pounder in the stew.'

'Capital, capital,' enthused Wilson-Stacey. 'Be a good chap and put it in the pool at Horseshoe Bend about noon. We'll be there after lunch, so keep the trout happy on floating pellets. Not too many, mind! I want the fish to be hungry. Worth a bob or two to yourself of course.'

'Very good Sir. I shall arrange my timetable accordingly.'

'Stout fellow, Crouch. See you in a few hours then.'

Mr Wilson-Stacey and Sir Basil arrived soon after 3p.m., the latter having enjoyed an almost entirely liquid lunch.

'Well Stacey, where's this monster trout?' boomed Sir Basil.

'We'll see him move soon,' answered his host. 'He starts rising about now. The rods have been after him all season without success, but, of course, few of them possess your skills of presentation and fieldcraft.'

'Quite so, quite so,' slurred Sir Basil. 'Take a Tups d'you suppose?'

'Something a little larger I fancy,' answered Wilson-Stacey. 'We get a strange beetle in these parts, a brown insect like these clipped deer-hair patterns in my fly box.' He knotted one on, having taken the precaution of attaching a ten-pound leader point.

'Match the hatch, eh? That's the ticket,' said Sir Basil. 'Now let's see him rise.'

From his position among the reeds, Crouch flicked a brown object onto the water. The great fish came into view and engulfed the pellet, causing the river to rock from bank to bank.

'Goodness what a trout,' shouted a flushed Sir Basil as he tottered on the brink, waving his rod over the pool. His end tackle landed in a heap on the water, the surface erupted, and before he knew it the rod bent double and the reel screamed like an angry bee. The fish clearly had more fight than the befuddled angler, but Wilson-Stacey saw it coming. Just in time he grabbed Sir Basil amidships, while Crouch pulled from the rear. Like a tug-of-war team they strained, puffed and perspired, eventually bringing the great trout tight against the margin where the keeper, with admirable foresight, had left an open reservoir-sized landing net partly submerged. Crouch heaved the net with its exhausted occupant ashore and announced a new club record of 9 lb 2 oz.

'A copybook capture,' cried Sir Basil modestly. 'Concealment you know. Right fly, placed inch-perfect. Tight line, rod up, give 'em no quarter. That's how it's done. Native fish I imagine?'

'Either wild or grown on from the fry stage, sir,' lied Crouch.

'Well look here, my good chap, put my record down in the game book won't you. And here's something for yourself.' Sir Basil passed across a number of crisp ones.

Turning to Wilson-Stacey he continued, 'Fieldcraft and presentation you say? Well, yes, some of us have it and some not I suppose. But I'd like to thank you for coming along to help with my gear. Any man who offers this quality of fishing must also be a true and honest sportsman with whom I can do business. Now about that contract . . .'.

The young man at the bar whispered to his friend 'That's Sir Basil Ormsby-Geech just come in, the well known financier. His reputation as an angler has spread far and wide. Always outwits the biggest trout in the water wherever he fishes as a guest. Got a nine-pounder today at Horseshoe Bend – using some secret fly, Crouch says. He's a true expert. The best fisherman in Berkhampshire by far – and an inspiration to us all.'

༄ 57 ༄
Wasted Years?

If I ever get around to writing my autobiography I can count on the readership (ownership at least) of those to whom I present a complementary copy, and one or two near relatives who will hold it up as a warning to their offspring. 'If you don't watch out you'll end up like Uncle G,' I can hear them saying. 'He threw away golden opportunities, chose to ignore influential contacts, and shunned close friendships. He could have gathered moss, but like a stone he just rolled along, content to let the currents carry him away to some secret backwater. Fishing indeed! What a worthless existence!'

I make no attempt to deny the charge, yet when confronted I maintain that each of us possesses a distinct personality over which we have little control – being the result of genetic influences – plus our own understanding of values and the meaning of life. Lucky is the man who can identify these, for, unlike so many, he knows who he is and what his role must be.

For good or ill I am a man of the valleys, woods and downlands, a lover of flowers, insects and birdlife. I am a lover of fish, and a hunter and killer of fish. Naturalists will find no contradiction here, for wild stocks were high when otters, pike and herons made savage inroads. Now I have largely replaced those predators, and I know that if stocks decline the culler is not responsible, but those who harm or mismanage habitats. To me this seems quite obvious, so fundamental, yet I accept that people who lead different lives may hold another view.

As I see it, the wasted years were those before I took up serious fly fishing. The seasons since 1963, when I finally got my priorities right, have convinced me that if fishing runs strongly in the blood then it should never be a recreation, a once-a-fortnight indulgence, or a sport which is pursued only when we can fit it into a busy social or business schedule. Fishing demands precedence: a fact which some learn when it is too late. Others, though, a dwindling band, have been fortunate or far-sighted enough to see it coming and have shaken off the fetters of conformity just in time.

The diaries reveal that I have fished some 3,500 days or part-days on over sixty rivers and ten lakes. What's that, two average fishing life-times, maybe three? The total 'fish caught' column reads 12,338, of which 6,856 have been trout and 5,482 have been others (mostly grayling). Salmon, sea trout, roach, dace, chub and other species feature in the records, but my great delight is to pursue wild brown trout and grayling with the dry fly.

So it may be said that the sum total of a man's life is contained in one short paragraph. Yet this is to say nothing of the countless hours of undiluted pleasure, the peaceful contemplation, the wonder of natural things that the fishing world embraces. For most it offers occasional relief to punctuate the world of supermarket trolleys, nappies, road-rage, mounting debt and other horrors: the path which the majority must follow.

But the question remains. All right, I did it my way, as many others wish they could, but at the end of the day will I still be so sure that I was right? Is joy that much sweeter when experienced only seldom? Will the diaries and the memories they contain suffice, or will I pine for human companionship? Is what I see as the real, natural and fulfilling way of life merely an illusion? Readers will have their own opinions. For myself, perhaps the autobiography will come up with the answers, if I have the time and the ability to reach 'In conclusion'.

໙ 58 ໙

Man of the Riverside

It sometimes happens that when a great angling mind departs this life much of his work dies with him, especially if his thinking was 'ahead of its time'. This, I believe, has been true of Frank Sawyer, whose conclusions about natural trout reproduction may have particular relevance today.

Fortunately, valuable portions of Sawyer's tremendous contribution were brought to light by Sidney Vines, whose book *Frank Sawyer, Man of the Riverside* (Allen and Unwin, 1984) is still obtainable from libraries. Of special interest to wild trout enthusiasts is Chapter 20, in which Sawyer (writing in 1957) recalls that as early as 1930 there was little natural regeneration from the wild stock on his six-mile length of the upper Avon in Wiltshire. There were seasons when his detailed observations indicated that, of roughly one million ova from 1,000 breeding pairs, only some 200 trout survived to become takeable fish in their fourth year.

Contrasting this figure with what can happen when nature is given a chance Sawyer writes:

> When river conditions are satisfactory, the natural hatch could be at least 90 per cent. In that case, assuming as before that the eggs shed by 1000 female trout total a million, our calculations would show that [here he allows for natural losses in the various stages of development] . . . the actual production of four-year-old trout reaches to the remarkable figure of 40,500. These calculations are sufficient to prove conclusively that the real answer to trout production lies not in artificial hatching and fry-stocking, but in making the river do the work as intended by nature.

Sawyer estimated that not more than one per cent of the ova laid in the river in former years hatched into alevins, as compared with at least ninety per cent achieved later, and that the principal cause of the early failures was a lack of oxygen.

He maintained that a high success rate on chalk streams can only be achieved where the eggs are deposited in the purest spring water which percolates from beneath the river bed, a case amply supported by the trout's preference for spawning on the clean gravels of small, spring-fed winterbournes, where these are accessible. When trout make holes in a redd, they 'do so not with any idea of providing a nest or an anchorage, but simply because they want to cut through the hard upper crust of the river bed to try to find an upward water supply.' This upward movement of water, in addition to providing oxygen, helps to keep undesirable spoil in suspension so that the eggs remain clean throughout the period of incubation.

The major scraping, cleansing and breaking up of the riverbed which occurred on the upper Avon in 1954–5 brought about a dramatic increase in the numbers of wild trout present, so much so that Sawyer, clearly elated, could now write 'The time has come when there is no need for us to use the hatchery to maintain a stock of trout . . . we have found the answer to successful trout production . . .'.

The remainder of Sawyer's chapter 20 is devoted mainly to another vital aspect of chalk-stream management, the provision of a healthy, nutritious diet, in which, Sawyer discovered, regular applications of chalk broke down rotting vegetable matter, increased valuable food forms and added considerably to the trout's weight and condition. Once again Sawyer had found the answer.

Yet, notwithstanding his lifetime's work on the river and the exciting discoveries he made, Frank Sawyer's words have largely been ignored. It is true that putting machinery into a river to break up the bed can be expensive – but some fisheries are prepared to pay several thousands of pounds each year for stocking with sizeable fish. A wide area of shallow can be dug over in a single day, and the operation repeated at intervals of three or four years, and the large quantities of chalk thus dispersed would be deposited on the reaches below. Maybe what is lacking is simply the will to do it, or our increasing reliance on modern scientists and fish culturists whose overall knowledge of river ecology may not be extensive.

✍ 59 ✎

A Triumph of Nature

The little fishing club no longer exists but Richard, one of its past members, now rents the stretch for his own use. Back in the 1960s and 1970s the landowner leased a two-mile length to the club – which was composed largely of City gents seeking a bit of fishing not too far from home – that was productive enough to give them a brace or two most times they went out.

It was an amicable arrangement. The owner wanted the water maintained as a striking feature of his property, with nicely mown banks and the trees cut back to reveal the cascades and an old hatchpool, which were visible from the terrace; the members enjoyed relatively easy 'carpet-slipper' fishing with little danger of a tangle on the back-cast. The part-time keeper erected a comfortable fishing hut, riverside seats were sited at strategic points, and the margins were cleared of all reedbeds and bushes to expose wide reaches that were most pleasing to behold. The members, wishing to see their fly drift naturally on the current without drag had the water plants trimmed hard, with a number of open pools created to facilitate snag-free nymphing.

Most of the rods felt the fishery had improved significantly by 1969. The lack of shelter brought about a considerable reduction in fly life, it's true, and the resident trout moved off in search of a more suitable habitat; but 200 takeable trout were turned in each month, the average weight had doubled, and the fish were now less discriminating as to the pattern of fly they would accept. Come the mid-1970s, however, water levels and flow rates began to deteriorate throughout the region and this stretch, being far wider than most, suffered greatly.

By the end of July 1976 flows had become sluggish in the extreme, and the depth could be measured in inches. Silt had accumulated in unsightly mounds, weed growth was almost absent, and stocking was pointless, since newly introduced trout vanished within days. Unable to replace those who resigned, the club finally folded in 1978, and – after a long period of neglect during which no work was carried out on the fishery – the estate was sold, the new owners taking over in early 1985.

Richard had kept an eye on the water throughout, suspecting that this lack of attention was just what nature needed to redress the balance. He approached the owner and succeeded in securing a seven-year lease at a fraction of the original rental, and with few conditions as to improvements. When he rang me with the news I was delighted, and arranged to look over the stretch, which I had last seen ten years before.

The change was dramatic, the most notable difference being the size of the stream itself. Land encroachment had gradually made it narrower, so that it was now only half the width, with the result that the water flowed at a swift pace and at a much increased depth. Ranunculus fronds weaved gently in the current throughout its length, while the river was hidden from a distance by tall bankside vegetation. Bushes and small trees had sprung up here and there, already over-hanging the water in places. The stones and the aquatic plants which flourished amongst them were alive with insects, and trout went dashing to cover as we waded in the stream.

This was a magical transformation, and I waited eagerly for Richard to invite me for a day's fishing. We chose a date in early June, but neither of us in fact fished much. I watched him land three beautifully formed wild trout of between 1 and 1½ lb, while I approached two and missed both on the strike. Somehow the hunting instinct was curiously lacking, as if the mere sight of this natural miracle was sufficient to make the perfect day. 'You know,' said Richard, 'we really believed we were doing the right thing twenty years ago by cleaning out the stream and opening it up for better access. Just shows how easily man can destroy the very thing he wishes to preserve! But nature always triumphs in the end.'

⚬ 60 ⚬
Country Ways

When old Harry Perch finally went to meet his maker, his departure marked the end of a family line whose contribution to village life had spanned countless generations. There is evidence of habitation in this sheltered spot since pre-Roman times, and, as someone remarked, 'You can bet it was a Perch who got here first!' There were Perches who weaved and Perches who thatched, tended livestock and tilled the soil; Perch the woodman, Perch the drowner, Perch the cobbler. The name appears frequently in the parish registers, and in the churchyard you may trace the family back until the carvings are lost in the dark earth of centuries. Doubtless, in years ahead genealogists will return in search of their origins, but, now that old Harry is buried along with his ancestors the name of Perch has vanished from the village roll.

Such stories have become all too familiar as ancient skills become redundant, landowners employ fewer workers, capitalize by selling vacant properties, and release parts of their land for private development. Those moving to rural areas, into the Shepherd's cottage, the Blacksmith's and the Perch's old family home are a new breed of villager, their values and lifestyles sometimes very different from their predecessors'. You need no knowledge of country matters to be a 'countryman' today – just the wherewithal to buy your dream dwelling, and maybe the status car, the Barbour and the wellies.

Some people, who perhaps came from urban or suburban areas, believe that since there are more fields and open spaces in the country, there will be greater freedom to roam and more room for recreation. In fact the reverse is usually the case. In built-up areas we may walk the streets and common land at will, sail model craft and paddle in the water, or ride motorbikes on or off the roadway, and do so without causing serious comment. Much of the land is 'public' and therefore accessible. Our noise and our litter are as nothing when compared with the whole. To reprimand a child for dropping a sweet-wrapper in the shopping precinct seems ridiculous, for it is lost in the general chaos, as is the music from our radio.

In the village we lose our anonymity, and quickly discover that a seemingly innocent act that might go unnoticed in town can give offence to our neighbours. Codes are more rigid, and our behaviour is influenced by common guidelines. Yet for centuries the likes of Harry Perch needed no rules. They had learned as part of their upbringing to love all natural things, that it was important to show consideration to others, that consensus needed to be upheld and country traditions preserved. They respected the fact that most of the land belongs to someone, and that nobody has the right to be there, except on public footpaths, unless he has an agreement with the owner or tenant to pursue some lawful activity. The likelihood is that rights of access will have been granted – perhaps to bird-watchers or rabbit-catchers, anglers, botanists or shooting people – for which certain sums of money may have changed hands. They should not be surprised, then, if the man who confronts them is somewhat abrupt in his manner.

Some of us are blameless of any transgression no doubt – even the killing of birds as our GTis streak between the hedgerows – but increasing numbers of people are coming into the country for sight-seeing, sporting and other activities, who abuse nature and break the code – not least some of those who decide to make their homes here.

ઌ 61 ૭

Worker's Playtime

I may be an old half-wit in need of some serious counselling, but when it comes to a day's graft I reckon I can see off these upwardly mobile folk, no trouble. Take yesterday for example. I was up at 5 a.m. working on some new material for a magazine, this being the only time I can get my brain into gear before the clamour of dogs and DIY enthusiasts becomes excessive. Some four hours later I was cutting nettles on my stretch of the Ebble. They were head-high by now, and the job had to be done urgently if my colleagues with whom I share the fishing are to retain their good humour. The point of the scythe kept embedding itself in old logs hidden among the vegetation (a vexing habit, I can assure you), and the tough stalks meant the blade had to be sharpened several times during my three-hour stint.

I had time for a quick burger at the snack wagon on the A36 before hurrying off to Grovely Wood where I keep a regular record of species for Butterfly Conservation. The Society is concerned about the decline of varieties such as the Pearl-bordered Fritillary, Silver-spotted Skipper and Marsh Fritillary in this area, but I was able to report the sightings of over two hundred Silver-washed Fritillaries, fifty-plus White Admirals and Dark Green Fritillaries, a dozen Purple Hairstreaks and one Purple Emperor, along with large numbers of the more familiar Ringlets, Marbled Whites, Meadow Browns, and so on.

The Purple Emperor is the most spectacular of our woodland butterflies, yet its preference for sitting among the topmost branches of large oak trees means it is seldom seen, and then only by those who know how and where to look. But I laid a couple of dead rabbits on the track beneath a known 'master' tree so that next week, when the corpses pong a bit, one or two Emperors may be attracted down for a free lunch – unless the fox gets there first.

I chatted for a while with Colin, the area warden from the Forestry

Commission, who told me of his plans to clear further areas of woodland with butterfly habitats in mind. Even the rare Wood White, last seen here by Malcolm Lyell in 1990, could make a comeback, given the space to roam and breed. Malcolm told me that he found two adults nectaring on a single flower-head, raised his camera and clicked – only to discover he had run out of film! The estate owner is also keen on the clearance project, as he is on the improvement of two rivers running through his land. More co-operation of this kind goes on in the country than many realize, and tenant farmers, too, are trying to manage their acres in a more wildlife-friendly manner today.

The evening looked quite promising, so, after frying a trout with a few mushrooms and a tomato, I wandered out to the river half a mile down the road. It would be some while before the fish really got busy, allowing me time to unwind and contemplate the meaning of life, as I like to do on occasion. But there's no peace for the wicked; a trout started rising to sherries just a few yards ahead, and another over by the hawthorn bush. The first came well enough but I missed him on the strike. The second took the fly too far down his throat for my liking (or his, I guess); fortunately my scissor-points did the trick, and he swam away none the worse, although maybe a little wiser.

About 10p.m. I saw a big fish head-and-tailing close to my bank, where the current funnelled the blue-winged olives. Up he came at the first reasonable chuck, but he was a little on the lean side – about 1¾ lb for his 17 in. – so this trout went back too. Then, at last light, I got a couple of beauties from the shallows, each just under the pound, and a stockie of 1 lb 3 oz for the pot.

As I trudged back to the shack I reckoned I'd done a fair day's work all round. 'Work?' I hear you say. 'More like a labour of love.' You could be right there!

Trout Catches 1966–1989

When we analyse our catches over a span of years an interesting and possibly surprising picture may emerge. In my own case, I was aware that the total number of trout I had caught in recent years was fewer than it used to be, but it was an eye-opener to discover the relentless pattern the records reveal.

These lower catches may be due in part to a decline in the trout population on the waters I fish, but I believe they portray more clearly the extent to which my own approach to the sport has changed. And my development as an angler may not I think be untypical, when compared with that of others over a similar period.

The only years during which my annual catches actually increased was the period 1963–66 inclusive, when they rose from twelve (in my first season) to 103, 253 and 457. From 1966 to the present time the results appear as follows:

Four-year period	Total trout caught	Approx. ave. per season
1966–69	1,495	374
1970–73	1,449	362
1974–77	961	240
1978–81	764	191
1982–85	630	157
1986–89	378	94

Last season, 1989, I caught a total of 47 trout – my lowest return since that first season with the fly rod.

Examining the diaries more closely, I find that the number of days fished each trout season, rather than falling over the years, has in fact risen from approximately 75 in 1969, to 83 in 1979, to over 90 in 1989.

Against this, however, there is the fact that on average I now fish only for an hour or two on most visits, up to a maximum of perhaps five hours at the height of the season. During July and early August, for example, I now seldom begin fishing until well after sundown, and then actually fish for just 30–60 minutes – whereas on many summer days back in the 1960s and up to the mid-1970s I fished for six or eight hours on end.

The number of trout I address over a given period, and the number of deliveries I make to each, is fewer than hitherto. If I find a particularly large trout I may sit over him for hours or days, even weeks, just waiting for him to come well on the feed, and then present the fly only half a dozen times perhaps, before slinking away into the darkness, hoping to find him rising in the same spot another time.

Alongside this more leisurely approach, I have become aware in recent years of the need to conserve stocks on certain waters. There can be little doubt that the number of native trout in many streams (especially those where fees are high), is declining. Today I sometimes watch a rise in progress without making a single cast. Fifteen and twenty years ago, I felt free to fish hard and take a few brace on most waters I visited, because I knew those waters were well able to produce and the wild stocks could stand it.

In much of the West Country, Wales and the North this still applies, indeed trout may be so numerous here that a degree of culling can benefit the fishery. On some chalk streams, however, where native stocks are threatened – not least by the irresponsible introduction of hatchery fish in silly numbers and sizes – a wild trout may be something of a rarity.

The decline in my own catches reflects to some extent a personal aversion to fishing for stockies; in fact fewer than ten per cent of those recorded came from a stew-pond. But above all, I suppose, the main factor as I reach what is politely called late middle age, is laziness. After a long day or week at work, it is fishing which restores the tissues and preserves my sanity – not the labour of it, for I seek no prizes, nor the challenge which some say is an essential ingredient, but simply the peace, the tranquillity of flowing waters and the blessed release which our sport affords.

ᥧᥩ 63 ᥩᥤ
A United Front?

In response to the suggestion that fishing is the most blameless of the field sports, one reader raised the interesting question: 'Are then the other field sports in some way to blame, and if so for what?' He continues: 'If field sports are to survive ... all field sportsmen must pull together. Otherwise we will be picked off one by one by the antis, who show little distinction between one sport and another.' A number of contributors have voiced similar concerns, but many fishermen remain firmly on the fence – reluctant, it seems, to back this proposal wholeheartedly. While it is understandable that those sports which are more vulnerable than ours should seek the support of the stronger angling lobby, many anglers believe that each sportsman should decide for himself what he thinks is just and morally right.

This is a thorny issue, for, on the one hand, we would wish to present a united front, yet those who take part in country sports are themselves divided. Many of us harbour misgivings about aspects of one pursuit or another. There are anglers who are distressed, even outraged, by the prospect of an exhausted stag or grounded fox being mauled by hounds, or hundreds of pheasants being brought down at organized shoots. Such views are held by some, so it is better said. Nor should we expect anyone who holds such an opinion to champion a cause in the interests of solidarity if he believes that cause to be wrong. Indeed, might he not feel that in doing so he could be contributing to the eventual downfall of his own sport? We should acknowledge that hunting, shooting and fishing have precious little in common. Each must put its own case, and stand or fall by the standards it has set.

While the antis are often portrayed as louts and yobbos, we should remember that most are caring people whose views do not happen to coincide with our own. If we are honest with ourselves, we may even sympathize with parts of their argument. On this issue, few rational

thinkers can take a rigid pro or anti stance; sentiment and logic inter-
mingle, common-sense and emotion overlap. Hard persuasion seldom
changes someone's gut feeling about what is humane and what is not.
All the sportsman can do is ensure that the image he projects is one of
decency, compassion and moderation.

Hunting folk, some will say, have failed to do this. Likewise, those
who stand in formation and shoot down driven birds may have their
motives questioned. And anglers – certainly where they kill fish that
are virtually tame, or take those yet to regain condition after spawning, or handle them carelessly – may expect the wrath of millions to
descend.

The main criterion by which field sports are judged must surely be
that of fairness. The quarry we seek to secure must have a better-than-
even chance of evading capture. If the odds are heavily loaded in the
hunter's favour, then we are simply indulging in a wanton killing exercise, rather than a legitimate sporting challenge.

Fresh salmon and sea trout, wild trout, grayling and coarse fish –
possessing all their inherited instincts for survival, their natural guile,
caution and dogged resistance – provide fair game indeed for fair-
minded anglers. It is when we introduce means of markedly shorten-
ing the odds – either through highly advanced technology, or unnatural production and instant stocking techniques – that we lose respect
for our quarry, and angling comes under increased scrutiny. It is right
that it should, for if results are contrived and virtually assured there
are many who will want no part of it.

∞ 64 ∞
As Others See Us

If the day ever dawns when angling comes under serious threat of abolition we could well reflect, as might the hunting people, that we were our own worst enemies. Fishermen have little difficulty in justifying their own actions, and can give as good as they get in the verbal slanging match in the press, but do we pay sufficient regard to the perceptions of a silent non-fishing majority whose opinions, given a day of reckoning, would prove decisive?

The great mass of the British public are caring folk to whom moderate behaviour and fair play represent the basis of a civilized life. Few argue that the hunting of game is morally wrong, always provided the creature we pursue possesses all its naturally inherited instincts for survival, and that the hunter conducts himself in a decent, respectful manner towards his quarry.

Some years ago the image of the fisherman, as I recall it, was of a solitary figure in sombre garb merging quietly into the natural setting as he plied his gentle craft. To the passer-by he was a part of the country scene, and accepted as such; his appearance, his actions and his motives did not give offence. This was the sport of the contemplative man, whose very nature was as unassuming as his apparel. Media people, wise and true, sometimes portrayed the angler as a little crazy, often unsuccessful, even a subject for pity – but essentially a modest nature-loving soul with whom the public could readily identify.

Some of the messages we see today in angling magazines, videos, TV coverage and the like are still most tasteful, just as some fishermen have retained a certain humility and restraint. It must be said, though, that a new image has emerged, and fishing, particularly trout fishing, is now seen in a rather different light. We may wish the antis would go away, but I fear their numbers will grow as long as we continue to project that image.

In the eyes of many, our appreciation of the natural beauties and mysteries that surround us is being replaced by the trivial, the vulgar and the grotesque – as manifested by so-called flies that some feel are an affront to nature, and by gross, misshapen fish that disgust the caring observer. Many abhor modern fishery-management techniques, in which we tamper with genes so as to deny natural reproduction, induce abnormal growth and offer big catches all winter, in some cases by bait fishing. We stock small ponds with tame giants that are destined to be killed at once (the less fortunate will die of starvation) and tell ourselves that angler-demand, and the belief that fish do not experience our kind of pain and distress excuses what we do. Perhaps it does, but how do such practices go down with an impressionable public?

Influenced by the more flamboyant elements in the angling press, we have created a kind of 'designer angler' to whom a fashionable profile appears more important than attempting to master the fundamentals of delicacy, stealth and concealment. We don't wear red coats and shout 'tally-ho!', yet the emblems of conformity are no less apparent. We don't blow on hunting horns or blood novices, but our posture is no less ritualistic.

I do not suggest that modern put-and-take policies, or the wearing of emblazoned costume, or the use of outlandish lures necessarily breeds loutish, inhumane or greedy behaviour of a sort that plays into the hands of the antis. All the same, they may be seen by many as synonymous with those attitudes we seek to discourage.

Some people have made fat profits from games like golf, snooker and tennis. The stuff of champions lies in the shattering of records, competitive hype, brand logos and maximum exposure. There is a cultural urgency to produce ever more impressive results, to be seen as a highly skilled achiever, to win at all costs. But this scenario is the very antithesis of what our innocent pastime is all about. If we succumb to this, the notion that we sacrifice living creatures in the pursuit of wealth or to enhance reputations might indeed be a valid one.

๛ 65 ๑

Firing from the Hip

If I am a bit of a traditionalist, then I'm in good company, for the fishermen I meet are mostly a conservative lot, not given to flamboyance or striking a pose on the river bank. We feel, perhaps, that – unlike more strenuous outdoor activities, in which the projection of a dashing, colourful image is entirely laudable – ours is essentially an unassertive, more sober pastime. We study to be quiet, merging into the background, unseen by fish and passers by alike.

Since the very nature of our sport entails some contact with mud, rainwater, barbed wire, cowpats and fish-scales, the angler's attire – if he is a proper angler – is of necessity scruffy, usually old, and certainly less than glamorous. Indeed, because the whole purpose of fly fishing is so far removed from that of the leotarded fitness freak, psychedelic cycling enthusiast or follower of baseball games, I confess that my horror of its being likened to any such pursuit borders on the extreme. But we can agree perhaps that while the motives underlying these sports include a display of robustness, competitiveness or a desire to be recognized as a participant, the angler's dialogue is principally between himself and his fish. The fisherman should not need to make a statement, or advertise his presence to society at large.

It may be that the unskilled or inept can compensate to a degree by looking the part. Role models abound in the glossy pages, and sports outfitters benefit from those who mimic their heroes, yet those who are merely clones may exhibit some confusion as to their true identity. One angler of my acquaintance was so extravagantly decked out in brightly feathered headgear, gadget-strewn waistcoat and the rest that I suspected he would never be a successful fisherman. He spent considerable sums trying to be somebody he was not, and soon gave up fishing in favour of polo. (I believe he may have taken up morris dancing, too.)

Of course, our individual persona is under constant bombardment. We watch power-boat anglers and rock-hopping fly fishers on video, read of amazing exploits in British Columbia or the Antipodes, and absorb all sorts of visual messages from elsewhere. We can hardly wait to employ those strategies ourselves, to become those anglers, and to catch the fish they catch. Yet it seems to me that those who pay homage to the fashion designer and ad-man betray the fact that their roots lie in a different world: one which is increasingly out of touch with the rest of nature. Even the essentials of fly fishing – like moving slowly, observing natural signals, using cover and dressing sensibly – we ignore at out peril. We may cut an elegant figure on the street, but by the river we can stick out like a sore thumb, as wild creatures dive for cover at our approach.

Sometimes I have a delicious dream in which I'm sitting beside a crystal trout stream. Around the bend appears a strange apparition, quite unrecognizable in clownish hat and black goggles as it bobs down the current in a float-tube. A flashing rod with feather-duster flies in one hand and a mobile phone in the other, 'the thing' treads water before me; it has put all my fish down and shattered my tranquillity. But suddenly there is an explosive hiss. The rubber ring zig-zags wildly around the pool before sagging limp and exhausted in the shallows, its occupant resembling a cheap jeweller's display stand after a ram-raid, while chuckling author, shooting from the hip as usual, pens his next 'Random Casts'.

৩৩ 66 ৩৩

Stillwater Policies

Small stillwaters, man-made pools and 'holes in the ground' now serve a vital function in satisfying the huge demand for trout fishing, certainly in areas where little river fishing is available and few large reservoirs exist within reasonable distance. Most are privately owned, competition among nearby fisheries can be fierce, and the margin between profit and loss may be slender indeed. Yet it seems to me, from speaking to many stillwater anglers, that the almost universal method of trying to attract custom – that of offering ever more staggering average weights – may not after all be the main criterion by which such lakes are judged.

True, some anglers do measure their enjoyment principally in terms of how quickly they can fill the freezer, but, judging by the views of those I have met, such fishermen represent a small minority. All want to catch trout, of course, but most accept they will go home blank on one day in three or four, and that over a complete season they are likely to take around two trout per outing on average, maybe less.

As to individual weights, I believe most of us are delighted if we catch a three-pounder occasionally – although it is nice to know there is the prospect, if only a slim one, of something bigger. But for table fish, as opposed to trophy fish, trout of between one and two pounds are probably the ideal size.

One rod, however, summed up what I believe is a common view that many fishery managers overlook: 'I don't mind if I catch smaller trout, as long as I can fish in pleasant surroundings.' On this water, fishermen must walk between the stew ponds before reaching the lakes; many fish bore blotches of white fungus, while a few could be seen rotting on the bottom. The tractor, evidence of whose expeditions could be seen in deep ruts around the fishery, pulled up alongside. 'We're just about to put in some more big ones,' said one of the workers, presumably thinking that would whet our appetites. Fortunately I had waders with me, and I needed them as I stumbled through the mud around a small, deep pool where little vegetation was in evidence and no trees grew. The one rainbow I captured had a stunted pectoral fin, red-raw at the tip, and, although I killed the trout as the rules stipulated, I could not bring myself to eat it.

One young fishery manager I met elsewhere showed me plans which should bring the customers rolling in. Inspired by the beautifully landscaped setting of top golf courses, he aims to plant weeping willows and exotic shrubs, clumps of colourful flowers in profusion amid well-kept lawns, with little streams chuckling in their descent through the sloping gardens. A lodge is to be erected, with a tackle shop and the most comfortable lounge-cum-fly-tying room that will overlook the main lake through french windows leading onto a wide veranda. Small fishing huts around the lakes will provide shelter and plenty of space for spare tackle, while garden seats and tables will be placed at strategic points, with well concealed litter-bins.

My friend plans to maintain a higher trout density than other smaller fisheries, with mixed sizes from 12 oz up to 2 lb, and a few larger ones. This will enable rods to see more fish and catch more. Anglers will be able to return trout if they wish, but the average weight, though fluctuating according to the time of year, should be around 1–1½ lb.

We shall see when the project gets under way, but my guess is that this new idea of providing more opportunity, with smaller trout, in a truly glorious setting, will appeal to the large number of caring fishermen who have become disenchanted with the policies pursued on some stillwaters.

❦ 67 ❧

On the Beat

The authorities have to remain pretty vigilant in rural Wiltshire, what with itinerant ravers, sun-worshippers and decrepit motor-homes. Farmers erect barricades, police mount roadblocks, and country folk are apt to lock up their daughters against marauding Moonrakers, Druids and the like. It was around Solstice time that I invited Graham Swanson to fish on the Nadder, quite forgetting that his less-than-elegant vehicle might well arouse suspicion when parked by the stone bridge in Burcombe. Indeed the constabulary were so quick off the mark that they pounced soon after Graham's arrival – to my lasting regret, for I missed the incident. But I can well picture the scene as described by my friend afterwards.

You must understand that we have watched Graham's commodious camper, which he purchased some twenty-five years ago, gradually become tattier each season as it nudges its way along overgrown tracks and byways, across undulating fields and into the most unlikely parking spots. As cracks appear in the structure so its owner applies more sticky tape, and any dents in the bodywork or ill-fitting doors are simply treated to a dose of the hammer. Nor does its owner inspire too much confidence – Graham's fishing clothes have provoked many a haughty comment on up-market waters.

Doubtless the two policemen had agreed, 'we've got a right one 'ere' before my friend greeted them warmly with the offer of tea and biscuits. He explained that he was only here for the fishing ('a likely tale'), but, after peering around the interior of the van, 'the Bill' appeared satisfied that Graham was no drug-pusher or would-be squatter, and let him go on assembling his tackle. 'Come by later this afternoon,' called Graham. 'I'll have a trout for you.' But they must have been called to more urgent duties elsewhere.

A few days later, my friend Mike Kelly and I were trying to find a hidden stream which flows behind a fairly chic housing development. We parked among the desirable residences, watching the curtains twitch, and proceeded to wander about the estate looking for a foot-path between the houses that might lead to the river. We must have presented a fearsome picture in our muddy raincoats and waders. Perhaps these good people thought we were burglars, for the curtain-twitching reached a new intensity – or were they perhaps expecting somebody from the Water Company? Eventually we found out, for a nice old gentleman emerged from one of the doorways. 'At last,' he exclaimed. 'We thought you would never get here. You are the council rat men, I take it?' We tried to look dignified as we informed him that we were actually fly fishermen, but almost at once we broke down in a fit of mirth.

One evening I went to the upper Avon, close to Stonehenge, to find considerable turmoil occurring on the bridge where I had hoped to fish. At least twelve police vans were stationed on the roundabout, ready to ferry people away, while a multitude of freedom-lovers jostled with uniformed officers. Tempers flared, colourful language drifted on the air along with a cloud of sherry spinners, and numerous projectiles hurtled towards the advancing gendarmerie.

I attempted to cross the bridge with my rod held high, but soon became trapped in no-man's land between the opposing camps. This was not the best spot to view the proceedings from – or come to that to watch the evening rise – so I inched my way forward until I reached the comparative shelter of the far parapet. From there I was able to survey the scene in its entirety; on my left sad *homo sapiens* was displaying all his fury and raw aggression; on my right a growing band of excited onlookers stood, revelling in man's obscene activities and urging them on to yet more violent deeds; just four yards below me two fine specimens of *salmo trutta* were rising happily in the calm of a summer night, quite oblivious of the uproar overhead. 'What price civilization?' I asked myself, and, in terms of living our respective lives, 'Which species has got it right?'

ೲ 68 ೲ

Appliance of Science

Why is it, I wonder, that so few modern trout fishers are able to identify even a handful of natural insects, yet those same anglers often know the names and the dressings of numerous bizarre confections whose likeness to any recorded species is remote. The essence of trout fishing, as I understand it, is to deceive our quarry into taking a faithful imitation of the insect currently engaging their attention, yet how many fly-tying instructors, and how many of those who publish these fanciful creations, encourage their pupils to study the food forms that trout actually eat? By failing to do so, are they not deterring newcomers from exploring that fascinating world of aquatic flies and their life cycles which is so fundamental to trout angling, as well as denying them the chance to meet the challenge before them? Clearly, if the angler has little understanding of natural insects, he has no alternative but to ring the changes *ad infinitum* in the hope that he may happen on an artificial which, on this occasion at least, proves acceptable.

One wonders how many experts themselves possess any knowledge of natural flies. I recall being introduced to a so-called entomologist at a recent angling fair, whose green eyeshade, magnifying lenses and angled lamps all looked very impressive, as did the colourful array of capes, tinsels and beads strewn about. A large diagram depicting the trout's optical mechanism enhanced the effect, yet when I asked him what species of fly his current brainchild represented he simply replied 'I don't go in for all that scientific stuff.' Doubtless any awakening interest in entomology shown by budding fly fishers would be snuffed out at birth!

Scientific is it? Well let me ask this. Which is easier to learn, the names of six or eight olives and pale wateries, plus a few sedges and land-bred insects, or the hundreds of infinitely variable concoctions with names like Rat-faced MacDougal, Baby Doll, Mohawk and

Woolly Bugger (many of which originated thousands of miles from these shores and bear little resemblance to any aquatic species, let alone one found in the UK)? We have taken an essentially simple subject and woven a complex web of confusion, from which the beginner, once enmeshed, finds it virtually impossible to extricate himself.

Some justification for advocating the use of highly impressionistic patterns might exist if it could be shown that native or acclimatized fish succumbed more readily to these than to imitative dressings, but in my experience the reverse is almost invariably the case. Instant stockies may grab at anything, but established residents run for cover more often than not. Nor can we argue that wildly inaccurate representations make sense on the grounds that the trout's vision is different from our own. It may well be true, but speculation running riot to this extent does nobody any favours, except perhaps the commercial fly-tier.

So what should the newcomer do, when so few modern books and articles discuss natural flies in any detail? Should he join the bemused throng at the tackle shop, picking out a bit of this and some of that just in case a species may emerge that may perchance resemble something he has bought – and, if not, go back for another lucky dip? Should he buy a fly-tying kit and copy those fancy dressings as soon as they appear in the press, without really knowing what it is he is supposed to be imitating? Or will he, rather than simply following the crowd, prefer to think the matter through in a logical manner? If so, he may begin by familiarizing himself with the limited range of flies he sees in and on the water, or as a result of autopsy. He will study these duns, spinners, nymphs and the like, note their appearance, and then tie up his patterns accordingly. Thus when he finds a feeding trout he can make a reasonable deduction as to its current diet and knot on an appropriate artificial. Not too scientific is it?

ᥦ 69 ᥫ

A Lost Civilization

Tired after their long day spent in flower-decked meadows, the boy and his sister trotted down to the river bank where they stooped to drink from the sparkling stream. They marvelled at the brightly coloured butterflies flitting among the trees, the dozens of grasshoppers leaping away at every step they took, and the assorted notes of a hundred frogs croaking in the lush grasses nearby. The landscape all about was sharply defined, clear as crystal in the freshness of a summer afternoon as the two children took their fill of the sweet waters and laughed together for the sheer joy of being alive in a perfect world.

The scene was so idyllic that the strange story the boy had to tell seemed altogether incongruous. Millions of years ago, according to ancient letters, drawings and artifacts known only to himself and the Wise One he had consulted, there had been a previous civilization which had lived upon this land, whose number was so vast that some families lived above and beneath one another in 'stacks' of twenty or even thirty homes, reaching high into the sky. The secret documents revealed that each dwelling had artificial lights like the brightest stars, which illuminated the rooms at the touch of a button, and 'gas' was brought from deep in the ground through pipes to provide heat in the cold period and enable families to cook their food. Water came out of pipes, too, so they could drink and bathe while remaining indoors.

This curious, long-vanished people had no need to hunt. Food, sometimes already cooked, was distributed widely throughout the areas of habitation and was obtained by handing over pieces of material called 'money'. This money was given to people in exchange for their labour, which was carried out in separate buildings where they worked together for long periods each day. The harder they worked the more money they were given, and so they could secure more of the good things for their home and family.

When they went to their place of work or to the distribution points called 'shops', or just sought to get away from the packed centres of population, these folk sat in family-sized boxes which, using a liquid (again taken from deep holes in the earth), drove themselves along as fast as the birds can fly, and travelled along special hard tracks which ran between the houses and all across the countryside.

In the time they called AD 1950, about 2,500 million people lived on this planet; by AD 2000 the figure had risen to 6,000 million, and soon after that it had tripled, and the planet was not able to support them all. Not enough food could be produced or distributed, and the amount of gas, lighting and liquid for their boxes began to dwindle. So they fought over the remaining resources and had great wars, using weapons which could kill thousands at a time. Soon they destroyed the means by which food and water was purified, so they died of poisoning – and by now even the air was unfit to breathe. It had taken another ice age to rid the earth of its impurities, to heal the destruction that this insane race had wrought upon the world, and for new species to evolve. This particular area, the map had shown, was in the south of England and had been known as 'London'.

The two youngsters returned home. Their father and mother were showing great excitement, for their father had just finished making a wooden structure which would enable them to move materials about without the customary lifting and carrying. Proudly he displayed his new creation, and the circular revolving stone at the front which was his greatest discovery: he had invented the 'wheel'. Yet he was puzzled by the reaction of the boy and girl, who simply walked away in thoughtful silence as if somehow they had foreseen that this advance was inevitable.

৩ 70 ৫

To See, and to Hear

As we consider our uncertain origins and the multiplicity of genes which have produced twentieth-century man, we can appreciate how our wonderfully complex personalities have evolved. No man may be said to possess a distinct, individual identity; it is more an elaborate hotch-potch of largely inherited characteristics that makes up what we call his 'nature'. From an early age we learn to subdue certain instincts, often those of a more creative or mystical kind, while the worldly talents which will enable us to compete and to prosper are encouraged.

Throughout life, however, each of us longs for the happiness which is born of fulfilment. We seek it perhaps not primarily in social areas which have to do with wealth or position, for these are very often but surface trappings. We look for it more in the crowning of deeper, more primitive yearnings, which may express themselves in an appreciation of art, music or poetry, in stalking and hunting, in solitary communion with natural things, or in philosophical repose.

It is true, of course, that relatively few achieve this enviable state, for the thirsting soul is denied by the constraints of society, and by our own compliance. Even the ability to identify those latent desires within may have become blurred with the passing of the years. But still we sense an urgent, intangible energy, a 'something' that if we explore the psyche, we might yet rediscover. Or is it only undeveloped races which understand and nurture that vital force, and not advanced cultures, whose links with the past are more tenuous?

Most of us steer an unnatural course in an artificial, man-made world, as far removed from our roots as it is possible to be. And yet it may be because of this that many strive the harder to find peace and tranquillity. By design, or good fortune, some have so ordered their existence as to allow themselves the space and the solitude in which to contemplate and to search for deeper truths – in wild countryside, by fishing in unspoiled places, and by letting the glories of nature enter and renew the spirit.

Those living in Wessex, as I do, can hardly fail to be mindful of our heritage. As we fish beneath the great escarpments and chalk ridges, or in the wide valleys of the plains, we are surrounded on every side by distant echoes and relics of immense antiquity: Iron Age hill forts, Roman settlements, early field systems, burial mounds from the Bronze Age and Neolithic times (some 2,200 round barrows are recorded on the fringes of Salisbury Plain alone) and monuments which predate even the earliest Mycenaean civilization of ancient Greece or the first pyramids of Egypt. In places like this, as we sit among the resting places of our ancestors – watching the sun set over Stonehenge, or looking up at the rising ground of Old Sarum as fishermen have done since before the birth of Christ – we may experience something of the mysteries known to our forefathers.

Far-fetched though it may seem, there are times when it is as if a small voice whispers to those of us who can overcome our arrogance and disbelief. We may learn that each bird and tree and fish is as much a part of creation as we are, of equal importance in nature's scheme; that man has no right, simply because he has highly developed brain cells, needlessly to purloin or waste natural resources and poison the air and seas; that, if his race is to survive, it can only be in harmony with the earth's natural balance. If he fails to preserve a healthy ecosystem, the very life-force from which he evolved, then he will reap fearful consequences.

If we as individuals are to discover the purpose of our existence, and experience the heights of joy which that knowledge can bring, we might seek above all humility. For it is the humble person, who keeps an open mind and an open heart, who is best able to receive guidance, to hear, and to see.

⤷ 71 ⤶
Annie Alicia Oak 1898–1989

In the early summer of 1968, finding no room at the inn, I happened upon the cottage occupied by old Nan Oak. In near darkness, I was mindful of the landlord's words: 'She's old, mind, and she may be nervous. Used to have a lodger years ago, but he died long since.' As the door opened I kept my distance, and spoke in reassuring tones. Her husband Ted had passed on too, and not long ago her only son. Now, at the age of seventy, she lived alone with her memories.

I have wondered since whether there was something in my manner which reminded her of that lost son, or whether it was simply human chemistry, but right away I felt so at ease with Nan in her little cottage that it was as though I had come home at last, after being lost in some strange, unfriendly world. Maybe I sensed, deep down, some echo from my own past. From the outset I could never think of this haven as 'fishing digs', or of Nan as my landlady. I was accepted totally, encouraged to treat the cottage just as if it were my own.

Despite a hard life and some bitter blows, Nan possessed an uncommon fortitude, great wisdom, and a remarkable inner strength. From old English country stock, she displayed kindness, good humour and courage in such measure as I had not known before. Her name was so appropriate, for nobody was ever more like a solid and dependable oak tree than old Nan. Never, ever, did she expect anything in return for all the pleasure and comfort she so enjoyed giving to others.

My arrival at her door that night was to be the start of nineteen halcyon years in that heavenly fisherman's retreat close to Stoford Shallows, and I like to think it brought her a new lease of life as well. She was never happier than when doling out cups of tea and her famous rock cakes to all and sundry, seeing muddy boots on the back step or hanging up to dry, fly lines strung between the fir trees, fish strewn here and there about the sink and fishermen nodding drowsily at the hearth. There were no set meal-times, yet, incredibly, whenever I returned unexpectedly a dinner was waiting, and Nan always smiling her welcome at the door.

Nan Oak was a mother to us all – grown men from many walks of life, but little boys when we came down for the fishing. If you were dripping wet, dog tired, or fuming over the loss of a big trout, you ran to the cottage where Nan would make it better. Within minutes your humour was restored. As you sat with her you saw the futility of self-pity and could laugh at yourself once more.

The back garden slopes towards the cottage, and Nan, whose legs were not as strong as her spirit, would often be found on hands and knees, snipping the lawn with clippers – in latter years even household scissors. Once when I appeared she stumbled, trying to hurry, and came rolling down the hill between the runner beans and the flower-beds in the summer sunshine, roaring with laughter. She must have been over eighty then, and this is how I will always remember her, so full of joy and fun.

As the first cuckoo came to the valley that spirit left the old frame to join her husband, her son and the rest of her family, and some of our fishing friends who have gone before. We buried Nan Oak two weeks after her ninety-first birthday, in Ted's little plot at South Newton down the road.

As I tackle up by the churchyard gate of a summer night I will look over the ancient flint wall and remember all those happy days. Maybe I shall tell her of my troubles once more, and of the one that got away – and maybe, in doing so, I shall have the scales removed from my eyes and see life's underlying realities in clearer perspective.

ೀ 72 ೀ

First Trout of the Antipodes

It is astonishing to consider that the lakes and rivers of New Zealand, now thought by many to be the finest trout waters in the world, in fact contained no game fish when the early settlers were arriving a hundred and fifty years ago. Eels, lampreys, minnows and smelt were about the only fish present, apart from a mysterious species of grayling (*Prototroctes oxyrhynchus*) now said to be extinct. So there began the most remarkable acclimatization exercise: to populate with game fish a country the size of Britain, possessing thousands of streams and rivers, and situated 12,000 miles away across the globe.

While the names of Mr Borcius, Mr E. Wilson and Mr A.M. Johnson are associated with these first endeavours, it was Mr J.A. Youl, beginning his investigations in 1854, who finally succeeded in transporting fish from the UK, albeit with tragic initial results. In February 1860 he shipped thirty thousand ova in the *Sarah Curling*. From early literature we learn that:

The ice-house consisted of two rooms, one within the other, lined with lead; the space between was filled with powdered charcoal; a filled water-tank over the ice-house with a pipe leading into it allowed a gentle and continuous stream of water to pass over the ova as they lay in swing trays. The passage was long, the 15 tons of ice gave out, and the last of the ova was found to be dead when the ship was 68 days out.

In January 1864 he again tried. Boxes were made (of inch pine) measuring twelve inches by eight inches by five inches, with perforated top, bottom and sides. At the bottom was first spread a layer of charcoal, next a layer of ice, then a nest of carefully washed moss, and on this spring cushion were deposited the ova. Over them was laid a covering of moss, then a double handful of broken ice, and the

211

whole was saturated with iced water and screwed down. One hundred and eighty-nine boxes, containing 100,000 salmon and 3,000 trout ova, were packed closely on the floor of the ice-house, and upon them were piled blocks of ice to the height of nine feet. The *Norfolk* sailed on the 21st January, 1864, arriving in Melbourne (Australia) on 15th April. The State of Victoria retained 4,000 salmon ova, of which it is said 400 were hatched. The remainder were sent to Tasmania by a Government steamer. They were taken to the Derwent river, and placed in the hatchery provided. Mr Ramsbottom estimated that there were 30,000 salmon and 500 trout still living. On the 4th May the first trout was hatched, on the next day the first salmon, and by 25th May there were 300 trout and 700 salmon! At the end of 1865 the surviving salmon were allowed to enter the sea.

Most of the remaining trout perished, but about thirty were released into the River Plenty, while just six pairs reached maturity and spawned in the ponds. Their progeny were liberated in some rivers and streams of Tasmania, Victoria and New Zealand.

Numerous further introductions followed between 1865 and 1870.

From these shipments most of the trout found in New Zealand have come, for they not only throve in every stream into which they were placed, but quickly came to maturity and spawned so freely that it became easy to distribute them. . . . Mr W. Arthur, who investigated the subject more carefully than anyone who has written on it, states that the brown trout in Tasmania were descended from three lots from England. Of these, Mr Francis Francis sent one from High Weycombe (Wycombe), Bucks, and another from the Wey at Alton, Hants, and Mr Buckland sent one lot from Alresford on the Itchen, Hants.

While the precise origin of Mr Youl's first successful introduction in 1864 remains uncertain, it is known that he visited fish breeding establishments in both Scotland and Ireland while conducting his experiments in the early 1860s. We can be sure, however, that a large proportion are the descendants of English chalk-stream stock, distributed via Tasmania. After 1880 there was a constant interchange of ova and fry throughout both the North and South Islands, with, at a conservative estimate, 64 million young fish introduced up to 1921, by which time most of the 28 fishing societies in New Zealand were operating their own hatcheries.

ᦡ 73 ᦤ
Sleepy Old Town

Before the tourists arrive, Harihari looks something of a ghost town as it straddles Highway 6, the western route down the South Island of New Zealand. I was hot and tired after exploring the rugged country to the north-east in search of a legendary stream called Lost Creek. (It was nowhere to be seen on the map, and, after some hours of off-road work, I'd concluded not only that I would never find it, but the chances were that nobody else had either, despite all the tales of amazing trout. You hear stories like this on the west coast, where Irish blood runs in the veins.) Harihari boasts a motel, tea rooms, post-office-cum-store and Tomasi's cabin accommodation. Strapped for cash, I went for the last, taking my meals at the tea rooms, where I was pointed in the direction of the spring creeks which flow like crystal across lush farmland.

The tiny Thorp Creek running through the Levett's holding contained no fish I was told. A quick look from the bridge, though, revealed a big trout hovering near the surface in the first pool, another nymphing in the second, and a languid heave thirty yards ahead had me scrabbling through the willows that grew out into the stream. I could cover these fish, just, but playing them among the mass of branches was a heart-stopping experience. A hooked fish could not be allowed to take line. A doubled-up rod and twanging leader was the only answer, or the trout would be down beneath that fearsome tangle in a flash. I lost a couple and spooked some more, but my labours were handsomely rewarded with the capture of four magnificent fish weighing between 3 lb and 3 lb 4 oz.

I discovered another jewel of a creek a mile or so behind Berry's Farm, and came upon the deep pool where it suddenly increases in size from a shallow stream winding through the pastures. (This suggested an addition of fresh water from a large spring, as did the stream's extraordinary clarity.) I spent a day creeping and crawling after trout of up to five pounds, but they seemed to have sensed my presence long before I approached. I did catch two, of 2 lb 8 oz and 2 lb 2 oz, on a CDC Spinner in relatively broken water further down, but I reckoned the bigger ones could only be taken at nightfall. Crouching at the edge of the pool, I waited in vain until the light had almost gone.

Then it started. Losing their inhibitions, eight or ten trout began to rise, some literally under my rod. I hooked one so large there was no way I could stop him screeching across the pool, into some tree roots and away. Then another rocketed downstream with me stumbling over the rocks in pursuit. Like many of these fish, however, he fought like the very devil for a few minutes, then gave up completely. I couldn't see to net him properly, so with my torch clenched between my teeth I slid him into the shallows before heaving him ashore. This one went to four pounds, while others taken in that heavenly pool during the next few nights scaled 4 lb 2 oz, 3 lb, 2 lb 12 oz and 2 lb 10 oz, with a number of about 2 lb 8 oz.

I returned some of my trout but others were definitely 'owed' by way of thanks or apology. The helpful ranger didn't eat them; neither did the American who roundly scolded me because he'd seen a 'private fishing' sign of which I had no knowledge (I guessed he was a catch-and-releaser anyway – you can tell by their fancy attire). The Berrys and the Levetts enjoyed one or two, as did Charles Lucas at the store, Mr and Mrs Tomasi (whose cabin I succeeded in comprehensively flooding one day); and the policeman who allowed me to take breakfast in the tea rooms while he held a correction session with young offenders at an adjoining table. Life is pretty relaxed in this sleepy, one-street town nestling beneath the Southern Alps.

⊷ 74 ⊶

Magic Moments

Just occasionally the more fortunate among us may touch the uppermost peaks of joy that our sport can bring. It may be some seemingly minor encounter, a grand battle with a mighty warrior or simply the exquisite setting, but somehow it is that precious day that we recall whenever we dream of fishing.

My own special memory is of an expedition to the Motupiko river, a tributary of the Motueka in South Island, New Zealand. Sub-tropical downpour had brought the main river into raging spate, so I drove south over the Stanley hill towards Korere on the drier, eastern side of the watershed, to find the stream flowing like purest crystal. Over the centuries the river had carved a winding course through rock outcrops to form twinkling runs and limpid pools beneath a smooth cliff-face, shaded here and there by dark native beech and giant fern.

Clouds of purple and copper-coloured butterflies busied themselves among heavily scented flowers in the morning sunshine, while the liquid chimes of the bellbird and sonorous tui came ringing from above. This could not be the real world – surely I was in wonderland – but I was here to find one of the few big trout which come up to spawn and then linger in these magical waters throughout the summer months.

Approaching a deep grotto-like pool of breathtaking clarity I suddenly stopped in my tracks, for there on the shallow ahead hovered three large trout, each plainly visible against the sunlit river bed. Traversing the shingle beach on hands and knees, I crept into a less-than-comfortable casting position just as the nearer fish rose to intercept a drifting dun. My Pale Olive followed the same path ten seconds later but the fish, which looked well over three pounds, gave way as a heavier trout sidled across in front of him, rose, and missed my fly.

Sensing that something was amiss, the big fellow dropped downstream, came around in a wide arc below me and swam slowly along my bank. I flattened myself on the stones, but he knew I was there and faded from view. Further upstream, I spooked a monster from the margin, and felt a fierce tug in response to a speculative nymph before returning to my three friends. Instinct told me they were still a little wary however, so I sat beneath the red mistletoe amid a cascade of birdsong, happy just to savour this veritable Paradise.

By late afternoon the trout and I were well rested, and with the sun at my back I felt my approach would very likely go undetected. Crouching once again on the pebbles, I cast a small unweighted nymph towards the larger fish, only for the breeze to carry it three feet off target. Enter trout number three, which surged forward from nowhere, lifted, opened and closed his jaws and was on. The fish rocketed to the far bank, but I bullied him away from the perilous roots and branches, whereupon he shot downstream into the depths of the crystal pool. In twelve feet of water I could see every crimson spot, a delectable flush of gold along the flank, and the pristine fins and wide tail of a beautiful New Zealand trout. There were few snags here, and it was only a matter of time, provided the tackle held.

Fanciful notions sometimes enter my head I confess, but this encounter was particularly moving, as though a certain thought-transference was taking place. I looked directly into his eye, and he into mine. The trout weighed some four pounds, just right for a hearty meal with my hosts back at base. But a picture came to my mind of clean gravel beds, of the coming spawning season and the next. At home I would not have hesitated, but here I had the distinct feeling that I would return one day, remember and consider the possibility that the fish I stalked then were the descendants of this noble trout.

Something in that gentle gaze told me the cup was full to overflowing, and that I was so lucky to have lived to see this day, one brimming with every conceivable delight. I slipped my fingers down the leader and eased the hook free, standing spellbound for a moment as my onetime adversary, now a soul-mate, sank quietly out of sight among the boulders of the deep.

ᥦ 75 ᥨ
A Sweet Finale

Although I was assured that the Devine River was devoid of fish I nevertheless felt strangely drawn to her. It may have been the evocative name, or that my glance over the bridge revealed a scene of indescribable beauty, but there was also a curious beckoning, a siren influence, which so stirred the spirit that the urge to explore became irresistible.

A century ago a track had been cut along the top of the gorge, but by now nature had reclaimed it. Even so, I discovered two overgrown culverts and part of an old stone wall, along with a forlorn chimney-stack hidden among the trees. The river had created a deep, winding channel, a sheer cliff-face and mighty boulders polished as smooth as glass. Below, the music of the stream called urgently, yet I could find no means of descent.

Forcing my way through virtually impenetrable jungle I found the point at which earlier man had decided to go no farther. Literally, this was the end of the trail, yet as I sat exhausted beneath a blazing sun something caught my eye. Concealed among the hanging vines was the unmistakable outline of a small iron gate, whose rotten post and corroded hinges suggested that no one had passed this way for many a decade.

Beyond it a tortuous path led down through a dark gully and out into a cool, moss-clad cavern of pure delight. The sun's rays could penetrate only the centre of the ravine, highlighting the pellucid waters of an enchanted river, while the crags remained forever dank, covered with lush green lichens. Filled with awe, I wondered who had once treasured this secret haven; this fairyland fit for the innocence of childhood and possibly, before that, the worship of a long-lost race. Indeed, it was like some sacred place where nothing was beyond belief. One might imagine a voice coming from the rock, a burning bush, or a flash of light heralding some heavenly manifestation.

Yet all was silent save for the chuckling of the stream. No living soul was within miles, only the birds with their brightly-painted plumage and cascade of song, and the insects dancing over the virgin waters. I felt almost a sense of guilt, as if I was intruding in a spot so pure, so far removed from the tainted world from which I had come that I had no right to be here. Lest I should tarnish it, I moved slowly, softly, as I approached the sunlit pool. So clear was it that the depth appeared some two or three feet, but I knew it was more likely seven or eight.

Then I became aware of a new sensation. I was being watched. The back of my neck was tightening and the hair beginning to stand. I looked over my shoulder, along the rock-face, and to the tangled vegetation above. Although it was clear that nobody was there, I could still feel a definite presence. I shook myself, put the feeling to one side, and returned my gaze to the pool. Then I saw him. Below me, studying me closely from a position some three yards downstream, lay the largest trout I had ever seen. The sun revealed every spot along his magnificent flank, the great fins waving slowly in the current, the golden sheen of his rich brown back.

The fish appeared unafraid, friendly even. When I crept forward he came to within one yard of the bank upon which I crouched. For thirty, maybe sixty minutes we gazed on one another. I was becoming transfixed, mesmerized, as at the dawning of a beautiful dream; slipping into unconsciousness under that hypnotic spell, longing for the cool embrace of sweet water. Must I now atone for those years spent hunting trout to their doom? Was this to be some kind of retribution – even a reincarnation?

The harsh call of the kea jolted me to my senses. Conflicting emotions surged within: first a degree of resentment at the shattering of a vision, then by an overwhelming relief, and finally the joyous humility known to those given a new lease of life. I looked about me to find that nothing had changed. Even the hands on my watch had not moved, while of a fish or a green kea bird there was no sign.

I know now, though some years have gone, that my great trout awaits me yet. You can call it destiny if you will, but somehow, by begging, stealing or becoming a stowaway I must return just once more to that magical valley and a sunlit pool where time stands still.

∽ 76 ∾
Archie's Farewell

It is doubtful whether Archie had much idea of the path his future would take. All he knew was that a crossroads had been reached, as it had back in his twenties. The signposts read the same: pointing to the right he saw Job Security, Home Life, Social Acceptability; and to the left Adventure, Freedom, The Unknown. Thirty years ago the left had appeared the more appealing route, but it would mean taking a mighty chance, a leap into the darkness – did he have the courage? He turned to the right, for this way lay safety, friends and, eventually, a comfortable retirement.

Archie's work was interesting, stimulating to a degree, but after three decades it had become meaningless drudgery. In town everything had changed. People walked so quickly now, threatening to knock him down; he became confused by the flashing, bleeping crossings; public telephone kiosks, letter-boxes and toilets seemed fewer; there were no more cups of tea to be had in his favourite cafés, now it only came in pots, and when he lit up someone would point to a No Smoking sign. Piped music filtered everywhere, and he was startled by the strident note of reversing vehicles. Thrusting GTis with their shaven-headed occupants darted this way and that in Archie's rear-view mirror, while chip papers, empty cans and dog's mess littered footpaths and flower borders alike, as did a strange unkempt breed of humanity, the sight of which perplexed and frightened him.

This was not the friendly, comforting place he had known when he turned right all those years ago. He could no longer recognize some of his compatriots, law and order were declining fast, and he was sickened by the lies and platitudes of those he had voted into power. Under their guardianship, he saw greed and lack of concern spreading like a virus through his green and pleasant land. Even the old grass downlands, to their very summit, were golden brown with wheat, while rivers flowed as a mere trickle through his beloved valleys.

The rich were smug and self-satisfied, while the poor had become increasingly desperate. Belligerence and foul behaviour were rife –and were reported gleefully by media people in unnatural, lilting tones, along with shock-horror stories and the portrayal of the least savoury aspects of modern life. Wearily Archie realized this was a reflection of human appetites, and he no longer felt a part of his own society.

He was pushed finally towards that crossroad by a minor incident on the road close to his home. Already that year he had encountered numerous squashed hedgehogs and pheasants, a squirrel lying on his back with paws in the air, four dead blackbirds, an owl and a chaffinch. Meeting a partly stunned rabbit shivering and terrified in the roadway, Archie parked safely enough and got out to usher the poor animal back into the meadow. The air turned blue as motorist after motorist hurled a stream of invective and blared their horns on seeing him in the highway. Archie had not even impeded their progress, but he represented a target for their aggression, delivered from the safety of moving vehicles. 'Meet these people at a party,' thought Archie, 'and they would be as nice as pie. Underneath, in their hearts . . . is this what my countrymen have become?'

Archie knew just what he wanted to find. Somewhere where people were gentle and kind, where the hillsides were ablaze with flowers and butterflies, where he could explore wild country, safe and confident, free from the fetters of conformity; somewhere he could think clearly and find his true self, where people were thin enough on the ground to be seen as individuals, and where rivers went brimming to the sea as nature intended.

Of course he did not know whether his dreams would be fulfilled, but as he approached the junction he thought, 'living by the rules hasn't got me very far, and my present way of life will put me in an early grave anyway. You only live once, or so I imagine, and this is no rehearsal.' And so, well past middle age and with few savings, but with a happy song in his heart, Archie turned to the left, along that little-used track which leads to another world.

⨀ 77 ⨀
Archie and a Lone Bellbird

What became of Archie, whose disillusionment with modern society finally drove him from the accepted lifestyle and down that little-used pathway signposted Adventure, Freedom, The Unknown? He departed ten years ago, a lonely figure carrying a well-loved fly rod and his few possessions tucked into a battered holdall, from which swung the old black billy-can that was his constant fishing companion.

I knew Archie was heading south, possibly on the same route his father Tom had taken over forty years before. In his letters home Tom had told of a secret stream in South Island, New Zealand, which flowed as purest crystal through bush country near a tiny settlement called Moani Springs. I guessed that Archie's dream was to find that sparsely peopled Paradise, to settle forever where native birds and animals would be his only neighbours, and to discover the resting place of the father he had known in his youth. The Kiwis recalled that an eccentric Brit had taken a lift in Jake's truck a long time back, and 'Sure, he carried an old billy wherever he went. Wouldn't be parted from it for a second.'

Jake had dropped Archie near the mouth of the Moani river, whose watershed drained some four hundred square miles of heavily wooded country on the slopes of the Southern Alps. I reckoned he had journeyed upriver in search of the limpid tributaries, Moa Stream or Sunset Creek. The former, having its source close to the snow-capped mountains, was a rapid spate river; Sunset Creek, which rose at lower altitude in the vast Moani Forest, suggested a more stable habitat.

There were no roads, no tracks, just sixteen miles of seemingly impenetrable jungle before I could even begin to explore the creek. I would miss my flight for certain, but, as I stood wavering, a lone bellbird seemed to call with added urgency, before swooping in a wide circle and flying off upstream. Responding to this signal, I started four

222

long days of relentless slog through untamed bush, with its rampant thorn and clinging vine, resting only at nightfall beneath an upside-down New Zealand moon.

Late on the fourth day, torn and weary, I came upon a large clearing among the trees, where an area of springy grass led to the banks of a sweetly gliding stream. The remains of an old hut leaned half-hidden in the bushes, and nearby was a neat pile of rocks taken from the river bed, upon the largest of which had been etched the single word 'Tom'.

Part of the mystery was solved, but there was no guarantee that Archie had passed this way; perhaps a hunter or bushman had laid Tom to rest long before. Somehow, though, I knew my friend was close by. I moved on up Sunset Creek, marvelling at the wild flowers, the liquid chimes of the birds and the giant trout poised motionless in the depths.

I spied another clearing, with a ramshackle wooden building overlooking a broad shallow and the shaded pool below. A home-made bench stood on the grass, a plate lay on the upturned log which served as a table, while an empty rod-bag, unmistakably Archie's, hung on the handle of the open door.

I waited three days and three nights for Archie to appear, but my vigil was in vain. Just a lone bellbird kept me company, his golden tones cascading down from the green canopy. I turned, vowing to return, and as I did so something caught my eye. Beneath the tree was a small fireplace surrounded by blackened stones, the embers now cold and still, and an old black billy-can swung gently on the branch above.

᧵ 78 ᧷

Archie's Nirvana

You may recall that my old mate Archie, unable to stand the pressures of modern society, finally elected to withdraw into the magical valley of Sunset Creek, discovered some years earlier by his father Tom, and that I had made a number of trips over ten years in my efforts to uncover his whereabouts. The local inhabitants, remembering Archie's curly black hair, the ever-present billy-can swinging from a battered holdall, and his unmistakable nut brown eyes – the pupils curiously flecked with gold – were able to set me in the right direction. Four days' hard tramp in mountainous bush country had found me first beside Tom's last resting place beneath a small pile of stones, and then at the ramshackle building where Archie had made camp. His rod-bag hung on the door, the old black billy was suspended above the embers, but of Archie there was no sign.

This had looked ominous, but I determined to make one last attempt to unravel the mystery. It was clear that Archie never returned to base, since the rod-bag and billy were still where I'd left them two years earlier, and a tangle of vines now blocked the doorway. I calculated he would have moved up river, yet a strong sense of his presence seemed to pervade this place. Somehow I felt reluctant to travel upstream, but after searching over two days for some small clue I realized the futility of lingering further.

Four miles up the valley I came upon a set of footprints in the sand, and around the bend a fine plume of smoke rose from the forest canopy. Creeping forward, I spied a lean figure, the face deeply tanned by years of sun, but knew at once that this was not Archie. 'Sure thing,' the bushman responded to my enquiry. 'I remember the Pom with a billy, and the darkest brown eyes you ever saw. They had kind of gold tints like I've never seen before. Guess that was two, three years back. I've been in this upper valley ever since and he's not up here, that's for certain.'

After a welcome brew-up I accepted the bushman's conclusion that if Archie was alive he'd be somewhere in the area of Tom's grave and the old hut. I retraced my steps, feeling once more that strange sensation that my friend was close at hand. Then, attracted by the chimes of the bellbird in a nearby tree, I noticed Archie's cane rod leaning against a branch at the edge of the clearing. The line was threaded through the rings, with leader attached, but at the point there was no fly, only the curling 'pig's tail' suggesting the blood knot had pulled out.

So Archie could not have fallen into the deeps while playing a fish as I had feared. But had he done so as he tried desperately to land a trout which had broken free? After all, his net was nowhere to be seen. On the other hand, if that were the case he would surely not have had time to rest his rod against the tree?

Utterly perplexed, I sat down by the pool to think the matter through. A large trout rose gently to a passing beetle not five yards from me. As I watched distractedly, I felt there was something famil-iar about that fish. Was it the elegant movement, the inclination of the head, or the way the mouth opened? The trout came closer, pushing its neb clear of the water to engulf a struggling insect.

The prickling sensation at the back of my neck intensified. I shud-dered involuntarily, not with fear but in wonder and disbelief – a bedraggled artificial fly was visible in the upper jaw, and the eye that I glimpsed was of a dark, nut-brown hue, flecked with a hint of gold.

⸎ 79 ⸎

Wild Trout of the South Pacific

They say that dreams can be sweeter than reality, yet my adventures in South Island, New Zealand, from early November 1991 to mid-January 1992 proved more rewarding, and instructive, than I had ever imagined. Certainly, when I saw Norman and Jean Marsh standing on the balcony at Nelson airport I had little notion of just how exciting the fishing would be, nor how much I would need to adapt my style and approach to cope with these new and challenging conditions.

It was not my intention to pursue trophy trout on Taupo, Tongariro and the glorious Karamea, tempting though this was. I'd read about these fabulous waters, or seen them on video. Rather, my aim was to discover some of the little known, even unfished streams where I would encounter the resident descendants of those trout introduced from the UK during the latter part of the nineteenth century, to explore their natural habitats, and above all enjoy total solitude in pristine surroundings as yet untouched by the heavy hand of man. Only those able to blaze a trail through virgin bush country and camp out beneath the stars can achieve this ideal fully; even so, I reckon to have sampled the real New Zealand, at least in part, while avoiding those areas favoured by jet-set fishing parties on the international circuit.

As a taste of what was to come, Norman took me to Ngatimoti bridge over his home river, the Motueka, which flows from the towering snow peaks of the Mt Arthur and Mt Owen ranges and across fruit-laden plains towards Tasman Bay. Never had I seen such an astonishing array of large wild trout, all poised high in the deep water and nudging the surface with rhythmic ease. Eight or ten fish hovered in line downstream of the bridge, and a further half dozen above. Not one, we estimated, weighed less than two pounds, and several were between three and five.

Despite my terror at the prospect of making a hash of it in front of New Zealand's best known fishing author (and the group of onlookers who stopped to watch the fun), I yielded to Norman's insistence. 'Have a go,' he said. 'At least it will give us a giggle.' Electing to tackle two risers in the sharp run behind a boulder upstream of the bridge, my efforts to impress my audience came to nought as I stumbled down the steep rock-face like a young elephant. The trout must have known I was a visitor to their fair country, for both took the Devaux Olive first or second chuck, and both after a leaping, tearing fight found the inside of my net. We judged their weights at 3 lb 8 oz and 3 lb, but I was soon to discover that not many trout would be as co-operative as these.

After two nights at Norman and Jean's delightful home, I moved into a charming riverside bungalow close to the Motueka's confluence with a swift-flowing tributary, the Baton, in one of the most beautiful bush-clad valleys imaginable. My hosts were the Macleans, a hard-working farming family who offer a choice of self-contained accommodation, and somehow find the time to operate a guiding service for fishermen and hunters, and also riding holidays, gold panning, and helicopter flights to otherwise inaccessible wilderness. Dion Maclean, like Norman, is the most remarkable trout-spotter who knows every inch of these rivers. It was an education to watch the pair of them in action, both here and on the bustling Riwaka. Even in the restless water so typical of these mountain streams they could see fish which to my untrained eye were quite invisible.

On one sprightly little gem of a river, the Pearse, Dion pointed to a good trout lying right below our vantage point in the scrub. Try as I might I could not see it, but went in below and pitched my nymph upstream, following his instructions. 'Strike' called Dion, and I was into something big. The fish shot off downstream, my overfilled reel failed to run freely and, 'ping', that was that.

Soon, though, I was beginning to locate trout for myself, and felt more confident after netting a 3½-lb nympher unaided, from the Baton, while my lone expeditions to the Rai, Whangamoa, Motupiko, Mangles and Owen rivers produced several fine fish of between 2½ and 3¾ lb from stretches where I saw no trace of another angler. There are fewer trout in these streams than in similar rivers in the UK, and surprisingly their size became larger as I worked my way up into the smaller headwaters. They took up unexpected lies too, like the thinnest of shallows, where they were inclined to cruise among the stones in the very margins.

I was loath to leave Nelson province, which has the most pleasant climate in all New Zealand, but determined to keep to schedule and move on to the West Coast spring-fed streams and the rivers of Southland. My intention was to fish the La Fontaine creek while staying two nights in Harihari, but I was distracted by a wonderful discovery. Making myself known to the farmers hereabouts, it transpired that there was a tiny creek nearby, considered too small to be worth fishing. Yes, it held trout, but nobody had ever caught fish there as far as anyone could remember.

At first sight, I had the feeling that this was my special stream – as if it had been waiting all these years for my arrival. Not unlike some of my favourite winterbournes in the Wessex of twenty years ago, the creek was little wider than the length of my rod and full of crystal-clear water, with pockets up to five feet deep scoured out here and there to reveal pale bedrock. And in every pool lay a single trout that, had the sun been shining, would have been easy to spot against the light background. As it was, in somewhat overcast, windy conditions, the little creek nevertheless let me into her secrets.

In six hours of stealthy fishing over the two days I covered just three hundred yards or so, locating any number of trout over three pounds. Indeed, none appeared to be less than this weight, and some were a good deal heavier. Strangely enough, they were not as shy as I would have thought, as if this kind of predator was unknown to them. Some saw me before I spotted them, and swam downstream to investigate. They did not bolt, however, but sidled off to lie against a stone or under the bank, still quite visible.

I remember thinking that, had I been a more determined angler, I might have wreaked havoc among these gentle giants. I might have caught the bag of a lifetime, justifying my actions perhaps by putting them all back. I confess that, having killed one weighing 3 lb 4 oz for the nearest household and returned two other three-pounders, all on a weighted nymph, I felt that to carry on would have been overdoing it. I reeled in, had a cup of tea and made the mammoth eight-hour drive to my next destination. Lumsden lies close to the Mataura and Oreti rivers which flow from the Eyre mountains south of Queenstown. Here, the chap in the tea rooms warned me, it is perfectly possible to see all four seasons in a single day – and not just on one day, but for weeks on end. Burning sunshine, sleet and hail, raging gales and tropical downpour – I had the lot! The rivers were up and down, there was no rise, and most of the time it was too cold and windy to contemplate fishing. When I did, it was a three-sweater job, and the downstream wet fly brought me seven hard-fighting trout, mostly from the Irthing stream, although few weighed more than a pound. After an abortive trip to the exquisite Eglington river in Fiordland, I cut my losses and returned to the spring creeks of Harihari, this time to look more seriously at another unsung stream, Berry's Creek, in the lower reaches before it enters the mighty Wanganui.

This was the stuff that dreams are made of. The river varied from ten to thirty yards in width, with plenty of wadeable shallows, gentle stickles, and pools of amazing depth, so clear they took on an almost ethereal quality. If a trout was there he was often clearly visible, and usually he saw me. And some were big, very big: five pounds and more. It's hard on the knees and back when you are stalking trout in such conditions, but the combination of breathless excitement and blind panic, as with trembling fingers you tie the knot and make that single cast, can be thrilling in the extreme. The trout comes slowly, studies the fly minutely, and more often than not turns away.

Once in a while, though, you have a battle on your hands such as you will never forget. The line flies from the reel at an alarming rate, something huge leaps clear of the water and twists and turns and shakes its head like an angry dog. Each time you guide the fish towards you there is another electrifying run, and when eventually you get two feet of solid muscle into the net you hardly have strength to heave him ashore.

Although Berry's Creek lay just three miles down the road, my journey was quite an obstacle course, and took me twenty-five minutes each way. The boulder-strewn track, deep puddles, at least four gates and electrified fences to be opened and closed, and the boggy field where I had to park, to say nothing of the frogs and toads I encountered on the return trip, the cows, dazzled by my headlights, milling about the car and kicking it all made it a hilarious adventure. The windscreen became smothered in moths and sedge flies, and sometimes I would meet an opossum sitting on a gatepost – such friendly fellows, with pretty little faces; we had some good chats. They did not know we were supposed to be enemies (they damage trees to such an extent they are ruthlessly controlled), and, just for a brief moment, man and wild animal could share the joys of being alive.

I landed just fifteen trout from Berry's, Thorpe and La Fontaine creeks – and another tiny unnamed jewel which I christened Levett Creek – but they averaged over 3 lb, with the heaviest going to 4 lb

2 oz and 4 lb. I suspected that there are a number of spring-fed streams in Westland, south of Hokitika, which have yet to be discovered by the general angling public, but they would have to wait until my next trip, for I had promised myself a final fling on the magical Motueka and its sparkling tributaries.

By now, the evening rise was in full swing, and the holiday season was at its height. My previous reconnaissance work paid off, however, for I knew a number of hidden access routes to fine, lightly fished stretches, while most of the swimming, boating and fishing took place at more obvious spots. Around Christmas and the New Year I fished mostly in the mornings and late evenings, leaving some eight hours each day for other activities, like exploring native bush country with its fantastic ferns and heavenly birdsong, and searching for that elusive nugget to pay for my trip! I found gold fragments without difficulty, but only enough to have bought a few sedges. (Mind you, I could have done with them, for my stock was running low – torn apart by trout's teeth, barbs bent out by ferocious tugs, and a few snapped off by fish I was unable to stop.)

The morning rise was a more delicate business, involving the stalking of individual trout. Those I could creep up to without being seen were offered a little Olive or Pale Watery, or a nymph pattern. If the cast was a good one they often took without hesitation, but the resulting scrap inevitably disturbed a large area, and usually I caught only the one, if that. But the evening sedge rise could be spectacular. Beginning about 9.45p.m. it seemed to go on half the night. Indeed, looking at my watch on one occasion I found it was past midnight. I had fished eight minutes into Christmas Day.

Tall hills may cut out much of the surface sheen by 10 p.m. but with luck there is sufficient starlight or a rising moon to guide your fly to the rise. Now, the big trout cruise in shallow water, and you cast across or slightly downstream, twitching the fly towards you on a tight line. You strike gently, there is a sudden boil, and you must be ready for a lightning run and a series of whirring leaps. Sometimes the trout scorches towards some distant lie, or perhaps the fish remains close in on the shallows. The latter, I found were often the larger ones, and they included trout of 4 lb 10 oz and 4 lb 4 oz.

My two 8½-ft Hardy rods in carbon fibre and fibreglass were more than adequate, although there were occasions when a heavier line than my DT5 would have proved useful for covering distant trout. The extra shoot I could obtain from the Airflo Super line was extraordinary however, while my Drennan nylon points of 3 lb and 4 lb withstood all manner of abuse, like being sawn against boulders and submerged tree trunks. My greatest joy, however, was my Welly-Waders (from the Edington Development Co of Westbury, Wiltshire). I used them in wader form, rather than folded down into welly form, and they took an awful bashing from constant kneeling and crawling among flints, endless tramping over stony ground, and fighting my way through tangled thorns. They were so light and comfortable, the rubber remained soft and flexible throughout, and they never once sprang a leak.

Anyone considering a New Zealand holiday will be well advised to make contact with somebody who knows the ropes, or with a professional fishing guide. You will find there is a great deal to learn about fishing techniques, the seasons, natural flies and trout behaviour, as well as discovering the best streams and gaining access to the most productive spots. But, with the right kind of information, you too can make the most of that never-to-be-forgotten trip to the land of the kiwi, the bellbird, and a people whose charm, courtesy, and sense of fair play seem to belong to another age.

ᥴᥩ 80 ᥩᥝ
One Last Chuck

I imagine anyone who writes about fishing finds at the end of the day that he has said less than the half of it. Although this compilation represents a small proportion of the material available to me at the outset I feel I have failed, in some thirty years of writing, to portray more than the merest hint of the mystery and wonder that exists in the natural world, or to express the peaks of happiness that the fishing life has brought me. To say that fishing is a hobby or a recreation is not enough. It is a healthy pastime certainly, the most absorbing sport, an intellectual exercise, a refined art when performed well. Yet, no matter how we may attempt to define the essence of fly fishing, still we seem unable to touch the heart of it.

Perhaps this is because a day by the water is so full of fascinating incidents aside from fishing that we find our attention increasingly focused on the hundreds of minor dramas unfolding about us. New blooms burst forth as others fade, trees don fresh shades of green, the songs of migrant birds compete with homespun favourites, while the air is filled with all manner of insects intent upon mating and establishing territories. Some of us buy books which help us to identify the various species, and we note the particular conditions in which each flourishes. Although we may not be trained naturalists we become keen observers, amateur botanists, ornithologists and entomologists as we begin to appreciate the dependency of species upon species and the critical role of habitat.

The importance of such interactions is apparent in the case of the more localized blue butterflies which, according to species, may survive only in areas of original chalk downland, for example: ideally on warm, south-facing slopes that are closely cropped by grazing animals. Both the larval food plant and adult nectaring flowers must be abundant, and certain species of ant also play a vital protective role –

232

larvae being carried into the ant's nest over winter, and this hospitality is then rewarded by sweet secretions from the caterpillar's honey gland or through microscopic pores. Clearly, populations of Blues fluctuate considerably, spreading into suitable areas nearby in some seasons and facing possible extinction in others – all depending upon climatic conditions, the continued presence of sheep or rabbits (and ants), and the extent to which breeding sites may be disturbed by farmers and others. We could go on to consider the individual lifestyles of the Browns, Whites, Fritillaries, Hairstreaks, Skippers and the rest, but really, had I sufficient knowledge of the subject, I would need to sit down and write another book, and a thick one at that.

Such, then, are some of the complexities in the life cycles of terrestrial insects. So what of those we seldom see, which survive under water for most or all of their lives and whose patterns of behaviour have yet to be studied in detail? It has been estimated that over 100,000 species of diptera exist world-wide, some 6,000 occurring in Britain, and 2,500 species of aquatic upwinged fly (46 in the UK), to say nothing of the stoneflies, caddis-flies, dragon-flies, alder flies, water boatmen, crustacea and numerous lesser organisms, many of which remain undiscovered.

Man is sometimes arrogant enough to suppose that he can explain the intricate web of existence, and that it has little relevance to his own. Who is to say, though, that the many species of flora and fauna which have become extinct each year did not form some vital link in the chain of which we ourselves are a part? Do we accept the commonly believed, though somewhat speculative, theories about evolution, natural selection and the earth's origins? Did the universe just happen, or was it created, and what will be the effects upon our species of wiping out innumerable plant and animal populations? As we delve deeper into nature's mysteries the process becomes so mind-boggling that simple laymen like myself – and let's not kid ourselves that scientists have much greater understanding either – may realize the futility of trying to absorb more than a small fraction of it in one short lifetime.

So it is that the angler is more than one who simply catches fish. He becomes a student of nature, a recorder, a dedicated conservationist, a philosopher. As fishermen, of course, we have benefited greatly from the work of past generations of anglers, both in our understanding of aquatic life and the development of the tools at our disposal. We know more today about ecosystems, river management and fish breeding techniques than ever before. Information about where and when to fish is readily available in books, magazines and elsewhere (even on the Internet), while our state-of-the-art tackle and all-weather clothing is superb in every respect. We have fishing guides, casting and fly-tying instructors, and waters where results are as nearly assured as they can be. In short, we have the wherewithal to become instantly successful performers whose catches are greater than catches have ever been. And yet I sometimes wonder whether such advance has brought us closer to the core of what fishing is about, or does our progress actually divorce the fisherman further from the ultimate joy and satisfaction that he seeks? Is it not true that the gap is widening, for, as man and his technology march inexorably forward, the ways of the fishes he pursues, their habitat requirements and the food they eat have remained virtually unaltered over countless centuries? We may attempt to 'modernize' fishing and drag it into a new age, but we discover that nature stubbornly refuses to change with our changing times.

It is perfectly possible, if we become impatient with nature's pedestrian ways, to create the illusion of grand sport. We can simply turn in larger, fatter fish from the stewpond that are likely to gratify our desires whenever we choose to visit the water. We may even forget some of the natural laws: that trout take time to regain condition after spawning, that a one-pound trout is a good one for the water, or that native fish often remain inactive in the daytime during the summer months. True, the wild fish will then have to compete more savagely for food, they may fail to maintain weight, or be driven out of their hard-won lies, but the fisherman who is concerned more with quantity than quality perhaps will feel he has received value for money.

Nobody would deny that many lowland rivers and stillwaters must be stocked, if anglers are to have the chance of catching fish. This is generally because the prevailing habitat conditions are not conducive to the production of an adequate head of native trout. We welcome these hand-reared fish in the knowledge that, were it not for stocking, there would be no trout fishing. But there is a growing number of fishermen to whom the prospect of taking fish introduced in the recent past seems to lessen the essential hunting element, in which a degree of 'wildness' is implicit. We can pretend, but we know in our hearts that the capture of trout that are in any sense tame is not so challenging or rewarding, even if their dimensions are sometimes impressive. It is heartening to see that some fishery managers, certainly on rivers, are now beginning to heed this message by allowing trout time to become acclimatized, or by stocking with smaller fish which are able to grow naturally on the natural food available. The angler then knows that his trout, although it originated in the hatchery, is to all intents and purposes a wild fish.

There are, on the other hand, numerous rivers – more than most anglers and owners may suppose – which are well able to support fine stocks of native trout, provided we manage these waters in a sensitive way, so as to promote natural proliferation and growth, rather than inhibit them as we may do currently. Clearly the introduction of mature fish is an inhibiting factor, the significance of its impact upon native stocks being a matter of how many fish we put in and at what size. In order to encourage a balanced population of wild trout we must look to the provision of suitable spawning areas, optimum flow rates, adequate cover and, of course, a healthy food supply. If, in addition, the river provides luxuriant plant growths and stable flow conditions, as is naturally the case on many spring-fed streams, then so much the better in terms of increasing ephemerid life, crustacea and other food forms. Trout will grow more rapidly in such waters while in others they may, though numerous, remain relatively small.

Either way, there is in Britain at present a strong movement of opinion away from what has come to be called 'stockie bashing' and towards the preservation of natural trout fishing. Much work is in hand by such men as Dr Nick Giles and Simon Cain to increase water levels and flows on stretches that have fallen victim to the combined effects of dredging, water abstraction, bank erosion and silt deposition. Rivers are narrowed, lies created, spawning gravels are dug over, and much emphasis is placed on the reinstatement of bankside vegetation. Bodies such as the Game Conservancy, English Nature and the newly formed Wild Trout Society are active in these areas, as are the Environmental Agency and others, while individual anglers and clubs are lending their support more and more to the increasingly important matter of habitat improvement.

Although a number of stretches in the central south have been fully restored, it will take many years to improve all those requiring attention, especially since the cost of a major narrowing project can exceed £10,000 for less than half a mile of water. But it is immediately apparent on lengths where such work has been completed that native trout 'home in' as if by magic. Suddenly, a water that contained few wild trout is teeming with them, while all the insect life associated with a healthy stream reappears within months, even weeks. Nature, it seems, is just waiting for the right conditions, and she will do the rest.

It may rightly be pointed out, however, that much of this improvement work could be of relatively short-term benefit, for if borehole water abstraction is allowed to increase at the rate of demand it will eventually cause chalk streams as we know them (relying, as they do, upon constant spring flows from the aquifer), to vanish altogether. Many of those around London and the Home Counties have become denuded of all aquatic life in the past hundred and fifty years or so, or are no longer to be found. The construction of new houses alone looks set to increase by over four million homes nationwide by the year 2016, to say nothing of factories, shopping precincts, hospitals, schools, golf courses, and so on. Millions more baths, loos and washing-machines, thousands of green acres to be watered! And what of the twenty years, fifty years beyond? Already we have seen the quantities of water abstracted rise as much as tenfold in two decades in some southern catchments. No doubt water companies will succeed in repairing more pipes – currently some thirty per cent of the supply is lost through leakage – and new houses may be fitted with water meters; but again, these measures can only be of short-term benefit as long as demand continues to grow.

The current practice of sinking new boreholes and piping water directly into rivers to compensate for abstraction cannot be seen as a sensible long-term option, for aquifers are yet further depleted, while rivers must be maintained increasingly by artificial, man-made controls rather than by natural processes. Successive administrations have each 'passed the buck' to the next for far too long, while allowing some of our finest rivers to fade slowly away, as does human memory. Short-termism, political expediency, damage limitation – this is no way for responsible bodies to proceed.

In 1997 a new Labour government came to power after eighteen years of Conservative rule, and it seems – though words are not invariably translated into meaningful actions – that as a nation we may be prepared to bite the bullet. Clearly we will have to develop alternative water-procurement policies, such as desalination plants or the piping of supplies from northern and western regions, or from the lower reaches of rivers. This will cost great sums of money (and the longer we leave it, the more it will cost), but the consequence if we do not act is too bitter to contemplate. On the plus side we now have universal recognition that a living stream must receive its natural supplies of water if it is to remain such, and that any reduction inevitably causes a corresponding decline in aquatic life, including marsh-dwelling and wetland species. But we now have dialogue between government agencies, water companies and naturalists, all of whom are displaying real concern. From this point on – and it has been a long time coming – I believe we can look forward with a good deal of optimism.

It is understandable perhaps that some modern anglers, in their desire to see native trout protected, should have been seized by a conservation fervour amounting to a kind of missionary zeal. Some cannot bear to see a wild trout killed, yet it is easy to forget that it was deteriorating habitat, rather than rod pressure, which caused wild stocks to decline. We may have forgotten, too (or maybe we never knew), that, in a wholesome environment where predation is minimal, trout will thrive and multiply at an astonishing rate – so much so that the anglers' modest bag is of little account. Those who fished on the lower six miles of the Wylye back in the 1970s may recall that the trout population became so great, due in part to the keeper Norman Smith's successful onslaught on the pike (and in spite of increased rod pressure) that the average weight taken fell from over 1 lb (in 1953 it was over 2 lb) to around ¾ lb. Some may be horrified to learn that members were encouraged to kill six trout of over 11 inches when they could, so as to reduce the numbers and increase the average size. But we should realize that sensible culling levels vary from river to river, and from one period in time to another, according to a number of factors that affect overall trout density. Rod pressure is one of these, but it is a minor one, because bag limits may be set that reflect an individual river's ability to produce.

I know many rivers where any thought of adopting a catch-and-release policy would be absurd, yet there are others on which restrictions are necessary. These decisions should be made by experienced local fishermen, and always based on an intimate knowledge of the river in question, rather than on any well-intentioned though possibly inappropriate concept that may have originated in another part of the world.

So, while some of us may wish to use barbless hooks and return most or all of our catch, let us not view catch-and-release as some kind of moral crusade. We should not insist that others do the same, for it is every fisherman's right to enjoy the fruits of the river just as man has done since earliest times. Nor should we use the fact that we are returning our fish as the justification for hooking and playing excessive numbers; it may be argued that this practice is unsporting, since an undue proportion of the stock is likely to be damaged in this way, and it can make trout extremely difficult, if not impossible, for others to catch. Better, surely, to hunt sparingly and selectively, taking one or two for the pot, than to treat this precious sport as a game with the trout as reluctant playmates. Take one in its prime, and it is spared that inevitable, wasting end, the chomp of a pike or the thrust of the stalking heron.

Perhaps it is a mistake to be too sentimental about any wild creature. And yet, of course, we are apt to be, for that is our nature. Only recently I caught a trout that looked so happy as he rose in the summer sunshine, his spots so vivid and his fins so delicate I had not the heart to bang him on the head. I could have done with that fish for my supper, and the river was full of them, but emotion overcame reason as it so often does. Grayling and trout are winsome creatures certainly, but what of pike? Foxes and mink have pretty faces, though not so the rat. By what criteria do we judge which merit protection and which others will suffer as a consequence of the protection we try to provide? Cormorants can decimate trout and grayling populations – so where should our sympathies lie, with bird or fish? We may aim to achieve a harmonious balance among species, even-handed and without offending human sensibilities, but how can such a halcyon state exist?

Indeed I have said less than half, a tenth, a hundredth of it. For every question I address a thousand more remain. And when a century has passed, and another millennium, I suspect that fishermen will still debate these intriguing issues as we do today – and as our forebears did back in the mists of time. It was ever thus, for, learned though we may appear in our enlightened age, the angler's world is much as it always was. It is this sameness which brings such comfort – this knowledge that, no matter what burdens we must carry, there is a gentle valley to which we can escape, where the duns will always hatch and where agile trout will quicken to the fly.